W9-BZD-361

The Back Stage Guide
to
Stage Management

The Back Stage Guide
to
Stage Management

by
Thomas A. Kelly

Back Stage Books
An imprint of Watson-Guptill Publications, New York

Copyright © 1991 by Thomas A. Kelly

First published 1991 by Back Stage Books, an imprint of Watson-Guptill Publications, a division of BPI Communications, Inc., 1515 Broadway, New York, NY 10036.

All rights reserved. No part of this publication may be reproduced, stored in a retrieval system, or transmitted, in any form or by any means—electronic, mechanical, photocopying, recording, or otherwise—without prior written permission of the publisher.

Cover design by Bob Fillie, Grafiti Graphics
Book design by Publications Development Co. of Texas

Library of Congress Cataloging-in-Publication Data

Kelly, Thomas A., 1944–
    The back stage guide to stage management / by Thomas A. Kelly.
        p.   cm.
    Includes bibliographical references and index.
    ISBN 0-8230-7681-4 : $16.95
    1. Stage management. I. Title.
PN2085.K85   1991
792'.068—dc20   91-2490
                                                               CIP

Manufactured in United States of America

First Printing, 1991
2   3   4   5   6   7   8   9 / 96   95   94   93   92

To Robert D. Currie
my friend and mentor
and
Gilbert V. Helmsley
an artist and friend who died too young

Acknowledgments

I would like to offer special thanks to all the wonderful assistant stage managers I have had the good fortune to work with, especially Chuck Kindl, Grady Clarkson, Lani Ball, and Ken Cox. I would also like to thank: my wife Memrie and children Tom, Lydia, and William for their love, support, and patience over the years (and for letting me have the computer and quiet when needed for this book); John Istel, the editor of my ramblings here; and Bill Wilson, without whose guidance and example none of this would have been possible.

Contents

Foreword

It is impossible to make good theater without good stage management. I speak as a director who has occasionally endured bad stage management, and I know, believe me, what that means. I've also known bad productions with good stage management—and, alas, in these circumstances, however professional they may be and however hard they try, stage management cannot finally save poor writing, false acting, indulgent designing, or inept direction. But I have never known a really good production with bad stage management.

The trouble is that directors tend to take stage management for granted. When it is good, they don't notice it—like service at a first-class hotel. But if it is bad, they notice soon enough, because their job is made impossible.

What makes good stage management? I will leave the science to Tom Kelly and his book (he is one of the best I have encountered in thirty-five years of directing, incidently). I will take for granted the ability to cue shows impeccably, organize props with efficiency, and keep a clean and lucid "book" or record of the production. All this is the science. As director and head of the Royal Shakespeare Company and the National Theatre of Great Britain I have, I know, accepted these skills as the norm for many years. I will concentrate on the art—or, if you like, the intangibles.

The stage management team—and particularly the head of the team—establishes a mood and an atmosphere of work. The stage managers have to make a team of the whole theater staff—actors and technicians, and they must also liaise with the front-of-house staff. From them comes a sense of discipline: being on time, not wasting time, working hard. Yet this discipline has to be in the air and accepted by the whole community—not imposed by rules and regulations or by any kind of tyranny.

The stage management must think ahead. They should never explain why something doesn't work or isn't there as a justification for failure; they have to get it to work, they have to create an atmosphere in which everything is possible.

A director is particularly dependent on the stage management in order to organize the breaks in rehearsal. The various unions have organized the theater so that the break requirements are all different. They therefore increase the difficulty of getting on a play. If the day ever comes when the director and the designer *and* the stage managers are bound by breaks as well, it will be impossible to do a play at all. Or so I sometimes think.

Stage managers have to be diplomats. They have to deal delicately with actors, understanding the stress and strain of creation. And they must not treat the star actor with deference and small parts with disdain. An evenhanded understanding is essential.

They must have the confidence of the director and be able to tell him gently when he is being unreasonable or a fool.

And above all they have to create an atmosphere of enthusiasm and hard work and belief.

The most difficult situation for stage managers must be the need to be loyal to a bad director and a bad production. If they allow their own judgment to obtrude or even to show, they will undoubtedly make it worse.

Why on earth should anyone want to do such a job? I can only say that I am glad they do, otherwise I could neither create a production, nor know that it would be recreated loyally every night of a long run. Perhaps, therefore, ideal stage managers not only need to be calm and meticulous professionals who know their craft, but masochists who feel pride in rising above impossible odds. I thank them for making my work and the actors' work possible.

Peter Hall

Introduction

Tensions were high during the last days of rehearsal for the opening of David Mamet's play *Speed-the-Plow*. At one point backstage, Madonna, the pop superstar who was making her Broadway debut in the show, turned to her production stage manager (me), and said, "You were put on Earth for me to abuse, Tom."

This anecdote is an appropriate departure point for a book on stage managing because, basically, in their own way, most people share Madonna's attitude toward stage managers. If accepting lots of the pressures and responsibilities for a theater project while receiving little of the glory is not something you are willing to do, perhaps you should return this book before you crease it any further. However, if you are that rare person in the world of theater who has the talent, as Rudyard Kipling said, to "keep your head when all about you are losing theirs and blaming it on you," then read on.

I should note here that Madonna was speaking affectionately; she had come to understand and appreciate my ability to not only take her abuse but excuse it and let it go. I was able to do this because I, in turn, understood the pressures and insecurities that she was experiencing. This is a big part of successful stage managing.

In the simplest sense, stage managers create an environment within which highly volatile people can function freely, devoid of

1

petty distractions and stumbling blocks—other than those of their own creation. The stage manager must execute the creative vision of each production, supporting and assisting the directors, designers, writers, and performers in the achievement of their artistic goals. The stage manager's creative energies should be focused on finding as many ways as possible to make the theatrical process simple and enjoyable, and much of this book's focus will be on ways to do just that.

My hope is that this book will be read not only by prospective stage managers but anyone who ever comes in contact with a stage manager—whether director, designer, actor, or producer—and that each reader will enlighten others regarding a stage manager's functions. In this way all theater professionals will be able to take better advantage of stage managers as a resource and support system.

• • •

People backstage often ask me how I stay so calm, and like the musician asked how to get to Carnegie Hall, I answer, "Practice." I've been "practicing" the craft of stage management for a while, ever since I went off to summer stock in upstate New York with fantasies of acting stardom pirouetting in my head. After all, I had been the lead in all my high school plays, I had just turned eighteen, and anything was possible. My dream of becoming a successful actor continued for several years, in spite of discouraging signs to the contrary. But starting with that first summer in stock, I *always* seemed to find success and encouragement in the backstage and production end of the theater process.

Those first years of stock served as the ideal training ground for becoming a stage manager. I built scenery, hung and focused lights, ran sound and edited tapes, ran props, served as an electrician, worked in a box office, directed, and acted. I learned theater by doing it—all of it. These days such a regimen might be considered exploitative, and few would think of creating a training program like the one I found waiting for me in a small barn in upstate New York. But I have always been grateful that my first-hand knowledge of every production facet has made stage managing so much easier. I would advise everyone who wants to stage manage to try as many jobs in the theater as possible.

Gradually, more and more people asked me to work in a technical or production capacity while few even *hinted* they might want to hire me as an actor. I took up stage managing as a career, and I have now been at it for over twenty years.

In this book I will attempt to share not only *what* I have learned but also a little of *how* I learned. Of course, reading a book will not make anyone a stage manager. The more I stage manage, the more I know it is unteachable, unless the teaching includes hands-on training. Only the experience of taking a show from the preproduction-production phase through the opening night will give you the knowledge you will require. You will have to make your own mistakes. You too will have to forget to turn the house lights off one night or call the cue for a telephone ring instead of a scene-ending blackout. Every show, every rehearsal, every conflict resolved is one more lesson, and so your experience grows. All I can do with this book is attempt to spare you some pitfalls and help you identify some ideals and goals. And perhaps my practical experience will help make the concepts and principles you read about more real.

Stage managing has been a very rewarding experience for me. Personally, I find the discipline of calling a show and the all-consuming process of rehearsing a play or musical to be a profound source of satisfaction and, at times, a great escape. (It is hard to worry about much of anything else when you're calling cues for a big musical or feeding actors lines as they struggle through those first tenuous days off-book.) Stage managing has taken me to many states and a few foreign countries, has exposed me to some of the greats of our time and some of the lowlifes, but it has always kept its original promise that, unlike an office job, it would never be boring or the same every day. Best of all, if a show or situation ever seems unbearably bad, you're guaranteed relief: no show lasts forever.

If you are interested in becoming a stage manager, at any level of professional or community theater, what follows will provide some help and support. If you already are stage managing, read on, take what tips you like, and leave what you don't. I can't promise to answer all your questions—no book can—but by sharing my varied experiences, whether good, bad, or ugly, I hope to illuminate the many facets of this complex and constantly challenging profession.

1

What Does a Stage Manager Do?

Defining exactly what a stage manager does is difficult because the definition must include so many tasks and responsibilities. To be sure, a stage manager takes blocking notes, calls the lighting and sound cues during performances, and gives acting notes once the director leaves. But such a simple list of physical activities does not completely describe the stage manager's real role in a theater project.

After several hours of discussion on the qualities and requirements of a good stage manager in the stage managing class I teach at Rutgers University's Mason Gross School of the Arts, the students and I settled on what I believe is a good job description. It will serve well as a foundation from which we may explore the various aspects and responsibilities of the position:

Stage managers are responsible and adaptable communicators who have the ability to handle and coordinate diverse groups of artistic personalities with tactful discipline and a sense of humor. They establish a creative environment by combining the ability to prioritize and anticipate and solve problems, with calm sensitivity and grace under pressure. Their ability to do the above stems from organizational ability, acquired technical knowledge (sound, music,

5

lights, design and construction, typing, use of computers, and so on), familiarity with union requirements, and an inspirational personality that creates positive energy.

This is obviously an ideal definition. It includes a number of topics that will serve as jumping-off points for more completely defining and understanding the job of stage managing. Appendix 1 contains several other attempts at defining stage managers, including some by other theater professionals. You'll also find the Actors' Equity Association's definition of the duties and obligations of a stage manager, which will further help you to focus on exactly what a stage manager must and must not do.

It should be noted here that all professional theater stage managers in the United States are members of Actors' Equity Association. This alliance with the actors' union illustrates the collaborative and mutually supportive relationship that should ideally exist between actor and stage manager. At times, however, stage managers are placed in an awkward position because their managerial functions may involve to some degree the disciplining, hiring, and firing of actors. In television and movies, by contrast, those with a job description most resembling stage managers are members of the Directors' Guild.

Through my own evolving experience with the job I've come to believe that there is no fixed definition of a stage manager, only precepts and guidelines, because every show, every theater, every situation—whether it be geographic, contractual, or artistic—changes the scope of the job.

Of course, it is always a good idea to know what the person who hires you thinks the job is. That may seem like simple advice, but every director, producer, or general manager I have worked for has had slightly different views on the role the stage manager plays on a production or in the hierarchy of a resident or community theater's operation.

Usually, the higher the level of theater at which the stage manager is functioning, the more contained his or her job description is. For example, it is not unusual in some summer stock and Off-Off Broadway situations for the stage manager to run light and/or sound cues while calling and watching the show. At some resident theaters, the job of stage manager may include everything from casting to dealing with the transportation and housing of actors.

In each new production, a stage manager will have varying degrees of responsibility depending on his or her relationship with the director or producer. The stage manager may function as an assistant director on some shows and have broad artistic control. On other productions the producer or managing director may depend on the stage manager to be his or her eyes and ears, keeping firm managerial control over expenses and limiting the waste of time and money on artistic indulgence. At best, the job will fall happily into both camps and the stage manager will not have to take "sides" but will be able to best serve the director and the management by facilitating clear communication between the two.

Now let's get back to our ideal definition, take a look at some of the qualities it mentions, and see how these characteristics translate into actual tasks like scheduling, running rehearsals, and passing notes, all of which seem simple on the surface.

The definition begins by stating that stage managers are "responsible." This means that they are willing to take responsibility, and that they will initiate actions that will have a direct bearing on much of the production's ability to move ahead and succeed. Some people resist taking such responsibilities or find they can only function when given orders or directions by someone else. Sometimes it is better to start as an assistant stage manager or a production assistant until one builds up the knowledge and confidence to take responsibility. However, if it is totally outside the realm of a person's nature to take responsibility, then he or she should probably not seek stage management as a career. Taking responsibility presupposes that the stage manager knows the limits of that responsibility—the chart on p. 8 outlines it.

You will notice that the arrows on the chart flow in both directions, because most often the stage manager is the central clearinghouse of information between the creative and the managerial forces. It is important for the stage manager to communicate clearly the changing needs and requirements of the artistic and managerial personnel to all departments if a theater or a production is going to run smoothly.

A fairly standard example of this occurs regularly in the Broadway theater. Suppose that during a production meeting it is decided that the sound operator must set up the console in the house (the audience seating area) in order to hear and balance the

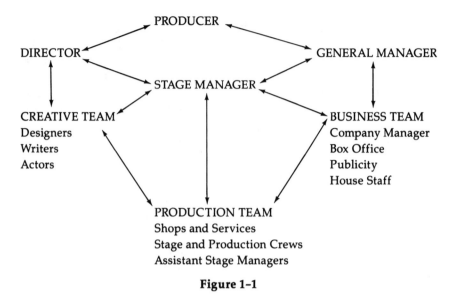

Figure 1–1

sound properly. The sound man and his equipment, therefore, will occupy a number of seats. Until the box office is notified of this decision by the stage manager, tickets could be sold for those seats. Box office personnel should also be informed of any obstructed or partial views that result from a certain set design choice. Catching these potential problems early will result in less aggravation later.

Stage managers should also double-check the performance schedule. Sometimes due to holidays or ticket sales patterns, playing schedules may change. If the actors and crew are not informed, it is possible to have either no one present but the audience for a performance, or a cast and crew sitting around an empty theater. This actually happened during the run of Howard Korder's *Boys' Life* at Lincoln Center Theater. Everyone in management thought someone else had told the stage managers, cast, and crew, but we all showed up for a Sunday matinee that no longer existed. Confirming schedules with management on a regular basis is a good idea.

Obviously, the chart is a simplified structural representation of the stage manager's relationship to all others working on a theater production. What should be immediately noticeable is that the stage manager is "in the middle" and that there are people to whom the stage manager is ultimately responsible, namely the director for all artistic and creative choices, the general manager for all business and contractual choices, and hopefully the producer, who will meld these two sometimes disparate forces into one clear direction. The stage manager, therefore, must be able to combine creative integrity with practical and efficient budgetary considerations. This means balancing the artistic vision of the director with the financial limitations imposed by the producer or general manager.

The chart also illustrates how crucial it is for a stage manager to be an "adaptable communicator," the next phrase after "responsibility" in our ideal definition. Since the stage manager holds the central position in the structure of theater production as shown by the chart, communication is as vital a part of stage managing as memorization is to an actor. There is, however, no one to feed the stage manager the line if he or she doesn't communicate fully. That makes expressing oneself clearly and without editorializing of vital importance. A stage manager who transmits a note to the design staff, for instance, in such a way as to reflect his or her personal feelings about the subject or sender of the note, will ultimately create a volatile and destructive (instead of constructive) creative atmosphere.

Let me give you an example. Suppose your leading lady feels her costume for a certain scene isn't right. After she discusses it with the director, they decide to go for something else. As the stage manager, you jot down a note about the objections and tell the costume designer at the next meeting.

"What do you mean, she can't wear the sweater?" the designer fumes. "Tell her she has to, and I don't care what she thinks."

Now . . . take a deep breath and then tactfully remind the person with whom you are speaking that you are simply the stage manager (i.e., the messenger) and as such are only imparting the wishes of the actor, director, or whomever. Most importantly, you must make sure that the costume designer understands exactly what the request was, and you should repeat it clearly and unemotionally. Lastly, if the costumer is still upset, you ask if he or she would like to speak to the offending party in person to voice his or her feelings directly. Usually, this will result in acquiescence, and two days later the idea to make the change in sweaters will have become the designer's, and everyone will be congratulating themselves on their creativity and ability to get along.

Although many do, stage managers must never take sides, play mind games, or call the personnel names. Transmitting a note with a preface such as "Guess what the nutcase-egomaniac-monster wants today?" is no way to get a designer or director in the mood to listen to a request that may have more validity than you imagine. There are enough short tempers and unbalanced egos backstage without the stage manager getting involved. A wise old stage manager with whom I worked for a long time, Robert Currie, once told me there are two rules of stage management: The first rule is that stage managers should have no opinions; the second rule is that they must know when to break rule one.

Adaptability is another vital part of this job. There is no "one way" to do something; each rehearsal may call for a radically different approach. A three-character drama does not go by the same rules or have the same rehearsal environment as a musical or large-cast Shakespeare, and the stage manager must be able to adapt. A comedy will require a different attitude and handling of rehearsal than a heavy drama. The former may allow for a carefree and easy-going environment whereas the latter may become so charged with the emotions being dredged up by the actors that the same jocular style would not be appropriate.

Adaptability is always required in dealing with the creative process because there is never a foolproof way to predict how long or how difficult certain work is going to be. Schedules, work calls, presets, running orders—all are subject to change at a moment's notice. It is the stage manager's job to organize and communicate the changes as quickly and clearly as possible. The stage manager must avoid editorializing or negativity, no matter how tempting, especially when he or she must tell a group of designers or carpenters who have been working like zealots to complete a project that the director has now decided to cut it. If at all possible, a stage manager should emulate Sgt. Friday from the old television show "Dragnet" and maintain a "Just-the-facts-ma'am" attitude.

I remember with some chagrin the first time I was faced with a tolerance tester of the highest magnitude. I was the original stage manager on *Sugar Babies*, the burlesque musical that eventually enjoyed a long run on Broadway starring Mickey Rooney and Ann Miller. It was the first big musical I had ever worked on as production stage manager from the first rehearsal straight through the initial technical rehearsals, when all the scenery, light, sound, prop, and costume changes are first worked out.

The pre-Broadway tryouts began in San Francisco, and I spent days and nights in my hotel room writing out cues for every department, figuring out where the many flying and moving pieces would be stored. At this point, a crucial task was to decide what traveler or drop would have to be onstage at each moment in order to mask the scene change behind it. (Travelers are the curtains that open and close on the stage level; drops fly in and out from above.) To complicate matters, there were about thirty-five different scenes and songs in the show.

I was then informed that over half the drops in the show would not be ready for the first technical rehearsal and that they might not even be ready until well after the first preview. Don't worry, I was told by the management, just use what you have. I was despondent; I felt I was the only one who recognized the impossibility of their request. Fortunately, the assistant designer was also aware of the folly of this notion, and as we commiserated and despaired a solution dawned. We both had friends at the San Francisco Opera, and we knew they had a warehouse full of drops. So we convinced our general manager to rent a bunch of them to substitute for our missing ones. In this way, at least we would be able to tech and open the show with some semblance of order.

As the afternoon of the first tech approached, I went over the cue sheets with every department head. They went off to lunch, and the lighting designer and I sat down to have a sandwich and put the first act's cues in my prompt book. We were about halfway through when the director arrived and announced that he had decided to completely change the running order of the show: songs from Act One were put into Act Two and vice versa. Whole sequences of costume changes were switched. All the scene changes that I had planned out so meticulously were now rendered worthless on what seemed like a whim.

Well, as I said, this was my first big one, and I lost my composure. An hour to go to the first big tech of my life, and whatever flimsy belief I held that I could pull it off vanished. I broke every rule of stage managing in about thirty seconds. I told the director off, told them to get someone else, and fled upstairs to the boxes to ponder why I had ever thought I could do this job in the first place. I felt very sorry for myself and very alone and very stupid.

Fortunately, the lighting designer on this show was Gilbert Helmsley, a friend with whom I had worked many times. Gilbert was also a teacher and a mentor, and in the next hour he taught me how it should be done.

The solution was simple: I would start with my first cue—house lights to half—and I would just rewrite every cue until I got to the end of Act One and not concern myself with the merits of the decision. I followed Gilbert's advice and the tech went beautifully, because as I settled down and did it I realized much of the work I had done was still sound. Since the crew had never run the show in the original running order, they weren't thrown by the new changes. Thanks to the miracle wonders of cutting, pasting, and photocopying, the cue sheets soon became as workable and valid as they had been a few hours earlier.

Adaptability. If this happened to me now, I know I would just smile at the director before setting out to make the requested changes. After that afternoon in San Francisco, everything seems simple.

The other key elements of the ideal definition are organizational ability and the need to prioritize; they come into play in almost every facet of the stage manager's job. Scheduling, laying out cues, and judging the need for rehearsals and techs can only be accomplished with these basic abilities, as we will learn as we investigate each step of production in future chapters.

2

Preproduction

Preproduction on a show at any level is an exciting time; on Broadway every show is going to be a hit, in stock and community theater every new show will be better than the last. It is also an important time for the stage manager to be functioning with every bit of his or her ability to foresee problems and work towards creative solutions. One must be delicate during these early days and not undermine the wide-eyed optimism and abounding creative energy with such statements as, "That will never work," or "You must be out of your minds!" It is better to work along with the creators, raising any important budgetary and logistical problems gently and clearly as you go.

Analyzing the Script

All stage managerial preproduction work begins with the reading of the script. If you have the time, it is a good idea to read it through once without taking any notes. This will give you an idea of the tone and style of the play before you start seeking out detailed information. Also, in reading a full play, you can save time and guesswork as you prepare lists and notes by knowing how intricate and vital to the plot various props and furniture pieces are and if they have any special needs. For instance, the first scene may require a chair for an actor to sit in, but in Act Two stage directions call for that same chair to be thrown or tipped over, and therefore it will need special attention in building and/or placement. Having read the script once to get a general idea of the plot and technical requirements, a good stage manager will go back through it like a detective, searching out every possible technical clue and every acting or stage direction that could cause problems.

At this point it is a good idea to do a production analysis. It will serve as a starting point for discussions at later production meetings with directors, designers, and the management or producer when trying to work out a budget. The more thorough the stage manager is at this point, the better for everyone. It is dangerous to allow designers and directors to go along assuming that everything in their script is possible technically and financially if you foresee problems that may crop up later on. For instance, the script may have been written by someone with a cinematic background and have lightning-fast changes that are going to require either advanced and sophisticated (read expensive) machinery or a larger number of stage crew and personnel than may be feasible under the theater or show's budget. Solutions and compromise can be reached more easily in the early stages of production, before the director has assumed that every instantaneous change will be possible.

The analysis will be of ongoing use to the actors and stage manager as they figure out the space required for costume changes, the time needed for crossovers, and so on. The analysis allows the stage manager to assist the director and actor in figuring out which entrances and exits may become complicated by a quick costume change or by the character's need to reappear from another side of the stage. The stage manager must keep his eye on all departments' requirements by constantly referring to the analysis; this attention will prevent members of the company wasting time and energy working on something that is later discovered to be technically or logistically impossible. With the help of this analysis, the director won't spend hours blocking a group's entrance from a wing space that must remain free for a large set piece.

Creating a Production Analysis

Another of the major purposes of a production analysis will be to assist in creating the agenda for production meetings. Therefore, it is important to include all areas of the production in the analysis.

Take a legal-size yellow pad or a stack of 8½-by-14-inch paper and turn it sideways. That should provide enough room for the eight columns you will need. Your column headings should look something like this:

ACT/SC./P.#	CAST/COST.	SET	LIGHTS	PROPS	SOUND	SPECIAL EFFECTS	SPECIAL NOTES

The first column designates the page in the script where a certain technical requirement arises. This column will keep you "on the same page" with everyone else as you discuss the show. It will also help clarify where the bulk of the show's technical requirements will fall, as well as where actors make entrances and exits. This is crucial in the preparation of schedules and scene breakdowns. Use a Roman numeral for the act, an Arabic numeral for the scene, and "p." for the page. For example, the sixth page, which is in the second scene of Act One would be written I/2/p.6. This is also the style used to number pages in a script.

The second column should contain all the information you need for the costume plot and for an actor-scene breakdown. The latter will be useful for scheduling rehearsals and will form the basis of any discussion of understudies or covers. As you read you should carefully note every entrance and exit of each character and include a basic description (age, character type, etc.), pointing out whether this changes at any point. For instance, if a character ages or becomes extremely wealthy between scenes, this will no doubt require costume and makeup changes for which plans must be made.

Indicate where costume notes are provided by the writer ("elegantly attired" is a favorite), but also be aware of the costume changes not specifically spelled out. Passage of a day or more will probably indicate a change of costume, as will any change in season or weather. Also note any action that an actor must perform with a costume. A fight, a fall, or the use of stage blood are examples of stage business that must be discussed and planned for artistically and financially. You should also look out for more subtle uses of costume. Does the character need any pockets or lots of pockets? Does a shirt or coat have to be taken off or put on during the action? Does one actor use a costume piece to tie or blindfold another performer? Does a costume have to be torn or ripped off? These are just some of the things to be watchful for in preparing your analysis.

The cast and costume section will also show right away if there is a need for quick changes that need to take place in the wings. By using this eight-column, "across-the-page" approach, instead of a continuous list, you will be able to look directly over to the set and prop columns and see if there will be any traffic problems. If there are scenery or prop changes happening simultaneously, plan adequate room for both at the production meetings.

The next column is for the set, and it should have each setting and all scenery shifts marked here. Be thorough: it is from this initial analysis that you will get an idea of the size of running crew you'll require. The designer will work out a lot of the shift problems with you, hopefully, but think ahead. For example, try to determine what scenery and furniture could be put on a palette or winch and what could be flown, if you have a fly floor. By bolting one or two large pieces of the furniture to the palette floor and putting some sort of glide strips on the bottom of the palette, two people can push off a whole living room of furniture instead of running around moving each piece. Wagons are larger variations of the palette and often contain whole sets with walls and furniture. These are often moved by winches, which allow one man to turn a crank, reeling in a cable that has been attached to the wagon, and due to the laws of physics, move far more weight than one person could pushing or pulling.

The stage manager should be aware of the following elements of the set:

- Doors and their locations
- Whether or not the door frames are large enough to allow costumes, hats, trays, and other props to fit through
- Any indications of a raked stage (a stage floor that slopes down toward the audience)
- Anything that moves onto or off the stage during the course of the action that will have to be handled by actors
- Any playing areas that are elevated and that may require railings and escape stairs so the actors will be able to exit

- Any flying pieces that come in or out during the action
- Any curtains or blinds pulled by actors.

Mainly, the stage manager should be ready to discuss and plan for anything about the set that will affect the actor. From the outset, safety should be a primary concern so there are no unfortunate surprises once on the set.

The light column is fairly self-explanatory. Look for changes in the time of day and season. Keep an eye out for practical lights, mood or effect lighting like lightning, and so on. The lighting column should also denote the position of any blackout. This is a time when the stage goes completely dark, and the stage manager has to plan ahead to assure that all backstage and house lights are out. If a blackout is indicated, the across-the-page form will be very helpful in ascertaining what else is going on in the dark: what actors have to get on- or offstage and what scenery or props have to be moved. All of this must be carefully discussed and planned in ensuing production meetings.

The prop column should contain every prop mentioned or indicated by the script. For instance, if the actor says, "Why don't you mix some drinks while I whip us up some dip for the crackers," there are a whole lot of props indicated by this line of dialogue that may not appear in the stage directions.

Carefully look at how any prop is used (or abused) in the script. A book or a newspaper seems simple enough, but a book or newspaper that is thrown, used as a weapon, sat on, or manipulated in some way makes the prop's requirements a bit more complex. (That's why you must be a detective while completing this analysis.) This fifth column will form the basis of your preliminary prop list, so try to include preset positions wherever possible and some indication of whether or not a prop is a "perishable." (Preset positions are the initial placements of a prop on- or offstage; perishables are those props that are eaten, beaten, or destroyed every performance and will have a great bearing on the cost of the props for the show.)

The sound column should include every audible effect, whether doorbells, phones, sirens, cars honking, doors slamming, or what have you. Also note any offstage voices that may require actors using microphones. In many large theaters, the question of whether or not to amplify the actors arises for every production. It should be dealt with as early as possible, and especially when body mikes are being considered since they will effect the use of costumes and the ease of costume changes.

Try to indicate, wherever possible, the source or location of a sound effect, so the necessary speakers and size of equipment can be accurately budgeted. Let's say a play calls for a radio that must broadcast a news report from stage left, a car horn that must be heard when the front door is opened stage right, and a dog howling in the back yard, up center. This may necessitate at least three speakers.

It is also important to note any mention of music, either practical (onstage sound emitted by a real radio or music that is sung, hummed, or whistled by actors), or underscoring or effect music (offstage sound such as heralding trumpets or a band passing by). Two considerations are important here. First, if the song or music is copyrighted, you must alert the management so they can secure the rights to use it; secondly, you must find out from the author and director what music they envision as live and what will be on tape. This becomes further complicated if a character plays an instrument onstage, but the actor doesn't know how to play it—you will have to discuss and plan this in your production meetings. Of course, with musicals the question of sound amplification becomes larger and far more complicated, as levels must be set according to the orchestra size, and body mikes distributed according to chorus and/or principal designations, and many other factors.

The category of special effects covers a wide range of problems that are important to note when you prepare the initial analysis. Although weapons are usually under the jurisdiction of the prop department, effects people often handle charges or explosive devices—anything more complicated than a standard blank-firing pistol.

I stage managed a play on Broadway called *Accomplice*, a murder mystery by Rupert Holmes that ran briefly at the Richard Rodgers Theatre in 1990. The show had electrocutions, retractable knives, blood bags, a flaming umbrella, and an exploding lamp. All these effects required close coordination between the effects designer and the prop, electric, and set crews and designers. For instance, there was a scene in which a man took a foot bath and was then electrocuted when his wife tossed a hair dryer into the tub. The prop man had to find a bathtub big enough for all the wiring and effects to be hidden in. The set designer had to make sure there was a spot in the floor where a small trap door could be opened under the tub and that was also close enough to an electrical outlet to allow the wife to throw the hair dryer into the tub without pulling the cord out. And the electric and prop shops had to rig and wire the tub while still having it look believable as an antique that might be found in a quaint remodeled English farmhouse. Every element in the show had similarly complicated multi-department requirements, and throughout the production and rehearsal periods it took endless visits to the various shops and many, many phone calls and faxes to achieve the desired effects.

Rain and running water are examples of other stage effects that involve several production departments and must be carefully coordinated through meetings and discussions.

In the "Special Notes" column of your analysis, you should include anything that occurs to you that might involve extra planning, expense, or personnel. If there are accents or dialects in a play, there may be a dialect coach, and if so, when and how often does the director wish to give up rehearsal time? Or should you try to schedule the coaching around the rehearsals on the actor's free time? If there are fights, will there be a fight director? Are there any special cueing needs that should be discussed right away?

As soon as I read *Accomplice,* I knew there would have to be additional television monitors mounted in order to ensure the cast and crew's safety. These simple TV cameras, like security cameras in a bank, would allow the stage managers and crew to see the exact position of the actors during various explosions and when trap doors opened.

It is also important to note anything that might require special licensing such as open flames (torches, candles, kerosene lamps), explosives, or any scenery or effect that will involve the audience. On Broadway and in all New York theaters, every firearm used must have a permit, every open flame must have a permit from the fire department, and every pyrotechnic or explosive device must be inspected, approved, and operated by a licensed pyrotechnist. In whatever town or city you are working, it is a good idea to check what the licensing requirements are for any fire, firearms, or special effects that you may have in your show. Don't forget that it is much simpler to deal with these elements in advance rather than have an inspection after opening night and discover that implementing safety devices will take time and delay your performances.

ACT SC., P.	CAST/ COST	SET	LIGHTS	PROPS	SOUND	SPECIAL EFFECTS	SPECIAL NOTES
I, 1	Willy Loman 50's, suit, hat Linda Loman 50's-nightgown robe	2 or 3 level cutaway of house, w/ kitchen, 2 bedrooms	Dim/Night Practical lights in kitch. and B.R.	2 Heavy Salesman cases Refrigerator kitchen table 3 chairs	Music/Flute Car arrives door slam Linda/off-stage Does she need microphone?		
I, 4	Willy - slippers "-suit jacket on			Pens, etc. for Willy's pockets to empty on table			
I, 7				Milk bottle in refrigerator with milk			
I, 8				cheese in refrigerator			
I, 11		An exit from kitch. USC					
I, 12	Biff 30's Happy 20's in pajamas	upper level is Boy's B.R. - Note: Must be quick escape for fast transition + cost. change later	Moonlight thru window and bedside lamp	Cigarettes (period) ash trays, lighter			

Figure 2-1 Sample Production Analysis of *Death of a Salesman*

Figure 2–1 is a sample preliminary production analysis covering the first dozen pages of *Death of a Salesman*.

Once you have drawn up the eight-column form, photocopy a big stack of them, because a proper analysis will take many pages. After you've completed it, it will be easy to devise preliminary prop lists, sound effect lists, costume plots, rehearsal and scene break-downs, scene-shift plots, and initial rehearsal and tech schedules. More importantly, if done correctly, a production analysis gives you the security of knowing all the elements of a production as you enter into meetings and discussions with the creative and technical personnel. It will make them feel immediately secure that you are organized and capable of taking charge. There is nothing worse than a stage manager being caught unprepared or forced to play catch-up and fake it. As the executor of the creative vision, the more thorough a job of preparation you do, the more confidence and fun you can have in commencing the journey from printed page to production reality.

Meeting the Director

Often your first meeting with a director will be in the form of an interview to gain his or her approval of your hiring by the producer or general manager. Sometimes you may be the resident stage manager and the director is a guest director. In the best of all possible worlds, the director has asked for you, and you can cut through all the preliminaries and get to work.

If you don't know each other, the first meeting with a director is vitally important. The hardest part of these first meetings is being yourself and not trying to impress or overwhelm the director with your brilliance. The director needs to get a sense of the person with whom he or she will be dealing on a daily basis.

Listening is a good practice in a first meeting. Let the director tell you about the script and the concept even though you may be bursting with questions and hard-earned observations gleaned from your production analysis. Often directors will get into exactly what they expect from a stage manager and how they want things run. If not, it is important to ask your own questions. Here is a sample list of questions you should ask and issues that you should raise during your first meeting with the director:

1. At the beginning of the rehearsal process, how long will actors remain at a table reading and discussing? How soon does the director expect to start blocking? Does the director want you to call places and formally begin each rehearsal and scene, or would he or she prefer to ease from informal small-talk into the rehearsal work without abruptly shifting the mood?

2. What level of rehearsal props and furniture does the director expect and at what point?

3. Does the director want strict blocking kept from the outset or will there be a period of improvisation?

4. How does the director want breaks called, five minutes in an hour, or ten minutes every hour and a half? Does the director wish you to call a reminder ten or fifteen minutes before a scheduled break?

5. What policy would the director like to establish regarding visitors at rehearsals?

6. How would the director like to structure the basic rehearsal schedule and how should you break up the script—by scene, page number, act? Your production analysis should serve as an excellent tool to devise an actors' scene breakdown, detailing the acts and scenes and which actors appear in them.

7. Would the director like to establish any guidelines for prompting actors with their lines? How soon does the director want actors "off-book"? And should you correct them word-for-word or allow them to paraphrase at first if the scene is moving along?

8. How are rewrites to be handled, e.g., handed out and read through outside rehearsal or held to be distributed all at once by the director?

9. How much discussion and leeway does the director want to allow before you prod him or her to move on and stick to the scheduled work for the day? This is a delicate and very important point that should be agreed upon in advance, because there should be no sign of quarrel or

disagreement between the director and stage manager in front of the cast.

10. Establish a time when the two of you can talk privately each day so you continue working on the same wavelength while not having to discuss questions or problems during rehearsal periods.

The director and stage manager should emerge from the first meeting with a genuine feeling that they can work together. The basic ground rules should be set.

A stage manager should further inquire whether there is any research or background material the director would like in rehearsal. In regional theaters, dramaturgs will often provide these materials, and sometimes the director may have an assistant who will help with the extra research work. Find out if these positions exist on your show and set up a meeting as early as possible to discuss everyone's responsibilities. Clarify where the responsibilities and authority of the stage manager's position will overlap and/or supersede these often helpful, but sometimes meddlesome, additional staff.

Make it clear, for instance, that no schedule should be presented to the actors or crew by anyone other than the director and stage manager; that notes to the crew must be handled through the stage manager; and that any script or major blocking changes given to actors must go through the stage manager to avoid chaos. Often the director's assistants will give out the director's notes, thinking they are sparing you the trouble when in fact they are creating a nightmare by giving out information and changes that affect your ability to call cues and run the show.

It may also be useful to ask the director if he or she has any previous knowledge of the cast and any advice about the most effective and helpful ways to work with them. Finally, seek out any personal likes and dislikes—smoking rules, food and drink favorites to have on hand, or certain words that they may prefer using. (Directors often use different terms to describe the same thing. For instance, they may prefer that everyone use "company" instead of "cast" when addressing the actors.) Let the director know you are available to make life as pleasant as you and the budget possibly can allow.

Meeting the Producer

Presuming all is well with the director, and you want the job, it is now time to discuss it with your employer. No matter what kind of theater you may be working for, it is important to have a full and clear concept of what is expected of you, especially in terms of work hours and duties outside of rehearsal and performance. There are "traditions" in a lot of theaters that you should find out about ahead of time so you're not surprised when someone informs you that the stage manager always did the sound before, or drove the actors, or organized company parties or softball games, and so on.

There are fewer of these added-on responsibilities in a single-show, commercial-theater stage management job, but it is still valuable to set boundaries. Basically, I always try to convince management to allow me to handle everything from the curtain back—actors, running crew, dressing rooms—while they deal with everything and everybody from the curtain out—house manager, box office, concessions.

This is a good basic premise, but it gets complicated. Since you should try to divorce yourself from financial responsibility as far as possible, it is necessary for management to deal with actors and crew concerning salary and money for expenses or overtime work. However, the need for specific work or additional expense is often requested by the stage manager, so there is overlap in these areas.

There are many different types of management for which you may work as a stage manager. In a regional or resident theater there is usually a managing or producing director who is in charge of the business end of the theater and with whom you discuss your contract and the initial budget and contract necessities of the show. This position is comparable to the general manager in the commercial theater.

The general manager or managing director often has an assistant who may be called the company manager in the commercial arena, or the business manager or assistant managing director in a resident theater. These assistants are the functioning day-to-day business representative on the show, handling payroll, petty cash, and other financial matters, and through whom the stage manager will communicate directly to the producer, general manager, or managing director.

It is very important that this communication be clear, open, and devoid of misrepresentation. Work to establish a common vocabulary and be sure that the company manager understands when you are joking and when you are serious, otherwise confusion about a show's progress can abound in the front office. Remember that business people don't always fully understand artists' eccentricities and strange demands, and therefore may not always see things the same as you. What seems like a reasonable demand to an actor working under pressure for eight hours a day, like getting a check cashed since he or she is stuck in rehearsal during banking hours, may seem excessive to a business manager.

In the first meeting with an employer, the stage manager should proceed much as with the director, listening to the manager's description of how he or she wants the theater or show run. Then augment the manager's basic outline of responsibility with ideas and needs of your own.

Your first meeting with the producer or manager should also include a discussion of any unusual expenses you have discovered through the development of your production analysis and through your previous meeting with the director. Mention any hidden costs you have unearthed (the previously mentioned need for additional video monitors on *Accomplice* is a good example). If you feel the crew size will need to be larger than average, or if the casting or scene changes will preclude doubling or understudying within the company, make sure you bring it to the producer's attention.

You should also mutually establish the production's important preliminary dates:

- The deadlines for the submission of the designers' completed drawings
- The date by which the shops will bid and/or begin work
- The days of auditions
- Projected date of casting completion
- The beginning date of rehearsals
- The dates the company will move into the theater
- The date of the first performance.

As with the director, you need to establish your lines of communication with the manager. What are the forms and reporting systems he or she is used to? Is there a best time every day to talk and update each other on progress and problems? Producers and managers don't want to be burdened with everyday conflicts that you should be able to solve, but they do appreciate early notification of major problems or decisions that only they can handle or make. For example, in *Speed-the-Plow* we were constantly dealing with overzealous Madonna fans who would jump onto the stage in the middle of a performance. Fed up with their potentially dangerous interruptions, Madonna told me clearly, in her own inimitably forceful tone, that there had to be additional security men hired. I called the general manager immediately, so that by the time the songstress and her people reached him, he was aware of the situation and had agreed to hire more security men. It was far better for him to have talked to me first than to have had to meet her fury head-on, ignorant of the full details of the situation; in this case he already had a plan and a solution ready to calm Madonna.

Finally, you must discuss your own working requirements. This includes salary, billing, assistants, and the establishment of a petty cash fund for your purchases and expenses. You should agree on the limit and extent of this fund and how far you can go in terms of hospitality (coffee, tea, food, and other assorted sundries for auditions and rehearsals) and additional creature comforts (dressing room supplies, lozenges, varieties of juice, mineral waters, and so on). Every producer has different limits, and it is best to be clear at the beginning, so you don't do more or less than they want you to.

Production Staff

The next step is the selection of a production staff. The amount of input you have in the choice of production personnel will vary depending on the type of theater in which you are stage managing. Resident theater companies and a great many community theaters have long-term staffs; the job here is to meet with them and discuss how they function and how it would be best to communicate with them in terms of schedule, notes, and other information.

In any production situation, you must try to form as positive a team effort as possible. The stage manager is like a catcher on a baseball team, involved in every play, giving the signals, and positioning the players. It is the stage manager/catcher's responsibility to be sure everyone is working with the same signals and is very clear about the activities of the rest of the team.

In a theater where you are the new person on a team that has been playing together for a long time, be sure you learn their particular ways of working, but don't be afraid to introduce enough of your own methods to take charge. I don't mean that you should arbitrarily demand changes in a theater staff's work methods, but often people have fallen into habits that make no sense, and it is up to you to ease them into new routines that work better or ensure clearer communication for everyone.

For example, I once worked in a Broadway theater where the crew proudly told me they never looked at the callboard. To me, the callboard of a theater is the center of communication. If you post a schedule or notice there, then everyone who works in that theater will see it on the way into work, and everyone begins the day with the same information. More importantly, the stage manager does not have to explain the day's schedule a hundred different times. I explained this to the crew and showed them a sample schedule that would always indicate when they were involved, and they finally grew to like it. (They also began to notice that by checking the board, they could find out about free tickets to various shows, including our own.) Other resident staff people have told me, "I only take verbal notes," or "I only take written notes." This usually stems from past communication problems, and it is always best to suggest that perhaps you can improve upon whatever system fouled them up before. For a while, until trust is established, you may want to work with both written notes and a daily talk.

In the commercial theater, the general manager or technical supervisor often hires crew people that he or she has worked with previously. However, your input may be sought when the regular person is not available, and you could have the opportunity to suggest, or even hire, personnel for one or two departments. In any case, it is important to know the functions and duties of each backstage department. Let's look at an average production staff of a Broadway show and what each position entails.

Production Supervisor

This position is becoming more and more of a necessity, especially on big, technically complex musicals. Usually this person has functioned previously as a production person in either sets, lights, or props. To be clear here, a "production" staff member is someone who assumes initial responsibility for some aspect of the mounting and creation of a show. He or she works directly for the producer and with the creative personnel. There are also "house" staff members who work for the theater and execute the daily running of a show with those people in the "running crew," hired by the "house" department heads.

Production supervisors will take overall responsibility from the outset for the coordination of the technical elements of a show. They will help with the budgeting, scheduling, selection of scenic shops for the building of sets and costumes, and the rental of sound and light equipment.

It should be noted that in almost all commercial theater situations, the rental of the theater is on a "four wall" basis. This means literally what it says; you get the four walls, and everything else must be built or rented, delivered, and set up by the production. The production supervisor will usually oversee all the elements of the design and construction period and remain on the job until all the technical aspects of the show are running smoothly. Working closely with the production department heads, the production supervisor ultimately leaves it all in their hands.

Production Carpenter

The production carpenter will be responsible for everything having to do with the set and scenery for a show, including its rigging, hanging, and movement. He or she is also responsible for the hanging plot, which establishes where everything that must be hung will be flown above the stage—scenery, lights, curtains, special effects. The fly floor, a large grid above the stage from which these technical elements are hung, is usually divided by six-inch sections, each with a pipe, and the carpenter will work out which pipe gets what.

Basically, the production carpenter will run the load-in of a show, deciding in what order the work will be done so that everything keeps moving as swiftly and sanely as possible. The production carpenter may also be involved in the building and use of wagons and winches and will establish the need for a production flyman or winch operator if the complexity of the show demands it.

Production Electrician

The production electrician is responsible for everything that relates to the lighting of the show. Using the lighting designer's plot, this person prepares the rental order in the lighting shop, making sure all the instruments are to the designer's specifications and in good working order. He or she cuts all the color gels for the lights, checks that the theater's power supply is sufficient for the show's requirements, and orders any necessary lighting board equipment or ensures that the one in the theater is adequate and functioning.

The electrician also oversees the installation and wiring of the sound equipment, and usually is the one to hire a production sound person to whom the electrician delegates responsibilities for this area. The production electrician must coordinate the hanging of the lights with the carpenter, and supervise the internal wiring of any set pieces or installation of outlets for practical lamps and appliances.

On a musical, there will often be a production followspot operator who may also function as an assistant to the electrician. The followspot operator is usually chosen by the master electrician.

Production Sound Supervisor

The production sound person, often hired by the electrician, supervises the preparation and installation of all sound equipment. The stage manager must work closely with the sound person on the ordering and installation of the internal communication systems and headsets, all of which will be discussed later. On a show that requires lots of sound effects, music, or other aural elements, there usually will be a sound designer. The production sound supervisor's relationship to the sound designer is analogous to the relationship between the production electrician and the lighting designer: they are responsible for the technical execution of the design.

Production Property Master

This staff member works closely with the set designer on the location and procurement of all furniture for the show and with the director and stage managers on the hand props used by the actors. If there are special props that must be built, he or she will coordinate this with a shop and supervise its work. Props also include rugs, curtains, and upholstery, as well as all food and liquid requirements in a show.

Wardrobe and Hair Supervisors

The wardrobe supervisor coordinates all maintenance and changing of costumes in the theater. The designer and the costume shop construct or "build" the costumes; the wardrobe supervisor oversees their use. Often in a regional or resident theater these two functions will overlap more, and the wardrobe supervisor will manage the construction or rental and the running of costumes during the show. The supervisor will establish the need for dressers and hire them for each production. Here is another valuable use of your initial analysis. You can draw from it a preliminary quick-change plot that will help establish the need for dressers. The dressers will assist actors getting in and out of costume and coordinate the cleaning and washing of the wardrobe.

The hair supervisor will function much as the wardrobe person. He or she will hire those hairdressers needed for the preparation and running of the show.

Casting the Crew

Having done as thorough a production analysis as possible, the stage manager should be in a good position to help ascertain the desired number of crew in each department. Further, if possible, discuss with the department heads the particular needs and style of each show and how that might affect the choice of various production personnel.

Try to "cast" a crew a little bit. The work will go far more smoothly, and the end result will be more successful. Hire people wherever possible who have a track record in the type of production you are staffing. For musicals try to hire people who have experience with musicals or big-cast shows to do them; try to employ staff who are used to the detail and closer personal contacts of an intimate show to do a drama with a small cast. Pay attention to teams of people who have worked well and harmoniously together in the past; it helps under pressure. Recently Sir Peter Hall told me that the experience of mounting *The Merchant of Venice* in New York was one of his happiest ever. This resulted from the positive "can-do" attitude of the crew, who, because of the ease of communication and a shared respect and understanding of responsibility garnered from working together in the past, allowed no problems to get out of hand.

Assistant Stage Managers (ASMs)

Every cliché in the world holds true when discussing assistant stage managers (ASMs). Your success will be greatly affected by your choice of assistant and your ability to effectively delegate responsibilities. Sometimes the choice is yours and sometimes it is made for you. When discussing your job requirements with a prospective employer, one of your strongest requests should be choosing your own assistant. In some instances, your assistant will also head up or be part of the running crew, another reason you want someone whose diligence, tact, and reliability are unquestioned.

Now, let's look at the need for assistant stage managers. There should always be one assistant, and most of the time, on a musical or large-cast dramatic play, you must have two. If you look back over the analysis you made charting the entrances and exits of cast, scenery, and props, you will begin to get an idea of how many assistants are necessary. Ideally, every entrance, exit, and scene shift should have an ASM present, both to cue and help execute the change, as well as to alert you if there are any problems in terms of running the show: an actor missing for an entrance whom you will have to page, a piece of scenery that must be moved or adjusted necessitating a longer blackout, and so on. Your assistants are additional eyes and ears, and without them you are flying blind when calling a show.

Sometimes on a simple play, it is possible for a stage manager who is calling the show from the wings to also run and check his or her side of the stage, but it is better not to have to do this. One reason that this is not a good idea is that it eliminates the possibility of the stage manager occasionally watching the show from the front (a necessity that is discussed in detail in Chapter 7). Many newly designed theaters have booths from which the show can be cued and watched, but watching and trying to maintain a show directorially over a long run from the wings is impossible. So it is almost always necessary on a long-running show to have at least two assistants. Sometimes you open a show with one assistant and then add either a combination understudy/ASM after the opening or hire an additional outside ASM once the show is established, so the PSM can go out front to watch.

In allocating responsibilities, discuss with your assistants which areas they feel most comfortable with. Some ASMs may feel more confident about technical matters than they do about artistic ones; others may love working with the director and actors but feel intimidated by the technical side. Your rehearsal and technical period will function best if your assistants are confident and happy with their assigned tasks.

I try to divide the responsibilities into general areas, so that one assistant is handling all "actor-oriented" jobs, such as recording blocking, cueing lines, taking all costume and prop notes and routing them through me, and assisting me in the creation and communication of the daily schedule. If I have two assistants, I will ask the other to focus on the more technical functions. This assistant should watch for changes and developments that will affect anything in the areas of set, lights, and sound, and help me establish the proper cueing and scheduling of technical work and rehearsals.

From the outset of rehearsals, I will assign initial responsibility for one side of the stage to each assistant, so that as the production process unfolds, they learn what will be the offstage and technical requirements of their side during the actual running of the show. Some other responsibilities that need to be divided depending on the number of assistants and the complexity of the show are:

- Care and feeding of cast—providing and replenishing coffee supplies and food
- First-aid—keeping the kit stocked and remaining aware of actors' needs
- The maintenance of the script—tracking changes and rewrites, and dispersing same (more on this later)
- Security—supervising the storage of actors' valuables (wallets, jewelry, watches) and keys to dressing rooms
- Scheduling—typing and communicating rehearsal and fitting schedules

The more clearly you define each assistant stage manager's area of responsibility, the smoother the production will run. Remember, however, that in delegating areas of responsibility on a show, the stage manager does not relinquish full authority for them. It is important to work with your assistants constantly, checking on their progress, and sharing observations in every area.

There are other advantages to having ASMs. Because assistants will provide the production stage manager with better information, it will be easier to foresee and stave off potential problems. Furthermore, if much of the detail work is being handled by assistants, it allows the PSM to have more time with the director and other creators and thereby better understand and appreciate their needs.

As with every member of the production team, it is vital to keep communication open, easy, and honest. No one on the stage management staff should feel paranoid about making a mistake, asking questions, voicing an opinion, or making an observation. The more the stage managers are keeping up with each other, the better the whole process will flow.

Production Meetings

From the moment you are hired to stage manage a show, you should be pushing the major creative contributors to get together at the earliest possible time for a production meeting. Smaller design and casting conferences can continue, but until you bring together everyone involved in the creation of a show, many questions remain unanswered. Time is wasted because many people wait until this meeting to really begin thinking about and focusing on the problems of a particular project. The initial full production meeting becomes a "reality-check" for everyone, the point at which collectively everyone says, "I'd better get to work, because this looks like it may really happen."

A good stage manager functions as a combination of host and master of ceremonies at these meetings, always referring back to that valuable first production analysis to make sure that everything that needs to be addressed is properly discussed. Let's look at a list of who should be at the meeting:

1. **The Director.** Check his or her schedule first. Once you know the director's available dates, you have a starting point from which to schedule as many other people as possible.

2. **The Producer(s).** Often, however, they will just meet and greet everyone at the outset of the meeting and then leave, knowing the stage managers and general manager will fill them in on the details discussed.

3. **The General Manager,** or someone with full budget knowledge and authority. The presence of this person is vital lest much time be wasted coming up with design solutions and/or casting schemes that are well outside the realm of fiscal possibility.

4. **The Playwright** (play) or Librettist, Lyricist, and Composer (musical). Often in these meetings a difficult technical transition can be solved by the writer adding or amending certain material. Sometimes they must be present to answer casting or costume questions.

5. **Designers.** Every design decision affects each designer. For example, the colors of costumes, sets, and lights are all interdependent. Often designers work with assistants on a show, and it is important to include them, if possible.

6. **Production Heads.** The production supervisor, if there is one, and all the individual department heads should be there. Frequently, this is the only time the production staff gets to hear the creative ideas behind the project and to meet some of these people before the show is in the theater.

7. **Casting Staff.** These people need to have input from the creative team in order to make a realistic appraisal of casting needs, understand the creators' expectations, and determine their own staff's ability to find performers willing and able to do certain roles and/or understudy.

This is a basic list, and it will expand or contract depending on the circumstances of the show that you are stage managing. (Shakespeare no longer attends production meetings, for instance.)

Preparing for the Production Meeting

As you prepare your "guest list" and contact them, be sure to record the vital contact information—everybody's name (correctly spelled), address, and phone number—that everyone will need at the meeting. This information will form the basis for a contact sheet—the single most important tool that stage managers prepare. Its maintenance is essential to a production's successful communication. Accuracy and thoroughness are paramount here. The first contact sheet should include everyone attending the production meeting and list their job titles or descriptions and any other pertinent names and numbers, such as secondary offices, the scenery and lighting shops, as well as any known cast members.

The stage manager must also prepare a preliminary production schedule that includes days during the preproduction period when people are and aren't available for meetings, conferences, or casting. Frequently, designers and directors are working on other projects, so it is crucial that the stage manager take responsibility for gathering this information.

Once a date is set, everything will begin to fall into place. One week before the meeting, send out a reminder to everyone; this will also serve as a check on the accuracy of your contact sheet. A day or two before the meeting, telephone everyone to confirm their attendance, again working from your contact sheet in order to be assured of its accuracy.

Heading into the meeting, it is important to talk to the director and prepare an agenda with him or her, as it will be useless to try to discuss topics that the director doesn't want to approach at this point. Be sure you also agree on the formality of the meeting: does the director want to run it or have you handle it? Write up an agenda, and go over it carefully with the director and the producer/general manager to make sure it includes everything they want discussed. Figure 2–2 is an example of an agenda for a meeting. Check Appendixes 2 and 3 for samples of production schedules and contact sheets that I've handed out at production meetings. It is essential that you date everything you hand out, especially schedules, contact sheets, and script pages, so that people can readily know whether they have the most current versions.

AGENDA

I.   INTRODUCTIONS AND OPENING REMARKS:
     Rupert Holmes and Art Wolff

II. THE SET
     1. Progress report and any questions on construction/Roy
        Sears
     2. The Trap/All effects rigging and requirements
     3. Foot bath/Look, style, and effects coordination with
        lights, trap operator for electrocution effects 1, 2, and 3
        including sound
     4. The Wheel/Operation and use: How controlled on and off the
        stage; actor and operator coordination, etc.
     5. Fireplace/Practical? Revolve/How does it operate? Can
        actor just push, is it crew operated?
     6. The Chair/Discuss fully its use, operation, and safety;
        any provision for him getting stuck up there?
     7. Discuss AEA involvement and report to them in advance on
        all effects, flying, smoke, and knives, etc.
     8. Discuss all rain and coordination with costumes, etc. Will
        rain effect give enough sound or must it be enhanced?
     9. Rundown on load-in and coordination with the Luncheon, etc.

III. SPECIAL EFFECTS
     1. General progress and concept update/Greg Meeh
     2. Discuss each major effect (Foot bath, Umbrella fry, and
        "The Big Wow") and their relationship to all other
        departments—sets, props, costumes, sound, and lights
     3. Other effects: All blood problems and knives coordinated
        with props, costumes, etc. Include "Jacob's Ladder" lamp
        effect

IV. COSTUMES
     1. Progress report/Alvin Colt
     2. Discuss all blood problems and special rigging for effects
     3. Discuss understudies, also Hair and Makeup
     4. Quick-change booth necessities

Figure 2-2   Sample Production Meeting Agenda

V.   LIGHTS
1. General progress report/John Monaco
2. All coordination with effects, also rain, lightning, and sink
3. Board and racks location, Q lites, practicals, and coordination and schedule of load-in, etc.

VI.   SOUND
1. Discuss effects (thunder, electrocutions, etc.)
2. All music discuss with Rupert
3. Discuss operation and effect of onstage tape recorder and the cues played on it; schedule recording session
4. Communication systems and console location

VII. GENERAL AND MISC.
1. Everyone reminded of confidential aspect of keeping script's surprises a surprise/Rupert and Art
2. Go over schedule/All invited to 890 Broadway on Thurs. 3/15 at 4:30 to "meet and greet" cast
3. Run-thrus, discuss concept of cast on stage Sat. March 31 without "tech"
4. Discussion of all program and front of house coordination with Gel Gatto, etc.
5. Questions or additional information

NOTES:

In creating the agenda for the meeting you should draw heavily from your production analysis as well as from any notes taken during your meetings with the director or designers. Every department and designer should have a place on the agenda. This will also help keep the meeting moving, because everyone will see that they will have time to offer their input and ask questions and therefore won't be trying to get a word in before they are scheduled.

The temptation at these meetings is to move too quickly due to the time pressures of everyone present. The stage manager must gently try to keep everyone focused on the agenda and avoid endless stories and bad jokes that sometimes flow if people are avoiding facing the problems that exist. The stage manager should structure the agenda so that everyone necessary for any particular element of the production is present at the time it is brought up. Some people may have to come late or leave early, so make sure their department, and any others that will affect their work, are discussed while they are present.

It is helpful to start the meeting with introductions and a quick look at the preliminary schedule, and then have the director make his or her remarks before getting into the specifics of the meeting. I try to alternate the agenda so that somewhat routine matters are interspersed with the more complicated areas of discussion so that people don't get burnt out too soon. If possible, schedule a break before the most complicated or tense matter on the agenda so that people have a chance to meet privately before launching into messy waters. You may know, for instance, that the director and set designer want to radically alter the look of the show and need approval and support; give them a chance to talk to each other or other people involved before formally presenting the ideas at the table.

Casting is an area that will involve fewer of the people present, like the crew and some of the designers, so schedule those discussions before or after the bulk of the meeting. Keep careful notes or minutes detailing what is said, with exact quotes when possible, so that agreements, desires, and finalized decisions can be acted upon. It is a good idea to draw up these notes as soon as possible after the meeting and get copies to the principal people attending. Appendix 4 contains some examples of post-meeting notes that illustrate what I mean.

Basically, if a production meeting can answer more questions than it raises, and everyone emerges feeling a basic surge of positive energy, it is a success. Most often, it is the stage manger's diligence and thoroughness of preparation that will have proven a prime contributor to that success.

The Audition Process

Stage managers should be involved as much as possible in the casting and audition process. By listening to the discussions between the casting agent and the director the stage manager will gain important insights into the show. By watching the director's reactions to various actor's auditions and interpretations you will get a sense of his or her tastes and working style.

The primary function of a stage manager during auditions is to prepare the space, making sure the room for the audition is well lighted and that there is a place for the auditionees to wait and prepare or freshen up. The stage manager should also maintain accurate lists for the director if there are appointments, and make signs and/or notices that will help people find the entrance to the room, studio, or theater.

Remember that this is a time when everyone involved is nervous and on edge—the creators are anxious that they might not find what they are looking for, and the performers are often tense about their auditions. It is helpful to maintain a formal but calm air in your handling of both groups. If you can, provide as much information as possible for the auditionees. Perhaps print up a sheet that includes the production's title, dates, creative staff, and—most important to an auditionee—whom they will be meeting or performing for that day. Make sure you or your assistant checks each auditionee for name and contact number, and collect a picture and resume from every actor who hasn't submitted one previously.

Keep an accurate list of who is seen and in what order. Work closely with the casting director, if one is working on your production, checking for any changes on the audition schedule. If you are running an open call, keep an accurate list and schedule, collecting all information from the auditionees when they arrive and give them an idea of how long it will be before they are seen based on whatever time span you have arranged with the director (usually two to five minutes for each performer).

Throughout the audition process, whether it is at the highest level of agent submissions and appointments or a large group call, the stage manager can do much to help humanize and ease tensions. Have water, tissues, and plenty of change for the phone handy. Treat people as courteously as possible, and try to avoid condescension when answering their questions. Try to introduce each person individually whenever possible, after having checked the pronunciation of their name. Double-check that they are ready; sometimes that one extra breath or straightening of clothing is necessary to give them the confidence to go out and put themselves on the line.

If actors are reading from the script, be sure they are absolutely clear about what section is to be read. Sometimes the stage manager is called upon to read with the actor. If this is the case, always stand or sit to one side of the stage and face away from the director thereby keeping the focus on the actor. Try to avoid any excessive acting; remember it is the other person's audition. However, it is helpful to give some character to the reading so that at least it makes sense. Make an effort to stay in the tone or style of the piece. Listen to the directions and comments the director makes to each auditionee so that you can help people prepare as the day goes on. Two frequently asked questions at auditions are: Does the director want to hear an accent? Should the actor play older or younger if indicated?

Also indicate on the stage with tape where the actor should stand for the best light and acoustics. The audition process will be the first contact you have with the future cast of your show, so let them see from the outset that stage management is well organized, supportive, and aware of performer's needs.

Dance Auditions

On a musical, there will often be large chorus dance auditions. These take a great deal of organization to avoid chaos. It will be necessary to sign up a large number of dancers, and the best way is to have stacks of numbered cards in two different colors (one for men and one for women) and have them filled out and returned by the dancers after they arrive. The cards should contain names, phone numbers, height, weight, hair color, and not much else; initially they are a tool for you and the choreographer to organize large groups of dancers.

The next step will usually be for groups of twenty or thirty dancers to go into the audition space and learn a dance number with the choreographer. You can call for numbers one to twenty or thirty, based on their card numbers, collect their cards as they enter, and divide the cards into groups of six to ten each, depending on the wishes of the choreographer. After teaching the combination or dance to a large group, the choreographer may dismiss some people and then start auditioning the smaller groups. At this point it is valuable to have the groups line up in order so that you may line up their cards in the same sequence in front of the choreographer. He can then address them by name, work with the group, and hand you the card or cards of those he wants to keep for further auditioning.

This screening process will go on until all the smaller groups have been seen, then those who have been asked to remain will return to learn what is usually a more extensive combination or dance number and perhaps to be seen individually as well. Again you should organize the cards and the dancers so that the choreographer always knows who is auditioning in front of him or her. This may also be the time to hear them sing, and sometimes men will be called back in order to be paired with different women and vice versa. It is vital that the cards and lists be kept accurately so at the end the choices and their identification and notification match up.

It is terrible to tell someone they are chosen and then have the choreographer tell you he or she meant the one in the yellow shirt, not the red. Work as quickly as you can, but don't lose track of who's who. It is vital to have assistants and be clear with them and the choreographer exactly how the call is to be organized.

The Production Schedule

The single most important preproduction responsibility of a stage manager is the preparation of the production schedule. A veteran Broadway general manager and producer, Roy A. Somlyo, once told me that the test of a good production schedule was whether he could ascertain on a daily basis whether we were behind or ahead in every area and department. Therefore it is important to include deadlines, delivery dates and completion dates for everything involved in the production. By the time production meetings are completed and the work is progressing, the stage manager should have assembled enough information to accurately assess the time needed in the theater for the technical preparation of the show prior to the addition of performers (load-in, hang and focus time) and the directorial and technical requirements in terms of time needed with the actors (technical and dress rehearsal time).

In preparing a schedule for a professional theater, the stage manager will have to be aware of the rules of Actors' Equity Association. In a community or university theater, the stage manager must ascertain the basic time and energy restrictions of the cast and crew.

As the level of production goes higher, the number of unions with varying work rules escalates. On a Broadway musical, the stage manager may be dealing with time requirements of four or five different unions in making a schedule. (I will discuss all this in more detail in the section on technical rehearsals.) To demonstrate the variety of possible schedules, a number of samples may be found in Appendix 2.

It is the quality of the preproduction work that will either lead to a smooth, well-run rehearsal and creative period or a chaotic, hair-pulling experience. Every bit of preparation and planning will pay off ten-fold once rehearsals start. On a personal level, the stage manager will be much more relaxed and confident if he or she has done a thorough job. Because of the stage manager's knowledge of the script and familiarity with all the creative staff gained through production meetings and discussions, he or she will also be better able to answer questions from people new to the production. Most importantly, if the preproduction period has been well organized, everyone involved will feel secure with the stage manager, making the job far easier and more rewarding as rehearsals begin.

3

The First Rehearsal

As the preproduction process continues, the stage manager gets closer and closer to what should be regarded as his or her opening night: the first rehearsal. It is vital to the stage manager and the production's success that everything goes as smoothly and peacefully as possible on the first day. The tone for the production will be set, and the actors' willingness to trust the stage manager to look after all necessary details will be established at the first rehearsal.

The Rehearsal Space

Long before the actual day arrives, the stage manager should try to get into the rehearsal space (room, hall, theater) and familiarize him- or herself with the facility. Here is a partial list of items to check:

1. The location and accessibility of the men's and women's rooms.
2. The availability of drinking water (perhaps a cooler will have to be provided).

3. The adequacy of the room's furniture. Are there enough tables and chairs?

4. The entryway or lobby area. Is there a place for hanging coats, etc.?

5. The availability of dressing or changing rooms.

6. The adequacy of the lighting: bright enough, too bright, etc.?

7. The condition of the walls. If there are enough mirrors for dance rehearsals, they must often be covered for a non-musical play. This is most easily accomplished with rolls of brown packaging paper and masking tape.

8. The condition of the floor. Decide whether you will be able to use tape to mark out the set. Make sure it meets the requirements for a dance floor if necessary (see Appendix 11 for a description of an acceptable dance floor).

9. The size of the room. Make sure it is large enough for the set to be marked out on the floor, while leaving space for the director to sit a few feet away and for the actors to make entrances and exits. Ideally a rehearsal space should be ten feet bigger in each direction than your set; i.e., if the set extremities are 40' × 30', you need a space 50' × 40'. Sometimes it is possible to cheat on the depth or width if the set's playing area is less than its actual dimensions. For instance, if there is a porch that people will be seen crossing before entering an upstage front door, there is no need to mark out the veranda on the floor. However, it is vital to give the director some room to get perspective in front of the set.

10. The access to and availability of the space. Find out what time it opens and whether or not you will be allowed in early to set up. Don't schedule rehearsal to begin the minute the place opens; always allow at least a half-hour between the opening time and the first call in order to get set up and organized.

11. The size of the access to the space. Make sure there is a loading dock or freight elevator if you need to get large furniture or rehearsal set pieces into the space. Try to figure out what hours and manpower expense this may involve.

12. The adequacy of heat or air conditioning and how it is controlled.

13. Telephone availability. Find out where the nearest pay phone is or how the switchboard works if there's a receptionist. It often behooves the producer to install a phone for a long rehearsal period, greatly simplifying the stage managers' job.

14. The availability of copying equipment. If there isn't any at the rehearsal room, find the location of the nearest copy shop. Again it is wonderful if the production has their own rented or installed for the rehearsal period. On a new script, ask the management about the possibility of renting computers and possibly a fax (facsimile) machine. If a computer is rented, coordinate its selection with the principal writer on the show, so that it is either the same or compatible with the one being used for the bulk of the script changes. Having a computer with a printer and a fax will improve communication and clarity on a production about one thousand percent.

Of course, a lot can be achieved with carbon paper and a typewriter, too. Every situation will dictate different solutions; you may have to share a typewriter with public relations personnel or borrow one from your school or church. Try to strive for the most efficient means as early as possible; don't wait, thinking "they" will come up with a solution. The typewriter the producer says can be borrowed from a friend often has a way of having missing keys or faulty ribbons. Deal with the typing and copying situation early, even if you have to be an impossible nudge about it. If you don't, the same people commenting on your nudginess now will be criticizing your lack of planning ahead later.

Try to keep the main access door behind and to the side of the director's vision to avoid distraction. If you can, have the director or choreographer meet you at the space to see it and decide exactly how they want the room set up.

After the rehearsal room has been chosen and you have familiarized yourself with it, you can begin gathering the materials and information you will need to start using it. Once, while working at Lincoln Center's Vivian Beaumont Theater, the stage managers decided to tailor the space to the specific project we were rehearsing. The play was *In the Matter of J. Robert Oppenheimer*, a dramatic recreation of the trial of atomic bomb inventor Oppenheimer on grounds of treason and being a possible Communist sympathizer. As the stage managers, we immersed ourselves in the idea of "living history" theater as discussed with us by Gordon Davidson, the play's director. Because the play's subject was thick with paranoia and suspicion, we decided to make the atmosphere of the rehearsal environment as close to that of the actual hearing as possible. We made the waiting/lounge area cold and sterile, and covered the walls with pictures and posters of the period. The waiting room table was neatly stacked with *Life* magazines and newspapers of the period, as well as history and pictorial books on the bomb, the Communist threat, and other related topics.

When people arrived for rehearsal, they were treated as witnesses or government experts, as the case warranted, and were formally signed-in. They were then directed to wait quietly because "the hearings were in session." Overall, it was a very successful exercise that helped create the necessary atmosphere for discovering the play.

The Ground Plan

With the arrival of the ground plan of the set, the future of the production suddenly becomes more real. Stage managers learn a lot from the ground plan and must refer to it constantly. Basically, the ground plan is like an architect's floor plan, delineating the location and size of all walls, doors, windows, stairs, steps, and the other necessary structural details of the set. It is usually drawn in half-inch scale, which means that every half an inch on the drawing will represent one foot on stage. For example, a door that measures two inches on the ground plan will be four feet wide on the stage.

In order to work on the ground plan and figure out the dimensions of doors, furniture, and offstage space, it is necessary to use a scale rule. This is a triangular-shaped ruler that has different size calibrations on each face and from each end. By laying the side marked 1/2" (one-half inch) on the end alongside the lines on the ground plan, the scale rule will give the number of feet for any dimension, with fractional lines representing inches.

Study the floor plan for the show *Accomplice* (Figure 3–1) for a few minutes. Some of the first elements you should check for would include:

1. The actual playing dimensions of the set. For example, on the *Accomplice* ground plan, the Kitchen, Exterior Area, and Dining Room are all out of the playing area and would not have to be included in the floor marking in the rehearsal hall.

2. The offstage space. This will indicate whether or not there is a crossover, where there will be room for the stage manager, prop tables, quick-change booths, and the like. Notice on the *Accomplice* drawing there is no space between the scrim and back wall, so all crossovers had to be made through the basement.

3. Furniture location and size.

4. Different stage levels. Notice the indication that there is a "rake" to the stage. A floor that is raked usually is slanted or tilted gradually upwards as it goes upstage. This helps audiences see better and is often a standard feature on sets in theaters where the audience sits below the level of the stage, as in most standard proscenium houses on Broadway or in other parts of the country. Note the indication 6" in 10'0". This means that every ten feet, the stage will become six inches higher, so over twenty feet, an actor standing all the way downstage at the edge of the stage would be one foot lower than an actor standing all the way upstage. Other indications of level changes are shown by the indication of +9" or +27". These indicate how many inches from the deck or stage floor each level is, so looking offstage left, we can see there are two nine-inch steps leading to the dining room which is then twenty-seven inches high.

5. Location and path of any moving pieces. In *Accomplice*, there was a moving fireplace downstage left and a trap door stage right. These had to be carefully plotted and laid out in the rehearsal hall so that the placement of furniture and the movement of the actors didn't impede these moving

Figure 3–1 *Accomplice Ground Plan by David Jenkins*

pieces. It is vital that these measurements be accurately plotted in big musicals where large sections of scenery are tracking on and off and could run over people or other scenic elements. Imagine the wasted time and energy if the director stages a scene or musical number only to find out that he or she has to redo the work because a traveling piece of scenery or a moving wagon wasn't indicated on the rehearsal room floor. The stage manager must carefully mark such paths and be sure to point them out immediately to the director or choreographer in rehearsal. Then, if there is not enough room to stage a large chorus or crowd scene, the stage manager can suggest that the director and designer meet and solve the problem while changes are still relatively easy to make.

6. Location and size of any rugs, carpets, or other floor coverings. This is important for actors to know in rehearsal. For instance, a woman can walk quietly on a carpet in heels but will start to "clack" when she crosses onto wood. This may make a difference in the staging.

7. Location of all practical lamps that will be turned on and off by the performers. Also check with the designer on the type (pull chain, switch, button), as this will effect actors' blocking and timing.

8. Location of the "act curtain" (the curtain that closes to signify the end of each act). It is always a good idea to mark this on the rehearsal floor, so the director and actors know where they must stand to allow the curtain to fall.

Marking the Floor

Having thoroughly examined the ground plans, the stage manager should proceed to lay out the floor of the rehearsal room or rooms. This means that the set's outlines must be replicated on the rehearsal room floor. This is one of the most valuable functions a stage manager performs and should be executed with a lot of care and thought. It is helpful to have the following:

1. Three 50-foot tape measures, two 25-foot tape measures.

2. A ball of string (for making circles if necessary).

3. Three or four rolls of cloth tape, one inch wide, and in various colors.

4. Knee pads (for crawling around on the floor).

5. At least two assistants.

6. Scale rule, copy of the ground plans, and pencils.

7. A T-square.

Frank Hartenstein, the original PSM of *Starlight Express* and *Into the Woods*, among others, taught me a time-saving device that you should make for yourself: a sheet of clear acetate the size of the ground plan, marked with a grid of one-half-inch or one-inch boxes, depending on whatever scale the designer used. By placing this transparent grid over the ground plan you will be able to quickly plot points that would take a good deal longer if you measured every line with a scale rule. Instead, you can simply count boxes. The acetate then serves as a good way to keep the ground plan protected and available during rehearsal in case the director needs to refer to it or make additional measurements.

If the design calls for more than one level or set unit, before plotting or marking any specific points, choose different colors of cloth tape for each. Now place one of your 50-foot tape measures down the middle of the room, so that it extends from what will be downstage to what will be upstage, and secure it firmly: it will serve as the center line of the room or floor plan. Give your director the maximum amount of room by placing the "0" on the tape measure as far as possible from where the director will sit, while making sure there is enough room to lay out the whole usable set in front of him or her. Make sure this line is square and straight, or all your other marks will "drift."

Now place another 50-foot tape measure horizontally across the front of the playing area (with the "0" stage right), lining up the 25-foot mark with the "0" on the vertical tape measure or center line that you have already run up and down the stage. Check that it is square and fasten it securely to the floor. Secure another 50-foot tape measure across the floor in the same manner half-way up the center line so that the 25-foot marks on both tapes cross. Your floor should now look like Figure 3–2.

You and your assistants are now ready to lay out the floor. With the ground plan in front of you and either the acetate cover or your

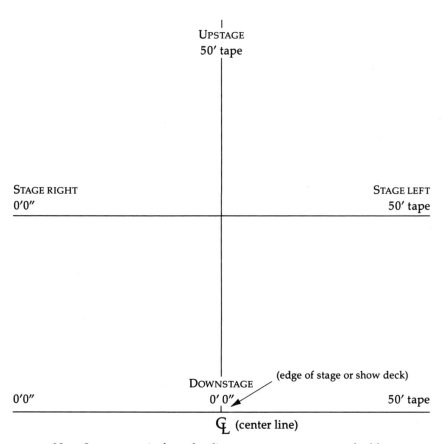

Note: Leave room in front for director, stage manager, and table.

Figure 3-2   Preliminary Rehearsal Floor Layout

scale rule, you can find each point necessary to transpose what is on the paper in front of you to the rehearsal floor. Basically, you are going to create a floor full of dots, that when connected with the cloth-backed marking tape, will render the outline of the set. (Never use masking tape to mark a floor as it will never come up.)

Your assistants should each have a 25-foot tape measure and rolls of the floor tape in a variety of colors. They can work together or individually to place the marks you call out. Every mark will be taken out from the center line, up from the base line, or up or down from the half-way line, whichever will make the measurement shorter. Typical points for a chair that plays center stage might be,

"At four feet, six inches on the center line, go out seven inches stage right, and at five feet, two inches on the center line, go out one foot, three inches stage left." This would pinpoint the two upstage legs of a chair straddling the center line at about five feet from the edge of the stage and facing slightly to stage left. Every set will require different markings, but these are the most important:

1. The beginning and end of every wall and the point where it joins the next.
2. The openings for all doors and windows.
3. The upstage legs or edges of every piece of furniture.
4. The four corners of any platform, rug, or other floor covering.
5. The four corners of any steps, staircase, or riser.
6. The four corners of any trap or other opening in the floor.

Different levels should be in different colors; so the bedroom in *Accomplice* would be outlined in a different color than the dining room, and the tapes would cross each other. Musicals and multi-set shows require different and more involved techniques but always begin with the same basic concept.

If a play has many unit sets, it may be better to have ground cloths for each set, with the different wall and furniture markings on each one. Then on your basic floor only the upstage corners of each such cloth need be marked. A ground cloth should be a sturdy material like canvas that won't tear when actors rehearse on it and should lie flat for safety. On the sides of the rehearsal room in their proper position the masking wings called portals should be marked. Any drop that will be flown in and out should be indicated by a mark with a piece of tape on the side so that you can point it out to the director or choreographer during staging.

These are some of the basics of laying a floor; every stage manager has different methods and tricks of the trade discovered through trial and error, and every show will have different demands. The floor should end up looking a lot like a big version of the ground plan in terms of shape and relative sizes and dimensions. After the job is complete, it should be possible to walk around the rehearsal room and get a spatial sense of the set's size and feel. Be sure you and your assistants check everything quite carefully before the actors or director get on it, so if a door ends up being six inches wide, you discover your own mistake and correct it.

When doing complicated tasks in the theater, remember the basic rule or axiom: If you don't know, ask. When I was young and relatively new at stage managing, the production manager at the Vivian Beaumont Theater asked me to tape out the floor for rehearsal. He asked me to do it as if I would obviously know how, and being eager to please, I didn't want to disillusion him by telling him I didn't. He gave me an assistant who also took it for granted that I knew what I was doing, and away we went. However, I had never marked a floor before, or helped anyone else mark a floor. I didn't even know how to read a scale rule. Basically, I didn't have a clue.

In retrospect, what we produced on that floor was hysterically funny. We "eyeballed" the measurements, making rough-estimates of the dimensions and tried to make it look as much like a big version of the floor plan as possible. But we ended up with steps three inches deep and doors less than a foot wide. Finally, we realized this could not be faked. We confessed, got a lesson in laying out a set properly, and started again. The result was far better, and we both learned not only how to lay a floor but how much easier it is to ask how to do something than to waste everyone's time faking it.

Many people starting out make the same mistake. In our desire to appear knowledgeable and on top of the job we take on tasks that are way over our heads. Today, I have no compunction about asking for help and appreciate when assistants ask me questions instead of plowing into work that I will either have to redo myself or have them do all over again.

Before taking up the tape measures, it is a good idea to mark the center and the front of the stage with a piece of tape in whatever color you used for the ground or deck level of the set, putting small pieces at each foot mark for quick reference later on. If you are doing a musical, the choreographer will probably want each foot in large numbers across the front of the stage for staging purposes. These should be absolutely accurate for spacing purposes in a dance and can be done with tape or stencils bought at most stationery stores. If you have several rooms or are moving a lot with a musical, it is handy to make a roll of canvas with the numbers that you can easily and quickly spread out anywhere. Often, those are the only marks a dance rehearsal will need.

Rehearsal Props

Props are one of the first items that actors will need in rehearsal. The timing of stage business as well as the meaning and memorization of lines is contingent upon their use of props.

The stage manager should create a preliminary prop list, which may be drawn from the original production analysis and any further developments and notes from staff meetings. This prop list should be written up in the preproduction phase so that it can be used in preparations for the first rehearsal. If a computer is available, prop lists should be kept on it. This will greatly facilitate additions and corrections, as well as simple preset changes, and make it possible to keep completely up-to-date at all times.

The first prop list should be as thorough as possible, as this will make it easier to keep up-to-date later on. Set a meeting with your prop master or prop department as early as possible to discuss rehearsal props. Try to cajole, beg, and demand as many of the actual items as possible since this serves the actors the most. However, there is great reluctance on the part of prop people, designers, and managements to have actors use real props in rehearsal. The reasons are understandable; they feel props will get lost, stolen, misused, broken, or otherwise damaged more easily in rehearsal than in the more directly controlled environment of a theatrical performance. There is also the jaded belief that if you give an actor or director a prop too soon, they will get bored with it and change it. I have listened to these arguments often, but the few times I've worked on shows that had real props in rehearsal, none of the arguments seemed to hold water. More often, problems were solved early, and inexpensive, well-thought-out solutions were found that would not have occurred to people while in the heat of a tech week.

Once you have established what actual props are available, the remainder must be duplicated or in some way mocked up as "rehearsal props." Use every bit of ingenuity and care to make these props as much like the real ones in form, style, weight, and function as possible. It is a frustrating waste of time to have a lot of business and action worked out with a rehearsal prop, only to find out the real one is bigger, doesn't open the same way, or work the way it was supposed to. A good stage manager makes sure whatever rehearsal props and furniture are used are close in every detail to what will be used onstage. This simplifies everyone's transition during the move to the theater and during technical rehearsals.

The stage manager's greatest ally in getting props early are star performers and directors with clout; they can make demands that would be laughed at by the prop department if made by a stage manager. For Mike Nichols' Lincoln Center production of *Little Foxes*, every prop was in place for the first reading, which is extremely unusual. This allowed the actors to immediately feel the environment of Southern elegance and style that is so strongly present in Lillian Hellman's play.

The Actors' Information Packet

As I have emphasized before, the first day of rehearsal is the best opportunity for stage managers to gain the trust and confidence of the cast. As they arrive, you should hand each of them a folder, with their name correctly spelled on it, and inside of which is every bit of information that could be helpful to them, as well as all the forms they need to complete. More often than not, they will be greatly impressed by your organization and consideration. Each actor's folder should include, but not be limited to:

1. The cast list. This item should detail each actor and the character he or she is playing. It will help the cast get to know one another more comfortably, without the awkwardness of having to ask "Who's playing the butler?" and so on. This list, if done in the form of Figure 3–3, may then be used for a myriad of other purposes: you can give it to the costume people for size and fitting information; to the press people to check off who has submitted their bios and headshots for the program; the stage managers and company manager can use it to check off who they need to collect paperwork from or distribute it to; and with a few additional lines, it serves as your sign-in and first-call sheet for rehearsals.

2. A contact sheet with every conceivable number needed (see Appendix 3).

3. Two schedules: one in calendar form and one a more detailed day-to-day plan. Be as specific and complete as

ACCOMPLICE

W/E

CAST
in alphabetical order

JASON ALEXANDER									
PAMELA BRULL							·		
MICHAEL McKEAN									
NATALIA NOGULICH									

UNDERSTUDIES
in alphabetical order

PAUL DEL GATTO									
MARGOT DIONNE									
JOHN HICKOK									
MARY KANE									
SAM MAUPIN									

Note: Each column may be used for a variety of purposes: to check off receipt of materials (bio, W-4, picture); for time of first-call; or as a sign-in sheet, in which case each actor would put his or her initials in the box under appropriate date.

Figure 3–3   Sample Cast List Form

possible. If the director has committed to certain calls, spell them out in detail. Include first run-throughs, deadlines for script memorization, completion of fittings and costume calls, and any other relevant events. Also be very clear about the days when attendance is mandatory. Try to indicate how committed the director is to keeping to the schedule in terms of days the actor is not called initially. Include on every schedule the address and phone number of the rehearsal hall, theater, and production office, as well as your own. Also date all schedules and indicate that they are always subject to change. Sample calendar and linear rehearsal schedules are in Appendix 5.

4. All forms that the actor must fill out, with as much of the information already entered as possible. If this is an Equity production, Equity insurance cards and membership information sheets must be included, as well as whatever employment forms the company manager might need. Fill in blanks like the producing company's name and address, the date of the first rehearsal, type of contract, etc., not only to save time and endless questions and repetition, but also because it is a nice thing to do for them. Make sure you have many pencils on hand.

5. Basic information sheet. This will vary in every situation, but some of the facts it should include are, once again, the stage manager's phone numbers and those of the rehearsal hall and theater, a guide to how to get places: subway and bus information to the rehearsal and theater, any tips on dining and entertainment in the area, any rules you want to formally set about lateness, use of the phone, refrigerators, smoking, and any other information that might be valuable. Recently I stage managed the Broadway production of *The Merchant of Venice,* and because half the cast was from England, we really went to town and prepared a "visitor's kit" that included subway and bus maps, visitor's bureau brochures, etc. This is also a good idea on tour. The more thorough you are, the less members of the cast get lost, and rehearsals and performances are less apt to be delayed or messed up by absenteeism and lateness.

6. A wallet phone card. Laminate wallet-size cards with the phone numbers of stage managers, theater, rehearsal hall, and production office.

The style and artistic level of these information packets can run the gamut, but there are always folders with two pockets in them on sale at stationery stores that can easily be labeled with everyone's name. Give packets without the specific actor forms to all production personnel, and make sure everyone's is complete and the same. A good test of what to include in the packets is to think of every question you have been asked on the first day of rehearsal or can imagine anyone asking, and see if it can't be answered from the information you hand out. The more times you can say the first day, "It's in your packet," the more you will be able to deal with unforeseen problems, and the higher regard everyone will have for your professionalism and caring.

Preparing the Contact Sheet

Somewhere in the great mysterious tradition of "it's how things are done," the stage manager was given the responsibility of the contact sheet. It probably began when some well-meaning stage manager, frustrated by the out-of-date and inaccurate contact sheets issued from the producer or general manager's office, suggested he or she take it over. Actually, it is practically impossible for anyone else to do it as well as the stage manager, because he or she, as the liaison between the technical, artistic, and management staffs, is the only person who has constant access to most of the people on it and is therefore best equipped to get the latest address or telephone number changes, additions, and corrections.

I discussed briefly in the "Production Meeting" section the basis of the contact sheet. This is a document that should go on computer if at all possible, as it will make changes and updates so much simpler. Everyone has their own format, and the stage manager should always check with the producing office to see if they have a particular style they prefer. It is also very important to have the management and producer check the contact sheet carefully for correct titles and order of importance. One producer I worked for solved the ordering problem by doing all contact sheets alphabetically; others like to carefully divide management and office personnel from creative staff.

Another careful consideration on the contact sheet is privacy; the stage manager should check very carefully about the inclusion of stars, directors, and producers, many of whom prefer to have only an office or agent's number listed. It is often necessary to create two contact sheets, one for a select group including the producer, the general manager, and the stage managers, and another for everyone in the company.

I always make two different types of contact sheets: one is a formal, long-form sheet that contains everyone and every bit of information necessary; the other is a "wallet" or "refrigerator" list, that in one or two pages contains the cast, crew, management, and other phone numbers and addresses needed on a more daily basis. Examples of both types are included in the appendixes.

On the formal list, I always begin with the producer and management personnel, partially because they are usually established first and change the least. Secondly, there is the "Creative Staff" section: the director and author and their assistants; all designers and their assistants; and any additional writers, composers, choreographers, fight directors, etc. The "Production Staff" section should include stage managers, crew, and all assistants, interns, and volunteers. The next section is the "Suppliers" section: the names and addresses/phone numbers of all shops, unions, rental agents, cleaning companies, and trucking companies. The "House Staff" is the listing of people employed by the theater for all shows: the house manager, the box office personnel, ushers, and doormen. In a regional repertory theater or a community theater, these listings would be in the first section, as the theater is both producer and management, but in a commercial situation, they are usually distinct. Finally, keep the "Cast and Understudies" list completely separate, because most likely it will change more than any other due to the normally nomadic nature of the performer. This section, as with the creative staff, should include the actors' agents and managers, along with the cast's home and service numbers.

These divisions have grown out of use; the people who you combine in a group are often people who have to be contacted at the same time, so you don't have to keep flipping back and forth. Two warnings: Be sure that everyone's name is spelled correctly; and be certain that their title, position, or character role is right. These mistakes cost more in terms of morale and goodwill than almost any other; identity is so important to everyone in theater.

Before distributing a contact sheet, try to confirm the information, either by calling the phone numbers or double-checking it in directories, old contact sheets, or with agents. If you can get through the first rehearsal without anyone telling you that you messed up their name, address, or title, you will have gone a long way towards unifying a company's trust and confidence in you as a stage manager.

Preparing the Script

The stage manager is often responsible for obtaining the show's scripts and putting them in the proper shape for all company members. The easiest is of course a revival of a play that has already been published, such as those by Samuel French, Inc., or Dramatists Play Service. In this case the stage manager can assemble the scripts and/or see that copies are made at a duplicating studio. If the play or musical is to be done "as is" with no changes, then the job is basically just counting up the necessary number of scripts and ordering and distributing them.

If a script is going to be reworked or cut considerably, then it is a good idea to re-enter the script in a computer with all the changes and cuts in it, so everyone starts working with the same manuscript and rehearsals won't get bogged down with some people having some cuts and others not. Once on computer, subsequent cuts and/or changes can be made easily and new pages printed and distributed. All pages of a new or evolving script should be numbered and dated for clarity. On movies and television, they use different color pages for different versions or rewrites, but often with a play or musical that is being worked on, you would run out of colors all too soon. Figure 3–4 is a sample page from the working script of *Speed-the-Plow* by David Mamet, listing all the rewrites made during the rehearsal period. Fortunately, due to the small cast of this play, it was possible to update everyone daily with new pages and corrections and keep the rehearsal process running smoothly, with a minimum of comments like "But my script says. . . ." It is also necessary to keep updated scripts available for all design and production people. I usually keep the new pages and rewrites in folders on my desk in rehearsal marked for designers, sound, and prop people, as well as anyone else who needs periodic updates. When they come by, they can sit down and update their scripts.

It is also a very good idea to keep one script completely up-to-date that belongs to no one and is not used for anyone's notes or

GOULD   I wanted to do Good . . . But I became foolish.

FOX   Well, so we learn a lesson. But we aren't here to "pine," Bob, we aren't put here to mope. What are we here to do (PAUSE) Bob? After everything is said and done. What are we put on earth to do?

GOULD   We're here to make a movie.

FOX   Whose name goes above the title?

GOULD   Fox and Gould.

FOX   Then how bad can life be?

END.

SPEED-THE-PLOW

DRAFT JUNE 1987

Copyright © 1987
Copyright ©, by David Mamet
Revised 2/23/88
Revised 3/9/88
Revised 3/15/88
Revised 3/17/88
Revised 3/20/88
Revised 3/22/88
Revised 3/26/88

Note: Last revision date should appear at the top of every script page.

Figure 3-4 Example of Script Revision

blocking. This script can then be copied for anyone in its entirety or may be referred to by one of the actors or creative staff to help them update and insert new pages in their scripts. Often during rehearsal, the most up-to-date script is needed by people outside of rehearsal like the producer, publicity department, or designers, and it is good to have a free one to copy or lend briefly. Too often, the stage manager ends up being the only person with a totally accurate script, which can't leave the rehearsal because of all the other blocking and cueing information that is included in it.

If a play is still being written while rehearsal is going on, it is invaluable to production to have the playwright and the production office have the compatible computers. The cost of renting or even buying these will be a worthwhile investment because of the time, money, and energy saved by not having to do endless mailings, retyping jobs, and photocopying. It also means the playwright can work right at rehearsal or at home and instantly have access to his work as well as the ability to pass it on to the stage manager for printing and distribution to the cast. This will eliminate the awful hours of rehearsal sometimes wasted waiting for rewrites that then need to be copied and distributed before rehearsal can continue.

Too much efficiency in this area can squelch some of the fun, too. For much of the rehearsal period of *Speed-the-Plow*, Mamet was in Vermont, far from a fax machine or computers. He would write on his typewriter, call me on the pay phone at rehearsal, and read me sections of new dialogue. I would dutifully write the new lines down and read them back to him with as much of the flavor of the cast's current performances as possible. He would listen, make sure I had it right, and make some changes. I would read them again. As anyone who has seen or read a Mamet play knows, his dialogue is often colorful and full of epithets and euphemisms. Often when I got off the phone, the theater doorman would be laughing or shaking his head in wonderment at what he had just overheard. Little did he know that he had become our first critic.

It is important to have plenty of scripts. The list of the people who need one varies from show to show, so it is a good idea to do a script list for each show and mark down the number of each script and the date it is given to each person. Scripts are expensive, and sometimes it is easy to lose track of where they all went. There are people who may only need to read the script once and then can give it back, so if you keep a record of the people who have taken one, you can occasionally call in the extras. Here is the beginning of a list of people who will need initial copies as well as copies updated with changes (it's only a start, so be prepared with plenty):

- The producer and any of his staff or backers whom he or she might indicate
- The director, choreographer, and any assistants they might have
- The writers (playwright, composer, lyricist, book writer) and their assistants
- The publicity department
- The general and company managers
- The designers and their assistants
- Various crew members, especially props, sound, followspot, and wardrobe supervisors.
- All actors and understudies
- All stage managers
- The house manager
- The rehearsal pianist and conductor on a musical.

The Stage Manager's Script

There are many different ways to prepare a stage manager's script, and most stage managers eventually develop a technique that is best for them. Usually, the stage manager will require several scripts. I like to keep one with blocking/staging notes, acting comments given by the director, and any other notes of a creative and directorial nature. This script may also include comments on specific lines that I jot down during run-throughs or rehearsals, and my own timing and pacing notes. This is generally the book that I use in rehearsals, before and after opening.

I also immediately start a second book that is far more neat and formal, which will evolve into the "prompt" script. In this book I will begin to note any cues or technical descriptions that the director might give regarding mood or sequencing of house lights, curtains, sound effects, and so on. I also will keep track of everyone's exits and entrances in this script for warnings and checks later on.

Finally, I will enter important, finalized blocking and stage groupings so as to be able to help the lighting designer and wardrobe people prepare for technical rehearsals.

Some people do all this in one book, combining the blocking indications and acting comments with the technical notes and the cues, but I find it far too messy and confusing. In the end, I want the prompt book to have only the information I need for the running of the show, and the other book to have everything I need for the rehearsing or staging of the show with the actors.

Stage managers' scripts should always be on three-hole paper in a binder so new or additional pages can be easily added and taken out. I always keep a large stack of blank three-hole paper with the script so I can quickly put notes on cueing or new lines of blocking into the script without erasing and changing everything. If you are handed a small booklet-sized script of a show you are stage managing, go to a copy shop and get them to enlarge it onto three-hole paper. Then, get it in a binder. Even if you have to pay for this yourself, do it; it's worth it! Your life will be far happier.

Try to start the cast off with some form of bound script that makes it easy to insert pages and changes as well. A folder-like notebook with three rings or posts is available at all stationery stores. A particular favorite of mine is a simple black three-ring binder made by a company called Acco International from a material they call Accohide. They come in a variety of colors, are sturdy, and make it possible for the actor to clip pages in and out with relative ease. Put the actors' names on their scripts for the first day of rehearsal.

Notification of First Rehearsal

Referring to your contact sheet, now notify everyone on it of the time and place of the first rehearsal. (This is an excellent opportunity to check the contact sheet for absolute accuracy.) If there is time, mail everyone notification with whatever other schedules or information may be pertinent, and then call three or four days later as a backup. Better yet, ask them to confirm receipt of the package and let you know if they are coming. If you write or talk to everyone before the first rehearsal, you should be able to correct any contact-sheet errors before the first mass distribution.

If you have an Equity company, the union must be notified at least a week in advance so they can send an Equity representative to the first rehearsal to go over AEA rules, collect unpaid dues, and hand out membership and insurance information. It is important to mail them a cast list, production schedule, and the date of the first rehearsal as soon as you have them. Many people on the contact sheet may not be able to be at the first rehearsal or they may not find it necessary, but everyone should be informed, and the stage manager should know exactly who is and isn't coming in order to supply enough chairs, refreshments, and other items that will be needed.

Hospitality

Check with the producer or general manager on how elaborate a spread you can put out for the first rehearsal. It is traditional in the morning to at least have coffee, tea, and bagels or rolls. Make sure there is enough. You don't want to have to keep making new pots of coffee or running to the store for food. Fruit is always nice to have, and more and more people are avoiding caffeine, so try to have both regular and decaffeinated coffee available. If there is to be a reading around a table, it is nice to have some mints and nuts on the table for snacking. Remember the point is to make everyone feel secure and taken care of at a point when their anxiety and vulnerability are most acute.

The First Rehearsal's Agenda

A lot of people will demand time and space on the first rehearsal's agenda. This is because the next few weeks may be devoted exclusively to work on individual scenes and/or musical numbers and the first day is often the most opportune time to address the cast as a whole. Also, many people need information or input from them. Of course, the director will always say that he or she needs to get going as fast as possible and cannot afford to waste a lot of time, so the stage manager's task is to schedule everyone as compactly as possible. On a professional production, there are three people who will often need to conduct business at the first rehearsal. They are:

1. The Actors' Equity Association representative. The stage manager must schedule about an hour for the "Equity meeting." This meeting is for all AEA members involved on the production and its main purposes are to review the pertinent Equity rules; to have the actors fill in any necessary insurance and other work-related forms; to collect any outstanding membership dues; and to elect an Equity deputy. Because this meeting is mandatory and all non-Equity members are excluded, the stage manager must try to make the meeting as undisruptive as possible. One solution is to schedule everyone else to come after this meeting or try to set up other necessary meetings simultaneously—between designers and the director or between the public relations people and the producer—anything that will keep the non-Equity attendees busy, hopefully in a separate room. Sometimes producers and press people will want to conclude their business before the union meeting, so they can get back to their offices. Another solution I have tried is having the AEA representative meet with the cast directly after lunch the first day of rehearsal. This means the cast can meet, greet each other, get most of the formalities out of the way, read the play, have lunch, and then have their Equity meeting.

2. The Producer/Manager. They usually like to address the company at the first rehearsal and also may have to collect last-minute contracts or employment forms. Include as much of the necessary paper work as possible in each actor's packet, so the cast must suffer through only one session of filling in forms.

3. The Press Representative. Often the public relations director needs approval of program biographies and will want to set up interviews at the first rehearsal. Try to have this happen during the time set aside for the actors to fill out forms. Remember that the PR person is often functioning under tight deadlines already and must have time with the cast if necessary.

With the business taken care of, the company can move on to the "art." Often the director and writers will want to talk about the show and then have the designers present set drawings and models, costumes sketches, and any other elements of the production that are ready. Plan ahead for this by talking with the director and designers before the rehearsal, asking them how much time they would like and whether they will need any assistance. Stage managers often help with the designers' "show and tell," setting up tables, clip lights, or whatever will enhance the presentation. Even with careful planning, however, unforeseen circumstances may intrude. When we did *King Lear* at Lincoln Center, the set model was so large that we could not get it into the rehearsal hall. It had to be disassembled and rebuilt for display to the cast.

If the director intends for the actors to read the script while sitting in chairs or around a table, check to see if there is any arrangement he or she prefers, otherwise use your own best judgment based on the characters' relationships in the script and use the labeled scripts as "place cards" for the cast. They will usually pick them up and all move around anyway, but at least you started with an organized concept in mind. Along with their scripts should be the aforementioned packets of information, a pencil or two, and maybe a small pad for taking notes, as well as anything else you feel would be helpful.

Here is a sample first rehearsal schedule:

10:00	FULL CAST CALLED/COFFEE AND INTRODUCTIONS
10:15	EQUITY REPRESENTATIVE MEETS WITH CAST; DIRECTOR FREE FOR DESIGN MEETINGS WITH COSTUMES, SETS, AND PROPS IN SEPARATE ROOM
11:30	FULL CAST MEETS WITH PRODUCER, P.R. REPS., DIRECTOR/OPENING REMARKS AND GREETINGS
12:00	DESIGN DISPLAY OF SET MODEL AND COSTUME RENDERINGS
1:00	LUNCH BREAK
2:30	FULL CAST/READ-THROUGH OF PLAY
6:00	BREAK FOR DAY

Basic Necessities

Every theater production should have some essential items present at all times. Of primary importance is a first-aid kit that should be readily available during rehearsals and performances. The following is a list of necessary supplies to include:

- Headache relief medicine (aspirin, non-aspirin substitute), stomach relief medicine, throat lozenges
- Ankle, knee, and elbow braces for minor sprains
- Ice packs, assorted bandages, peroxide, and antiseptic sprays
- Needle, tweezers, and matches for splinters
- Eye wash and contact lens solution
- Orajel and Oil of Cloves with cotton swabs for toothaches
- Smelling salts, small oxygen tank.

It is a very good idea for all stage managers to take a basic first-aid and CPR (cardiopulmonary resuscitation) course. Almost all hospitals offer one. In New York, St. Claire's Hospital and St. Luke's/Roosevelt Hospital both offer courses to the public at various times, and they are very familiar with theater professionals and the problems they are likely to encounter because they get most of the emergency calls from the theater district.

Depending on the circumstances of the production, a stage manager may have more or fewer resources. I always make sure to have the following rehearsal supplies on hand:

- Dozens of pencils (basic number 2 with an eraser); pencil sharpener
- Legal-size pads and 8½-by-11-inch pads of three-hole paper
- File box and file folders
- Scale rule and rulers
- Stop watch(es)
- Notebook dividers
- Scotch, masking, and cloth-backed (floor) tape
- Push pins
- Scissors
- Extra three-hole binders, paper, and a three-hole punch

- Answering machine for rehearsal phone (if possible)
- Computer set-up (if possible) with printer, paper, diskettes, and any other necessary supplies
- Calculator
- Basic stationery and stamps.

This is only a start, and most stage managers will add and subtract items, tailoring the list to their own needs and requirements.

Finally, while the first rehearsal is happening, the stage managers and assistants should be able to be the most relaxed people in the room if they have anticipated everything correctly. Arrive at least an hour before the first call to make coffee and handle any last-minute details. Thereafter, full attention can be turned to the production's participants as they arrive. Again, the more the stage manager has prepared the information and assembled packets of needed forms to fill out in advance, the better the first day will go. People will be occupied with the information and forms, leaving stage management free to deal with the unexpected. Positive energy and good-natured efficiency and control will kick the show off to a strong start. In this way, the stage manager becomes the calm center of the storm of emotion that will inevitably arise as the creative process begins.

4

The Rehearsal Period

The rehearsal process of a show is a period of constant exploration, readjustment, improvement, and accommodation. The stage manager must be responsible for keeping track of all changes in the script, any new technical requirements, and the development of the staging. The stage manager is also a primary source of help, support, and confidence for the actors and director during this time.

There are many varieties of rehearsal periods, and every director works in a different way. Generally, a rehearsal period lasts three to four weeks and begins with a careful reading of the text and some discussion. This may be followed by a period of experimentation, where the performers work through the material "on their feet." The director will then begin to set the blocking; the stage manager is responsible for recording the actors' movements. As the staging develops, the cast will approach the deadline for being "off-book," which means they will no longer carry the script around, because they are supposed to have their lines memorized. The stage manager will facilitate this transition by providing lines from the script when the actors "go up" on their lines. Thereafter, rehearsals are devoted to a combination of act run-throughs; detailed work on specific scenes, character relationships, and transitions; and full run-throughs. The stage manager's tasks will vary slightly from one type of rehearsal and one type of show to another.

Rehearsing a Musical

On a musical, it is very important that the stage management team divide up responsibility, because there are often multiple rooms in which rehearsals are taking place, with actors and dancers running from room to room. Usually there is a "book room," where the director will work with the actors on scenes. One stage manager must always be in these rehearsals watching blocking and noting all entrances and exits in order to determine where costume changes will be made, props placed, and so on.

In another room the dance and music elements will be rehearsed. In this room the main stage managerial function will be to maintain order, call and monitor breaks, and watch the entrances, exits, and staging of large groups, checking that there will be sufficient wing and stage space for the movement being developed. Quite often there is a third room where singers can work on solo and duet numbers with the composer, or the room is used for the composer to work out revisions as well as new material. At least once a day there are rehearsals in one room where dancers and soloists are put together, or sections of the show are run, and all stage managers should be together at these. The scheduling and coordination of the various rooms is the responsibility of the production stage manager, and the assistants take whatever room they are assigned to and run it, calling all breaks, and communicating changes, technical problems, and developments to the PSM. In this way, the PSM should be free both to communicate with the outside world, giving notes and getting information from shops and designers, as well as to travel from room to room watching as numbers or scenes are staged in order to learn their timing and to note any technical or cueing problems for later.

Rehearsing a Non-Musical Play

On a straight play, the director may want to spend several days doing "table work" where the actors spend rehearsal time around the table reading the script and exploring meaning, character, and perhaps familiarizing themselves with an accent or style. Other directors want the actors to get right on their feet and make all these discoveries during the staging. The stage manager must know which method the director is going to pursue and be prepared for it. Going from the table to staging is a delicate moment, and the more the stage manager has prepared the taping of the floor and supplied rehearsal props and furniture, the smoother the transition can be for actors and director.

The beginning stage of rehearsal is also the period in which to check with the actors about how they want rehearsal props, furniture, and costume items set. Remember that they have to be out there in front of the audience, and whatever they need to feel comfortable and safe, within reason, is your job to provide. Some actors will never be satisfied and some are easily pleased or don't care, but never assume, and always double-check; it will pay off in the long run.

The stage manager should always sit facing the stage playing area so he or she can cue actors when they forget a line or some blocking. Once an actor begins to learn lines, the stage manager must be very alert and stay "on the book," which means watching the text carefully and being ready to "cue" the actor with the forgotten line. It is vital that this be done clearly and without judgment of the actor's success. It is also very important not to give line readings or performance values to the cueing or prompting. The stage manager should simply provide the missed line clearly and with as little emotion as possible.

The stage manager must pay careful attention to everything the director says regarding character interpretation and jot down the most salient points. Notes should be taken as well of any requests or changes the director chooses regarding the design or running of the show. These notes must then be passed on to the proper designer, crew member, or department head (more about this later).

As rehearsals progress, the stage managers and assistants should be able to develop an accurate prop and furniture preset list for every scene. Then, at the top of every rehearsal, all props and furniture for the scene to be rehearsed can be set by the assistant and checked by the PSM.

Rehearsing During the Director's Absence

Sometimes the stage manager will be called upon to run rehearsals while the director is in a meeting or otherwise engaged, and these can be very valuable for the cast. This time may be used to drill certain scenes in which the cast has had trouble memorizing their lines. Sometimes, a stage manager will be asked to lead a "speed-through," a rehearsal in which the actors run through their lines in order to make sure they know them. The actors usually sit while running the lines and concentrate on accurately speaking their roles as quickly as possible rather than conveying emotional truth or performing.

In the director's absence, the stage manager may choose to go over certain staging that is tricky or that demands perfect timing. Have a clear idea of the areas the cast should be working on, but also ask them which aspects of the show they feel need attention. There are always scenes that end up getting less rehearsal time, so try to include them. Remember that you are not the director, that the purpose of these rehearsals is to drill and refine the director's work, not redefine it, and remind the actors of this.

Once the routine of the day-to-day rehearsal process has begun, two of the stage manager's most important functions begin— recording the blocking (the actors' movements) and facilitating script changes. Stage managers often handle these tasks their own way, but there are certain standard rules and customs that apply.

Blocking Notation

There are some basic terms and symbols that everyone uses to denote areas of the stage: *upstage* (US) refers to the back of the stage, the area farthest away from the audience, and it derives from the Greeks, who always raked their stages, making the back of the stage literally "up"; *downstage* (DS) is the area closest to the audience; *stage right* (SR) and *stage left* (SL) are the areas to the left and right of the performers as they stand facing the audience (downstage), so that *audience right* would be the same as stage left, and vice versa; *center stage* (CS) is the center of the stage, anywhere on the center line that runs perpendicular to the first row of audience seats.

Given these basic directions, a form of shorthand has developed that simplifies the recording of blocking in rehearsals. Here are some of the areas and their symbols:

USR	upstage right	**USL**	upstage left
DSR	downstage right	**DSL**	downstage left
USC	upstage center	**X**	cross
DSC	downstage center		

Thus, if a character named Bill were to cross from one corner of the stage to the other, the stage manager might write "B X USR to DSL," meaning Bill crosses from upstage right to downstage left. Figure 4–1 is a diagram of a stage with all major areas indicated. These areas define a basic proscenium stage well, but thrust stages or arena (theater-in-the-round) theaters require different ways of indicating staging. Sometimes it is based on aisle numbers, or clock or compass positions in the case of theater-in-the-round. No matter the type of situation, the key is to use whatever system is clear, consistent, and used by all departments and designers. It does little good to work out a brilliant symbol system for your blocking and preset lists only to find out the theater staff uses another. This is particularly difficult when touring a show that goes into a lot of different round and semi-round theaters, as they will all have different names and numbers for aisles and positions. Try to develop a key that you can translate for any theater. Figures 4–2 and 4–3 show some basic stage shapes with possible symbols and abbreviations for staging.

Armed with the shorthand symbols, the stage manager must transcribe the actions, movement, and stage business the director is giving the actors. (As discussed before, the stage manager should place the script in a three-ring binder and have plenty of blank three-hole paper available.) If the script pages (those with the dialogue) have type only on one side of each sheet and they are placed on the right only, then the paper on the left side of your notebook will be the blank back of the previous script page. Blocking notes can be written on this back and if the page gets too messy, neatly copy the blocking notes onto a clean sheet of three-hole paper and insert it into the binder. Some right-handed stage managers find it easier to set up their books with the text to the left, leaving the blank page for blocking and notes to their right. On a new script that is

USR Upstage Right	USRC Upstage Right of Center	USC Upstage Center	USLC Upstage Left of Center	USL Upstage Left
SR Stage Right	SRC Stage Right of Center	CS Center Stage	SLC Stage Left of Center	SL Stage Left
DSR Downstage Right	DSRC Downstage Right of Center	DSC Downstage Center	DSLC Downstage Left of Center	DSL Downstage Left

C_L

Figure 4-1 Basic Stage Diagram with Blocking Abbreviations, Proscenium Stage

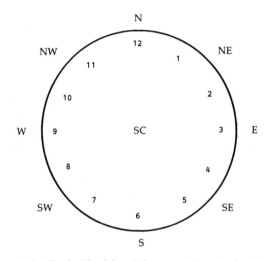

Figure 4–2   Basic Blocking Diagram, Theater-in-the-Round

evolving and going through frequent changes, write the blocking either on a new, blank sheet of three-hole paper or on the script page itself (the reasons for doing the latter are discussed below).

Either way, the blocking should be taken by putting a number by the word or line on which the action happens and writing the action down on the blank page across from the number. Start with numeral "1" on each page, numbering each action or bit of stage business consecutively. For each new page, start numbering from "1" again. This is very important, because if you continue numbering past the page, and then one day the director cuts out some blocking, your numbering system will be thrown off.

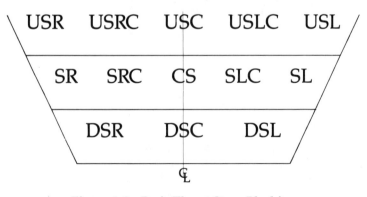

Figure 4–3   Basic Thrust Stage Blocking

HARLEY: Harley is a totally acceptable name. *(XDS to Hal)*

HAL: Not when your last name is Davidson! Look: yes, if you had a *, XDR*   *— X back to her*
     lousy body or lousy looks, you would not have gotten this
     part, but that's not your fault. In this business, the
     free rides, the lucky breaks will never compensate for
     all the inequity.   *— She sits*

HARLEY: I'm in equity!   *Lean into her*

HAL: Harley, you are not the only person who will be standing
     naked in front of the audience . . . symbolically
     speaking. Should we fail, Erika will be doing "Same Time
     Next Year" this year; I will be the permanent punch-line
     XDL *(* of the great backstage joke about how Erika's
     of bed *(* "manager-husband" has written a thriller that would rise
     and fall on the summer-stock market if Erika wasn't
     taking the lead and footing the bill . . . and Brian
     will return to the role he created: 'Understudy' . . .
     standing by for the upcoming national tour of "Love
     Letters," which Mandy Patinkin will no doubt be
     presenting as a one-man show. It seems to me that, of all
     of us, you have the very least to lose.

HARLEY: I just . . . I had thought . . . {SHE breaks down in
     tears}   *Hal wander UL*

HAL: Harley . . . lets you and me make a bargain, okay. I want to
     Sit w/ use your body in my play, (which I think should make you
     her after feel better than if I wanted to use your body outside my
     crying play), but I in turn have a legitimate two-act thriller
     "in New Haven prior to Broadway," we should all be so
     lucky, with a legitimate cast, of which, I might add, I
     am prepared to consider you a full and equal member; and
     in which you, (as Janet's accomplice), and later, (as
     Jon's accomplice), Harley, you are the title character.
     (pause) Okay?

HARLEY: Okay.   *LAMP*

Figure 4-4   Preliminary Blocking Script Page Sample

Early in the rehearsal process, before the blocking is finally set, it may be better to write the stage directions right on the page in the margins or in the space above or below the lines. Figure 4–4 is an example of how I've done this in the past. This will make it is easier to follow the script, feed the actors lines, and correct their blocking when they are still learning their roles. Also, if you are working on a new play where the script is constantly changing, don't write any blocking or directorial notes on the back of the previous page—if it is cut you will have to transcribe all the notes on it to a clean sheet of paper. However, for neatness and clarity, it is best to transcribe the blocking to the opposite blank page at some point later in the rehearsal process when the script is fairly frozen.

Often it is helpful to make small, rough stage diagrams of the set in order to record blocking, especially for large crowd scenes and for the positioning of chorus and tableaux in musicals. Actual dance staging is taken down by the dance captain or the choreographer's assistant, and they often employ a system of dance notation called Labanotation. However, it is the stage manager's responsibility to record the positions they reach, their entrances, and their exits. This can be notated in the same way that regular stage blocking is indicated, by placing numbers next to the song lyrics where various movements take place and showing the beginning and end positions on the facing page or on a roughly sketched stage diagram.

Script Changes

Script changes come fast and furious sometimes, and they must be carefully and accurately recorded as they happen. If a line or speech is cut after discussion between the actor and director, and it is rehearsed and run that way in a rehearsal, it is best to bracket the cut in the stage manager's script and date the cut. If the author later confirms the cut, the page can be retyped and new pages handed out.

Sometimes, the actor, director, or playwright will later decide that all or part of the cut line or speech must be reinstated, so always keep a file, dated, of all script pages that are changed and amended, so you can retrieve cut material easily. This becomes easier if a computer is used and every change becomes a new "document" or "file," always leaving the complete original text for reference.

The Rehearsal Script

As mentioned before, it is also necessary for the stage manager to keep an accurate record of directorial and technical notes in his or her script. In early rehearsals, I try to write down the exact quotes on character, motivation, and the meaning of the play as stated by the director or playwright during actor discussions or note sessions. These become invaluable later on when training understudies or rehearsing replacements. Even on a short run, you can arbitrate disputes or eliminate unnecessary arguments about changes by reading back an exact quote or a clear summation of the director's and/or the playwright's thoughts on the moment in question.

An interesting problem arises when the playwright and director don't agree. On *I'm Not Rappaport*, the Tony Award-winning play written by Herb Gardner and directed by Daniel Sullivan, the two often had completely opposite points of view about certain scenes and characters. They worked fine together, however, because their disputes had to do with different means to the same end, and they would work it out. But, when only one of them was present, the confusion could become astounding. In this case, I found it valuable to keep their conflicting quotes on the same page in different colors, so as I worked with an understudy or replacement, I could refer to Herb's broader, more intellectual position on discussions of character history and meaning, and Dan's more dramatic and directorial quotes on the actual playing of a scene, its pace, shape, and rhythm. Combining these viewpoints gave the actor a wonderfully rich perspective on the role, but balancing these two outlooks often proved a difficult and treacherous tightrope act.

As rehearsals progress, it is helpful to neaten and cut down on the number of notes you make in the book so that eventually your blocking script looks something like Figure 4–5.

① Jes enters R. on balcony.

② Lor hangs onto balcony;
Jes kneels down - kisses
him.

③ Lor drops from balcony.

④ Jes rises, moves off R.- gets
casket. Jes hands casket to
to Lor thru bars- (kneels)
⑤ Jes rises.

⑥ Lor x's L.to C.

⑦ Jes exits. Lor x's to L.C. -
puts down casket, kneels
down.
⑧ Graz x's L.to C. Sal x's
to below bench.
⑨ Lor opens chest, pulls out
jewels. Leo runs D. to L. of
Lor holding torch.

Man 2 + Viol move DS.

⑩ Man 2 gives torch to Graz.
Leo x's to Man 2, gives
him torch.

Figure 4–5   Sample Pages from Finished Blocking Script

Enter Jessica above in boy's apparel

JESSICA

① Who are you? Tell me for more certainty,
   Albeit I'll swear that I do know your tongue.
LORENZO ② Lorenzo, and thy love.

JESSICA

   Lorenzo, certain, and my love indeed,
   For who love I so much? And now who knows   30
   But you, Lorenzo, whether I am yours?

LORENZO

③ Heaven and thy thoughts are witness that thou art.

JESSICA

④ Here, catch this casket. It is worth the pains. ⑤
   I am glad 'tis night, you do not look on me,
   For I am much ashamed of my exchange;   35
   But love is blind, and lovers cannot see
   The pretty follies that themselves commit;
   For if they could, Cupid himself would blush
   To see me thus transformèd to a boy.

LORENZO

   Descend, for you must be my torchbearer.   40

JESSICA

   What, must I hold a candle to my shames?
   They in themselves, good sooth, are too too light.
   Why, 'tis an office of discovery, love,
   And I should be obscured.

LORENZO   So are you, sweet,
   Even in the lovely garnish of a boy.   45

⑥ But come at once,
   For the close night doth play the runaway,
   And we are stayed for at Bassanio's feast.

JESSICA

   I will make fast the doors, and gild myself
   With some more ducats, and be with you straight. ⑦   50

                                   Exit above

GRAZIANO

⑧ Now, by my hood, a gentile, and no Jew.

LORENZO

⑨ Beshrew me but I love her heartily,
⑩ For she is wise, if I can judge of her;

The Running Script

In a separate script, I begin to write the cueing and technical notes on a show, transcribing only that blocking which will actually affect a cue or that which will have to be carefully watched in the running of the show. For instance, if there is a fight or stabbing on stage, it is important to record how furniture may have been moved or if blood has spilled, even though that particular section may not have a cue. It is the stage manager's responsibility to know and foresee any problems that might develop during performance and work with the crew or actors involved to solve them. Carefully take down any stage business that might affect future cueing or staging so you are alerted to any possible problems. For example, make a note to watch that nothing falls off a turntable during the scene before it will move, or jot down a reminder to check if a door has been left open or shut incorrectly. (I will discuss the creation of the cueing script and offer sample pages in the next chapter.)

Fight Rehearsals

A whole book should be written about the creation and maintenance of stage combat. Even B. H. Barry, one of the theater's finest fight directors, must sometimes cajole and demand enough time from the director and producers to stage or rehearse the fights. In some productions, fight rehearsals are afterthoughts and stage combat isn't given adequate time to grow and develop creatively and safely. There is always pressure to produce results quickly due to time constraints, and actors may be pushed into performing maneuvers that are dangerous or uncomfortable for them. The result is a fight full of hesitancy and contrived-looking movements, making the moment seem artificial and staged.

As the stage manager, try to schedule plenty of time for fight rehearsals—I find they require about twice as much time as the director thinks is necessary at first. Best of all, see if you can set up an interview or meeting between the director and the fight instructor during the initial phase of preproduction meetings.

Also, make sure the fight director is present when the fights are first run on the set in stage lighting. Sometimes, a designer or director will sacrifice safety for "the look" of the show by having a fight scene staged on a set that is too dark or cluttered for the combat to safely occur. The fight director must be able to have this changed.

The fight director and the actors need time to themselves to experiment and discover what is possible to achieve together before they are judged or censored. In a show that has considerable fighting—sword duels, the use of other assorted weaponry, a big physical brawl—it is mandatory that some time be given to run the sequences every day of rehearsal and before every performance. Like athletes or dancers who must warm up, the actors involved must keep their fight moves and responses tuned to do exactly what has been safely planned, not what their normal reflexes might do to ward off a blow or repel a physical threat.

When I worked on the Broadway production of *Othello* in the early 1980s (starring James Earl Jones and Christopher Plummer), every fight was run before every performance. Even with all the duels and blows exchanged in the show, there were never any injuries. However, it was only after prolonged negotiations with the management and the unions that this extra pre-performance fight rehearsal was allowed. Technically, the crew and actors would have had to be compensated with overtime pay for this extra rehearsal.

After AEA's experience with *Othello* (as well as with other productions requiring extensive stage combat) the union decided to require fight rehearsals, as well as a fight captain. The fight captain must be a permanent member of the cast and is assigned to watch and rehearse the fights. It is his or her job to correct any stray moves, sloppy choreography, or extension of the original limits of the physicality of the fight.

Rehearsal Report Forms

It is a good idea to write up a daily rehearsal report. Try to get as much necessary information onto one page as possible. There are many forms the report could take. An example of the one I have used for the last few shows I stage managed is contained in Appendix 6, along with a completed form from *The Merchant of Venice*.

This form has many functions, for both the creative and management staffs. Its primary purpose is to serve as the only complete log of the rehearsal period. Therefore, its accuracy is essential. The stage manager should record the day's schedule carefully, especially the beginning and ending times of rehearsal, all breaks, and what scenes were rehearsed. This information is vital to resolving any overtime disputes or arguments about whether a particular scene, actor, or musical number received enough rehearsal. Often, the stage manager's log is used in insurance and arbitration proceedings, so it is crucial to be truthful, clear, and concise, without a lot of editorializing or cuteness.

This point was brought home to me while working on the Broadway musical *Cyrano*. Our stage manager's log was subpoenaed by an arbitrator who was searching for factual information about disputed events surrounding the firing of the conductor. Sure enough, all the salient facts concerning certain events and occurrences were there. But we had also included a lot of very colorful editorial comment on the day-to-day romantic and extracurricular happenings on the show. The arbitrator was a bit perplexed as he read through all these extraneous comments trying to find the necessary facts about the conductor during rehearsals. Needless to say, we were also a bit embarrassed to have our work read in public. This served as a lesson not only on the possible serious use of the stage manager's log, but also on the style and fitness of its content.

The log is also essential for bookkeeping. Often fittings and technical rehearsals will involve some overtime payment to actors, and it is important that an accurate record of all calls be kept, including start and finish times, to avoid confusion and debate later on. The log should record whether any actors are absent or late; Equity rules now allow management to "dock" or reduce actors' wages if they consistently don't arrive on time. It is also an important tool for informing the management, on a daily basis, of any growing problems that are eventually going to be costly or in need of control.

The log should give the highlights of all technical notes in a shortened form that will remind you upon review to refer to more detailed notes for discussion with the various designers or department heads and forewarn management of any additions or changes that will result in new expense. Leaving a space for "Notes and Comments" gives the stage manager a daily opportunity to add any particular thoughts, facts, or opinions on the day's work and progress that deal with anything outside the specific categories on the form.

Communicating Notes to Designers and Crew

Another of the stage manager's most important functions during a rehearsal period is relaying to the appropriate departments any notes, comments, and problems that crop up. It is a good idea to keep one daily sheet of blank paper on the rehearsal table, dated, with each department's heading on it, so the stage manager or assistants can add all notes to one specific place. These notes should then be entered in shortened form onto the daily report and kept in a folder for the designers or crew.

Various shows and theaters have different modes of note distribution, but the stage manager must see to it that it happens in whatever form as efficiently, accurately, and completely as possible. Often, in the commercial theater, notes must be phoned quickly to designers and shops to avoid costly progress on work that may have to be altered due to changes made in rehearsal. I try to update all departments at least once a day, and often two or three times daily in the case of props and costumes.

Some notes are easy and clear and can be easily passed on; others require an in-depth conversation with those concerned. Always try to get a clear idea of the nature and need for discussion before going back to the director with further questions. Try to assess whether there is a need for a meeting or phone discussion with the designer or crew member. Attempt to solve the problem with as little wasted time and emotion as possible but be sure not to avoid a conflict. It is always better and cheaper to have a designer and director have an argument and resolve it during the rehearsal/building phase of a show than to put it off until dress rehearsals in the theater.

The Golden Rule of Theater Production

When several different people on a production seem to be making conflicting demands that are impossible to fulfill, it is useful to remember a simple truism. It is the "The Golden Rule of Production" in theater and was first explained to me by one of the theater's finest designers, Douglas Schmidt. There are no exceptions to this rule, and the wise stage manager should be guided accordingly.

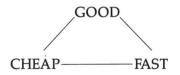

The rule here is that you can have any two, but *never* can you have all three. Let me give you an example. If the director demands a new set piece quickly and the set designer insists on a high-quality job, the producer will not be able to pay for it cheaply. If the producer absolutely won't pay a lot for the piece, than the director must compromise on the speed of delivery or the designer on the quality of its components.

A stage manager's priorities should be guided by this truth. This is why a show like *Sugar Babies* will try to set all its cues during a technical rehearsal even without all its drops; it is just too prohibitive to pay for the added overtime that on-time delivery would cost. In that case, the management opted for "good" and "cheap"; the company had to live with that decision as the drops arrived after the techs.

There are a variety of reasons why this rule might come into play: the creators procrastinate on finalizing the design concepts for the production; there are last-minute changes during the rehearsal period; the financing of the show lags behind the creation, so the construction shops don't get their start-up money until long after all artistic decisions have been made. The stage manager can positively effect the bottom line if he or she continually enhances communication and agreement among the creators by accurately transferring notes and efficiently scheduling meetings.

Scheduling

The stage manager must be in control of all scheduling by getting everyone's requests for rehearsal time, and balancing these needs with the union requirements and the energy resources of the cast and staff. All Equity contracts dictate the number of hours that their members can work each day and limit the hours that Equity members can work straight (usually five hours) before a break of one or one and a half hours.

Let's take a standard schedule and look at all the different ways of breaking it up. A basic rehearsal rule is that actors can work seven out of eight and a half hours, and five hours before a break of at least an hour must be given. This is optional, and every company votes on whether to make the break an hour or an hour and a half. If they vote for the hour lunch, then the day becomes seven out of eight hours, with the added half hour break at the end of the day.

Working with the rehearsal scene breakdown, the stage manager sets about structuring the day with all the required elements in mind. Often, a list of costume fitting requests will have come in during the day, followed by the director's desires for the day and, on a musical, the choreographer and music director's rehearsal time requirements. Frequently, the producer and press agent will request actors to grant interviews or make appearances. Because of all these needs, it is a good idea to establish a deadline for such "outside" requests. Then set a time later in the day to get the director's rehearsal request, as well as those from the choreographer and musical director.

Every day and every situation is different, but basically, the stage manager can now progress to the setting of the next day's schedule. First look at the rehearsal needs and see if there are actors who will not be called at all or only for small sections of the day. If these are the people needed for fittings or other appointments, then life is easy. This list can also be valuable when you go back to the costume people having found only two possible fittings they requested; maybe they can make use of the performers who are available.

If there are actors needed in two or three places at once, then the stage manager's job gets complicated. Before giving up and telling the costume designer, press agent, and choreographer that their requests are impossible to fulfill, look for easy solutions. In the spirit of a great compromiser, try to work out everyone's needs. For instance, a director may want to rehearse a scene that has a large number of people in it for two or three hours. However, only a few of the performers have a significant number of lines or amount of action. Suggest that the director divide up the rehearsal into three time slots wherein he or she can work with those with the larger roles first, then a period of time with the smaller parts, and finally a space of time to put them together. This will free up some of the people for other appointments.

If a leading player has only a small entrance in a particular scene, or only comes on at the very end, it is often possible to free him or her from rehearsal because the director would rather lose a lead from that rehearsal than be forced to let him or her go when work begins on the actor's big scenes. Most directors are conscious of the need for the cast to go elsewhere during rehearsal and will work with the stage managers and designers to make it possible. The further ahead the stage manager can make requests and work out the schedule with the director, the better. Some directors fix schedules in advance and stick to them, while others can't decide what they want to do until the last moment. The latter is more true with new plays or musicals, where the time usually devoted to discovery, experimentation, and changes makes it hard to estimate the time requirements.

Always try to keep the actors' energies in mind when scheduling, because it makes no sense to create a timetable on paper that is not realistically achievable by the performers. For instance, try to give a leading player a break between a long costume fitting and the rehearsal of a major scene or number. If possible, after a leading player's fitting, try to schedule scenes or songs that can be worked on without him or her, so if the fitting goes overtime, or if a lead needs time to rest after it, the rehearsal process can continue successfully. This is a good rule any time leading players are scheduled outside of rehearsal. Nothing alienates a company and the creative staff more than sitting around doing nothing, waiting for the star to reappear.

Try to get the schedule typed and posted (always in the same place or places every day) as early as possible. A sample of a daily schedule is included in Appendix 5. It is also helpful to attach a cast list (see fig. 3.3 in Chapter 3) with the time of everyone's first call next to their name so that you don't hear the frequent laments, "I didn't think I was in that scene" or "I didn't see my name, so I didn't know" when you phone to find out why someone isn't there the next day.

Program Information

The collection of much of the program information and the actors' biographical material has become a fairly standard stage managerial responsibility. Since the press agent is usually paid on a scale commensurate with the stage manager and is not involved in seven to ten hours of rehearsal six days a week, it is not clear why they can't handle this chore themselves. But the fact is they don't, and if they try, they usually make mistakes, so the stage manager winds up doing it.

Sometimes program bios will have been handled before rehearsal, but if not, get a list of all the bios needed by the press agent, the date he or she needs them, and the allowable length. I like to print this information out at the top of a piece of paper and make copies for every cast member. I make it clear that the bio requirements are set by the press agent so that any requests for more words or extended deadlines may be directed to him or her. Then simply keep a copy of the cast list upon which you can check off the submissions, before turning them over to the press department.

There are other components of the program that the stage manager is sometimes called on to provide: the cast of characters in order of appearance; the act and scene breakdown and descriptions; and the production staff and credits list. The cast of characters in order of appearance is self-explanatory, but check with the director and playwright about whether this should be done by visual or vocal appearance, because often characters appear long before they speak.

The act and scene breakdown should always be approved by the director and playwright. A fairly standard example is:

ACT ONE: The home of Mrs. Smith, an evening in winter, 1946

Scene 2: Later that evening

Scene 3: The next morning

ACT TWO: A hotel in New York, a few days later

ACT THREE: The same, moments later

The act/scene breakdown descriptions are more or less specific or poetic depending on the play and its nature. Of course, with a musical, it can be quite lengthy and complicated and is often connected with the list of songs in order. With new works, the proviso "Subject to Change" must appear until a play or musical is "frozen," which means the producer and creator agree that no more changes are to take place.

Careful attention should be given to the production staff and credits. The staff list should include everyone working on the production who does not appear elsewhere. Check and double-check with every department so that no one gets left out. The credits are for businesses and individuals who have provided services or donated props, costumes, or other production items. These credits should be carefully confirmed with every department as well.

Discipline and Order

The tone and atmosphere of the rehearsal process is very much in the hands of the stage manager. A good stage manager must walk a thin line between being the uptight and dictatorial disciplinarian who stifles people's joy and freedom of expression, and the lax, easy-going individual who allows the process to bog down due to wasted time and lack of control and communication.

Be as clear as possible about the basic rules of rehearsal with the cast. Ask for explanations of any lateness, but don't attack; just attempt to ensure that whatever caused the lateness will not happen again. Suggest that you will assist with wake up or reminder calls, and will investigate better transportation routes or provide numbers of car services if necessary. Always approach a person who is late as though they are more upset and concerned about it than you are, keeping in mind that together you can solve any problem to make sure it doesn't happen again. It does no good to get someone defensive or upset, because then you are further impeding their ability to get it together and get on with the work they have been called to do.

Make very clear the boundaries of rehearsal decorum in terms of smoking, food, and drink, as well as the rules on the presence of any guests. Try to always have a separate space in which the people who are not rehearsing can mingle, talk, eat, and so forth, thereby saving the rehearsal space completely for concentrated work. There should be a real contrast between the two spaces. If coffee or other refreshments are provided, try to keep them outside the work space, so breaks and socializing occur out of the way.

Try to give breaks of five minutes in an hour or ten minutes in an hour and a half. Announce the breaks clearly and give warnings when they are half over as well as when there is a minute left in the break. All too often, actors and directors stand around talking throughout a break and then go to the bathroom or make phone calls when you try to get them back to work. Try to discourage this, reminding them gently they are on a break, and that they should take advantage of it. Sometimes it is hopeless, so just announce the end of the break and wait. A favorite break-killer is the ten-minute discussion between the director and one or two of the actors about how destructive breaks are to the creative process, at the end of which, as everyone else is returning ready to get back to work, they take a break. No matter how much creative energy is flowing, after an hour and a half of work, almost everyone needs a chance to have a few minutes off.

Part of maintaining order in rehearsal is of course having it yourself. The stage managers should be friendly, accessible, and supportive but never the center of too much rehearsal frivolity and joking around. "A iron hand in a velvet glove" is a good model for professional managerial style; an alternative might be "easy-going perfectionism." If stage managers concentrate on functioning and communicating in a kind, clear, and supportive manner instead of trying to be everyone's best friend and the center of the company social whirl, they will be far more successful in the long run.

Visitor Policy

In general, rehearsals are very private work places. It is the only period of time in which a performer can experiment, taking creative risks in private, and experience failure that is not threatening or destructive. The stage manager has a responsibility to preserve and nurture that atmosphere. It is important to reserve judgment and criticism of anyone going through a rehearsal process; try to be supportive in every way possible. In the end, it is the actors who will put themselves on the line in front of hundreds or thousands of people, while the stage manager goes quietly about the backstage business, sheltered from public scrutiny. Always remember this distinction in dealing with actors.

I worked on one production that, unfortunately, made clear the reason why rehearsals should be private and closed to outsiders. The ingenue in this particular musical had a retired vice cop for a husband/agent, and he had never been around a show in rehearsal. Well, apparently he didn't appreciate the way his wife was handled in the show. He threatened to knock one poor chorus boy's teeth down his throat, and he was abusive toward the director, the producer, and me on several occasions. He was finally barred from the theater, and security guards were hired to enforce the ban. Needless to say, this was a particularly ugly exception. But be aware that anyone who is present in a rehearsal situation who doesn't belong may be a detriment to the whole creative process. Avoid it if you can.

Try to set aside a few moments at the end of every rehearsal day to catch up with your assistants and check each other's progress, as well as to divide any work that needs to be done by the following day. Go over notes, schedules, and share any personal insights or conflicts that you or your assistants may have become aware of or witnessed during the day. Often, you will return home to be greeted by phone calls about some problem that an assistant warned you about, and having had time to think it over, you will have a better chance of dealing with it constructively.

As the rehearsal period moves from basic staging to first run-throughs, back to detail work and then more run-throughs, the stage manager must be the instrument that allows this process to flow and develop. Whether by careful scheduling, by always having scenes preset, or by getting the accompanist ready, the stage manager should never let the day come to a screeching halt on account of something that could have been anticipated. This usually means working throughout other people's breaks and arriving early and staying late. This is *not* extra work; it *is* the work. Build a secure, creative environment for people to work in, and the process will be more rewarding for everyone involved.

5

Load-In and Technical Rehearsals

There is probably no more intensely involving and rewarding period for a stage manager than when a show loads-in to the theater and then goes through its technical rehearsals. The stage manager is at the center of every decision and the instrument of every bit of creation at this point. For a brief period of time, it makes him or her indispensable. However, responsibilities and pressures are also at their height.

All the preparation, planning, notes, and meetings now pay off—in an incredibly short, concentrated period of time. I have often thought that if the outside world could function at the level theater people do during this stage of production, we would have a far more advanced, organized, and communicative world. It takes a great deal of concentration and cooperation from many people to pull a show together successfully. And the stage manager is at the center of it all, juggling people's time and needs, prioritizing the artistic and technical requirements in order to keep both elements in balance, and generally keeping everyone focused on the common goal: the successful performance of a creative and professional piece of theater.

The Load-In

The term "load-in" refers to the act of moving the set, lights, costumes, and other technical necessities into a theater, and the ensuing process of setting everything up. It usually is a coordinated effort and is set for a specific day or days. In a university, stock, or resident theater, the scenic shop is often in the same building as the theater and so the "load-in" simply may entail moving scenic material within one building, and the lighting and sound equipment are rehung and rewired as opposed to being "loaded-in." In other cases, especially when working in the commercial realm, all the technical elements must be loaded onto trucks, carted to the theater, and moved inside. But in either case, this is the time that a large crew is called to help load and set up, and a lot of work happens in a short time.

The stage manager must stay aware of the progress, continually checking to see that the set is going in as planned, and that proper space is being left onstage and offstage for the actors. Problems do occur. Often the set requires bracing or masking that did not appear on any drawing and that may make a planned entrance or exit impossible. Or the sound department will suddenly appear with speaker stands and place them right where you and the wardrobe supervisor had planned a quick-change booth.

Quick compromise and adaptability is vital, and the stage manager must be the arbitrator of disputes concerning whose space requirement takes precedence. Always bring both parties together with you while you're trying to work out the solution. For example, sometimes a small speaker platform can easily be placed on top of a quick-change booth, and then both people's needs are satisfied. Better yet, you will have avoided the type of confrontation typified by comments such as, "He can't put his ------ change booth here if you want the show to have sound."

Preparing for the Load-In

To avoid as many last-minute glitches as possible, the stage manager and the technical personnel should get together at the theater at their earliest convenience in order to go over space allocation and plan the schedule for the load-in. There are a number of areas that should be checked with special care as you prepare to move a show into a theater:

- Dressing rooms. Carefully list the size and attributes of each one. Note the distance from the stage, the number and type of electrical outlets, number of spaces for actors, the presence of mirrors, showers, or any other amenities such as rugs, furnishings, and refrigerators.
- Wardrobe and hair areas. Check to see if there is an area with a washer and dryer, and the extra power necessary for irons, steamers, sewing machines, and so forth.
- Wing space. After you pace out the dimensions of your set, check that there is ample room backstage for scenery and prop storage, quick-change booths, lighting and sound equipment, and any other necessary controls (winches, special effects, for example). Often what looks ample on the ground plan turns out not to be. This may be due to peculiarities of the theater that weren't accounted for: fire doors, stairwells, various fire curtains or sprinklers, and so on. There are many creative ways to deal with cramped wing space, but decide how you will handle the situation in advance and thereby avoid bogging down the technical rehearsal process.

  Here are some pointers to remember when dealing with cramped quarters. Quick-change booths and prop tables that are necessary only for short periods can be made to break-away or may be flown. Large scenery or prop pieces that are only used once can be flown, or in some cases, taken right out the door until the next performance. One show I visited backstage had a set of prop shelves set against one wall that would fly in and collapse during the show, so as one shelf of props was used, it would stack on the floor, and the next shelf would come to preset level, until at the end of the night, a stack of shelves had piled up and could then be reset for the next show in reverse order.
- Crossovers. Be certain that there is ample room behind the set for the cast to cross from one side of the stage to the other. Often the ground plan may indicate space, but once

all departments run their cables, place their operators, and store their offstage presets, that space may be gone or rendered impassable. Always try to make an onstage crossover possible, but if reshuffling the set storage space or the placement of operators doesn't work, then the stage manager must make the director or choreographer aware of the time it will take for crossovers to be made. The usual alternative is to make the crossover under the stage or through the basement; in this case it must be carefully laid out (perhaps with a brightly colored tape) so that a safe, easy path is kept free at all times.

- Fly floor. If there are flying pieces in your show, check to see if they are operated from the deck (stage level) or from a bridge above. If they are run from the deck, be sure there is ample room allotted for the flymen to operate.

- Stage manager's console. The stage manager must find a place from which he or she can call the show. Optimally, a stage manager's console or desk should be near an access to the front of the house, the stage door, and the dressing rooms. If one of the backstage wing positions fits these criteria, and won't impinge on the space, sight, entrance, and exit requirements of your show, the placement of the console is easy. The key is to try to position the console where it is most central for communication with as many departments and actors as possible.

  In some cases, the desk must be situated on a raised platform backstage so that scenery can come on and off without interference (the recent Broadway production of *Into the Woods* had so many wagons and so much scenery tracking on and off that the stage manager ran the show on a platform above the deck). Other theaters may have a booth or front-of-house position for the stage manager. However, if you are to be backstage, it is important to decide where early so electric and sound cables can be run to your position with the proper lengths and numbers requested in the initial shop order.

- The deck. Be sure to check the condition of the stage floor, especially if a new show deck or floor is not part of the set. Also, check how level it is. When we arrived at the

Blackstone Theater in Chicago to load-in the set for the pre-Broadway production of *Death of a Salesman* starring Dustin Hoffman, we discovered that if you put a pencil down on the center line, it would roll toward the wings. Because this would severely impede the operation of the turntable and wagon that we had in the show, the load-in was extended two days so that, foot by foot, carpenters could level the stage. Meanwhile, the actors rehearsed in a hotel ballroom. We could not cancel any performances because the show had already been sold out to subscribers and the schedule precluded adding any performances at the end because of a commitment to moving the show to Washington, D.C., so we had to rush the first performance instead of having a relaxed technical and dress rehearsal period. We made it, but not without tension and frenzy that could have been avoided by one on-site inspection of the theater in advance by the designer, master carpenter, or myself. Better yet, someone on the theater's crew should have mentioned the problem in discussions prior to our arrival.

- Sight-lines and acoustics. Be sure to spend some of your pre-load-in inspection tour in the audience so you can advise the director and actors of sight-line and acoustic difficulties that could be better dealt with by adjusting the staging rather than making costly technical changes.
- Crew and staff. Try to meet and discuss the load-in and the production's requirements with the house or resident crew before moving into the theater. In this way they can make their plans, and you will have as few surprises as possible during the actual load-in.

Scheduling the Load-In

For the actual scheduling of the load-in, try to work closely with the heads of each department, getting their input and needs. Always establish the order of work so that there is little or no "battling for the stage." An old tradition has the electrician work from the front of the stage back, and the carpenter from the back of the stage forward. Sometimes it is better to schedule a separate day or days for the electricians to work over the stage before the carpenter starts setting up. This saves time because the electrician can more easily move ladders and enjoy greater access to the pipes for hanging lights. Then when the carpenters get the stage the electrician can work in the house and around the sides of the stage.

Every show will dictate different schedules and order of work, and of course touring will require a lot more simultaneous effort because the show must be set up in one day, or one and a half days at the most. Make sure the heads of each department meet with you and schedule the work together. Otherwise, the first two days of load-in will feature endless harangues, usually directed at the stage manager, which all boil down to something like, "You tell that ------ to get off the stage this minute or . . . ."

Of course, the most carefully prepared plans can fly out the window if various elements of the set are not ready, trucks get delayed, or any other unforeseen circumstance occurs. On the *Sugar Babies* national tour we had set the order of work that would allow us to load-in and tech within the time scheduled. In Chicago, however, the second truck of four didn't show up, so we tried to keep working around what was needed from that truck until it showed up a day late. Apparently, the driver had driven straight through from Los Angeles to give himself an extra day to "celebrate." Unbeknownst to us, he had ended up at a nearby motel, and after partying on his extra day, slept through the day he was supposed to arrive.

Needless to say, we were hard pressed to make the first performance. Everyone's patience and tolerance was sorely tested by having to interrupt the established flow of the load-in to compensate for the missing parts. Diplomatic negotiations between warring crew heads finally got the show loaded-in and set up, but not before one of the carpenters had threatened the sound man with a hammer, and the electricians were forced to focus the show while the audience was coming in. This incident illustrates the importance of establishing an order or schedule of work, agreed upon by all departments, that is adhered to throughout the load-in.

It is very important for the stage manager to arrange to be at the load-in even while rehearsals are still progressing. It may seem like there is little or no actual work for the stage manager to perform, but the crew needs someone to answer questions and keep work moving along. The stage manager also provides an on-site managerial presence and can help mediate any disputes regarding overtime. It is also the stage manager's job to keep a close, quiet, supportive eye on the progress of the set going in. The stage manager should work with the production carpenter to make sure that the precious inches and feet that have been planned for in the design to make the show function smoothly are not lost to a worker's decision to cheat a set piece forward a bit or hang a drop on another line. Conversely, sometimes you can make the crew's life easier by telling them they don't have to struggle to get some piece placed exactly where it is on the ground plan because fudging a few inches won't affect the staging. However, don't forget to check any change at this point with the lighting designer who has planned angles and lighting coverage by the original ground plan.

On tour this process speeds up, of course, and the need for adapting and changing is constant, so the stage manager *has* to be present. Also on tour, the stage manager usually lights the show and is therefore highly instrumental in the laying out of every load-in.

If rehearsals are continuing during the load-in, plan well in advance for your absence. Notify the director and other company members when you will be gone. Set up a contact schedule so that you and your assistant are in frequent communication. Sometimes it is possible to split time between the rehearsals and the load-in, being in each place when it is most important. Of course, this is impossible if the show is loading in another city and the company is still rehearsing in New York. However, as long as everyone is clear about what is happening, they will help you make it work.

Creating the Callboard

As the crew's work on the load-in progresses, take some time to organize and set up the callboard. The callboard should be as close as possible to the stage door or whatever other theater entrance the cast and crew uses. The stage manager should establish from the outset that the callboard is for schedules, the sign-in sheet, and other official company business only. It is not for restaurant notices, cabaret ads, or flyers from vocal coaches and acupuncturists. Try to establish a second board somewhere (perhaps in the greenroom, the room where actors rest and relax before, between, or after performances) for notices like the above, and keep the company callboard strictly for the business of the show.

A neat and organized callboard is a reflection of the stage manager's approach to the cast and crew, and it also keeps the necessary information clear and available, not covered up by a lot of trash. Place a nice sign on the board that asks that anyone who desires to post a notice should see the stage manager.

It is good to have the sign-in sheet and schedule always in the same place, as well as a place where any important notes or news will be posted. This can be achieved by sectioning off three areas of the board with black electrician's tape. At the top of each section write one of the following headings: "SIGN IN, PLEASE," "SCHEDULE," and "NOTES/NEWS, ETC." Date everything you put on the board, so people will know quickly if there are any changes or new information they need to check. Just this simple amount of callboard organization will enormously improve day-to-day communication and company clarity about what is going on throughout a production's run.

Assigning Dressing Rooms

While the crew is busy with the load-in, the stage manager can also use some of the time to finalize the dressing room assignments and make signs for the doors. Dressing room assignments should be posted on the callboard, and copies should be sent to the wardrobe department, doorman, house manager, prop man, and the office. Always check what contractual arrangements have been negotiated for each cast member in regard to dressing rooms. Sometimes actors have "first choice" or "nearest to the stage" clauses in their contracts. Sometimes they negotiate to have their own dressing room if possible.

Take all these factors into account, then work with the wardrobe and wig departments to get them intelligently situated. The object is to make the cast as comfortable and functional as possible. Try to keep people with a lot of changes and different scenes in dressing rooms closer to the stage, letting people with only one or two scenes travel further. Keep people with wigs closer to the hair room. Attempt to make "happy" assignments, keeping people who cannot and will not get along out of the same room. It is a delicate process and one that takes a lot of thought and diplomacy. Remember that contractual obligations and production necessities, as described, are the priority. Then if you're questioned about the assignments by disgruntled company members, you can offer firm reasons for the choices you made. Only deal with special favors secondarily.

Don't forget to find a place for the stage managers. There will be many people sharing this space as home base; the company manager, crew, hair and wardrobe personnel, and all your assistants, not to mention the director and designers and their assistants during the tech and preview periods. Furthermore, you will spend far more time in the theater over the course of the show's run than any actors, so don't feel bad about taking an adequately large room, even if it means doubling a couple of actors who would rather be alone. Unless they have negotiated such requirements into their contracts, your needs come first.

Don't think these assignments can be made easily and that everyone will be happy. No theater has ever been designed that will accommodate everyone perfectly; just do the best you can with the clear knowledge that everything was done with contractual and performance priorities in mind. If anyone wants to complain, explain that you understand their problem but due to certain show or contract necessities, you had no choice. You can suggest that if they want to complain further they should do so to their agents for not negotiating them a better deal, or to the management. The management can, of course, tell you to change someone's assignment, but hopefully they will have already approved and understood your choices and will continue to back you. There is usually nothing to be gained by being defensive or mean about any of this, just remain firm and clear and understanding. However, don't be so rigid as to dismiss an offered solution that won't make anyone more upset than they already are.

One actor in the 1989–90 Broadway production of *The Merchant of Venice* drove everyone nuts, becoming the perfect example of why it is often hard to get management or crew to help make actors more comfortable. (Their point of view is that actors don't appreciate anything anyway, so why bother.) This actor had to have his own dressing room, but there were limited single rooms available in the theater and, as with most Shakespeare productions, a large cast to accommodate. The first time he came to the theater, we took a tour of all the possibilities and showed him various options, explaining the drawbacks of each room, giving him the choice and promising to do whatever he requested to make his selection work for him. After he settled on a dressing room, which was usually a room for two or three people, the crew went about remodeling: it was painted, carpeted, fit out with shelves and furniture, and so on. Then, after a day in the room, he decided he would rather move a flight upstairs, which he had originally turned down and which by then had been fixed up, wired, and powered for the wig room. After much argument and misrepresentation of who had agreed to what, he was allowed to make the move. The hair department had to have electrical service run to their new room, and had to move all their appliances and other possessions.

Of course, after that debacle, any actor requesting anything in terms of dressing room amenities was greeted with understandable negativity from crew and management. This actor had gotten his way at the expense of that entire cast and probably many to follow. Dustin Hoffman, on the other hand, was busy trying to make everyone as comfortable as possible. On his own he supplied the cast with refrigerators for their rooms, cots, and radio/tape players.

As the load-in progresses, and after the dressing rooms have been assigned, the stage manager should spend more and more time on the stage as well as in the wings, so that he or she becomes a familiar figure to the crew and begins to feel at home before the onslaught of technical rehearsals and the arrival of the actors. Once the designer begins to focus the lights and the cues are being set the stage manager should be permanently on the deck or in the house, helping the lighting designer by showing him blocking, checking the furniture placement for focusing, getting scenery moved as needed, and handling any communication system problems. The stage manager should also watch and learn the light focus, because once the show opens, it will be the stage manager's responsibility to make sure it is maintained as the designer first set it.

Cue Sheets

Cue sheets are detailed lists that indicate what each person in each department will do backstage during the running of a show. Every cue sheet should describe the move involved, the approximate time it happens in the show, and the type of cue you will be giving them—whether verbal (on headset), visual (by cue light), or whatever (frantic hand signal)—and how fast or slow the cue is to be performed.

To make a cue sheet, divide a piece of paper into three columns: the left-hand column lists the type of cue, its number, and when it happens in the show; the second column indicates what the cue does; the last column denotes the speed or level at which the cue occurs. For example, one member of the running crew could get a cue sheet with the first row reading "END OF OVERTURE: FLY Q 1/RED LIGHT OFF" in the first column, "GATES FLY IN" in the second, and "ON A FIVE COUNT" in the third. This means that the flyman responsible for lowering a castle's gates onto the stage will execute his or her first cue—flying the gates in—on a count of five at the end of the orchestra's overture, once the red cue light is turned off. Make the columns and boxes large enough so that the crew members can write in their own notes.

Before the first technical rehearsal make two copies of all the cue sheets, keeping the originals for yourself. One copy should be distributed to every person who will be taking cues directly from the stage manager, and copies of all cue sheets to be executed by each department should go to that department's head.

The three department heads that should get copies of their area's cue sheets and the personnel to whom you give individual copies are (1) the production carpenter and all of his or her winch operators and flymen who are responsible for moving and flying scenery, and/or moving curtains or travelers; (2) the production electrician and any of his or her sound and special effects operators; and (3) the production property master and any of his or her crew that must move a specific prop, fire a gunshot, or adjust props in any way.

The sound designer often provides his or her own cue sheets. If the sound operator will be listening for cues on the headset, make sure all the cues on the sound designer's cue sheets are designated by letters, instead of numbers. This system will help the sound and light operators distinguish their aural cues during a performance. In some stock and community theaters, when sound designers aren't necessarily a permanent part of the staff, the stage manager must write up sound cue sheets as well and give them to the crew member running the sound. Sometimes, the stage manager may even have to execute the sound effects—

ringing doorbells, telephones, sirens, and so on—from his or her own console or desk.

Today, with the easy accessibility of word processors and computers, constant corrections aren't as much of a problem. If you set up the basic form for each department's cue sheet in a computer file or word processing document, you can quickly and clearly update changes every day. However, if no computer is available, it is best to print all cues with plenty of room for changes to be written in during tech week by you and the crew. Then, when the cues are set, a new clean version of the cue sheets can be made. Appendix 7 has some sample cue sheets.

In the best of all possible worlds, all cues—except for those given to the light board operator—should be non-verbal, i.e., by turning off a cue light. Confusion could result if a stage manager called "Q 1 . . . Go" during a performance, and three different people moved into action when only one was supposed to. Limiting verbal cues to the light board operator (and perhaps the sound operator) will make the running of a show smoother. An example of how to set up a cue-light board, write out the appropriate cue sheets, and then transcribe the cues into a script may be found in Appendix 10.

The Cueing Script

As discussed in the rehearsal section, it is a good idea to keep two scripts: a cueing/running script, in which all the cues necessary to call the show are written; and the blocking/rehearsal script, which contains all acting, staging, and interpretative notes. This allows your assistant to have the blocking script in rehearsal as you work on the cueing script. Try to pre-write as much of the cueing script as possible before the technical rehearsals begin.

Several different types of cues must be included in the running script: light cues, sound cues, actor warnings and cues for entrances, and all the cues from the cue sheets. The most abundant usually are the light cues. Meet with the lighting designer and he or she will tell you where the light cues are to be placed in the script. Number each cue consecutively from the beginning of the play to the end. The most common shorthand for writing a lighting cue is "LQ" followed by the number. For example, the third lighting cue of a play may be a scene ending blackout; it would be written "LQ3." If a new cue is added between LQ2 and LQ3, number it LQ2.5. An example of this appears later, in Figure 5.2, where you'll notice the first lighting cue for *Speed-the-Plow* is numbered LQ.7.

When entering the lighting designer's cues in the script, pay particular attention to the sequencing of the production's opening. The stage manager and the lighting designer must carefully coordinate the extinguishing of the house lights and presets. As the designer and stage manager go over the cues prior to a technical rehearsal, their relationship is at its most collaborative. They are basically trying to set the rhythm and appearance of the lights—before the director and actors arrive—in an effort to stay ahead of schedule, anticipating how the director will want the lights to look.

The next step in preparing the book is to go to the sound designer and get their cue sheets, as mentioned above, and transcribe them into the running script, numbering them by letter. Next, get your cue sheets, copies of which you have handed out to the sound, special effects, winch, wagon, and fly operators, and make sure you have all these same cues in their correct places in the running script.

Check that you have written warnings—whether verbal warns to the light board operator or the visual warning of turning on the appropriate cue light—for each cue in the script, allowing plenty of time between the warning and the cue's point of execution. Always begin by giving warnings far in advance and then shorten them as the show begins to get finalized.

Everything written in the running script should be in pencil! Nothing changes faster than cues, and the only way to keep up is with a good eraser and a lot of sharp pencils. I always keep a large supply of unlined three-hole paper handy so I can write out cueing sections on pages separate from the script and then insert them facing the page with the appropriate dialogue. A sample page from my cueing script would then look something like Figure 5–1.

Once the technical cues are all written, go back through the script and make sure that all warnings for actors to take their places are written in. Include a note indicating who is to check each actor. Always at the start of an act, list everyone who has to be ready, in every position, and check them visually or by communicating with an assistant on the headset. The opening page of a show's cueing script might look something like Figure 5–2.

Figure 5-1 Sample Pages from Final Cueing Script

And fair she is, if that mine eyes be true;

And true she is, as she hath proved herself;   55

And therefore like herself, wise, fair, and true,

Shall she be placèd in my constant soul.

Enter Jessica below

What, art thou come? On, gentlemen, away.

Our masquing mates by this time for us stay.

Exit with Jessica and Salerio

Enter Antonio

ANTONIO

Who's there?

GRAZIANO   Signor Antonio?   60

ANTONIO

Fie, fie, Graziano, where are all the rest?

'Tis nine o'clock. Our friends all stay for you.

No masque tonight. The wind is come about.

Bassanio presently will go aboard.

I have sent twenty out to seek for you   65

GRAZIANO

I am glad on't. I desire no more delight

Than to be under sail and gone tonight.   *Exeunt*

[Flourish of cornetts.] Enter Portia with Morocco and   2.7

both their trains

PORTIA

Go, draw aside the curtains and discover

The several caskets to this noble prince:

The curtains are drawn aside, revealing three caskets

(*To Morocco*) Now make your choice.

MOROCCO

This first of gold, who this inscription bears:

'Who chooseth me shall gain what many men desire.'   5

```
┌─────────────────────────────────────────────────────────┐
│                                                         │
```

SPEED-THE-PLOW   June 1989
Kennedy Center

Opening Sequence

As audience enters, the stage is open with the first act set draped in drop cloths. (See preset diagrams)

AT THE PLACES CALL:
    1. Actor playing Gould SR with one red script
    2. Actor playing Fox SL with Filo Fax
    3. 2 prop men SR, 2 prop men SL
    4. All worklights and running lights out
    5. Electrician ready for board and houselights
    6. Monitors on (Show program and TV)

ALL READY: HOUSE TO HALF

House at Half: HOUSE OUT
LQ.7

IN BLACKOUT, PROP MEN STRIKE THE COVERS FROM THE DESK SR AND THE COFFEE TABLE SL, AND GOULD SITS AT DESK

Gould sits: LQ 1

Figure 5-2   Sample Opening Page From Cueing Script

As you can see, there is a lot to check before starting the opening sequence: every crew member and performer's presence, as well as the position of key prop and set pieces. There is nothing worse than taking house lights down to half and then having to bring them back up because you realize you have to wait for an actor or crew person to show up. If the script is prepared to this extent, the tech will go much faster and smoother. Do not ever try to start a tech and write cues as you go.

Scheduling Technical Rehearsals

By the time the stage manager has spent a load-in period with a crew and seen all the pieces and elements in person, a meeting can be held to draw up a realistic tech-week schedule, based on what is achievable each day. Some directors will avoid this like the plague, desperately afraid that they will either be pushed to keep on a schedule that is too fast, or that if they get ahead they will have nothing to do. The director needs gentle guidance through this period, and the stage manager can be a great ally by showing the director clearly what needs to be achieved on a daily basis in order to make the first public performance with as many run-throughs and dress rehearsals as possible.

The schedule at this point should be realistic and inclusive, so that every department will know exactly when their deadlines are. There may be rehearsals with partial costumes, rehearsals with full costume and makeup, and so on. All such rehearsals must be carefully thought out and clearly planned. If the director thinks actors are going to be in costume, but the wardrobe people have taken costumes to be fixed or altered, you will have a problem. If the director wants to concentrate on acting, but the designers are all over the stage trying to look at lights and different sets, friction can mount. As the stage manager, be sure to double-check that you and the director are clear about each step, then clearly outline and schedule those wishes and expectations for the cast, crew, and designers. The tech-week schedule that is included in Appendix 9 should give some idea of the complexities involved in its creation; it also makes clear the necessary information the schedule must contain.

In the professional commercial theater there are three basic unions whose overtime and break requirements have to be factored into the creation of a schedule: Actors' Equity Association (actors and stage managers), American Federation of Musicians (orchestra members on a musical), and IATSE (the stage hands). In Appendix 11, I have included AEA's work rules concerning rehearsal hours during a technical rehearsal. All the performing unions have different work rules for the periods before and after the opening or first paid public performance of a show. Basically, these rules outline the hours that can be worked without incurring overtime, both on a daily and weekly basis, and they are wildly divergent from one union to another. Of course, in a college or community theater production, the only restrictions are the time and energy of the show's participants.

During technical rehearsals, Actors' Equity Association members are allowed to work a seventy-hour week before going into overtime, as long as they only work ten out of twelve consecutive hours in a day and are given an hour-and-a-half break at the end of five hours. The stage hands, however, enter overtime scale after forty hours in a week and eight hours in a day, so they do very well in the tech week (or weeks) in which they work the same hours as the actors mounting the show. A careful perusal of the sections of the rule books in the appendix will give the reader an appreciation of the complexity of trying to mount a show under union contracts. This is further complicated when touring, because every city has different rules, and a schedule that was fast, cheap, and efficient in one city may be financially ruinous in the next.

I always try to keep working in five-hour chunks, so if the crew has been working in the morning, I schedule their hour break while the actors are getting costumes and makeup or having notes. This can often make a half-hour of otherwise wasted time productive. Similarly, at the end of the afternoon, the crew will have a half-hour of time without the actors to fix, correct, or run things. Better yet, if all is well, they will have an extra half-hour to rest.

Breaks are the hardest element to keep unified during tech week, especially because the unions have varying requirements. If you can remember to give the orchestra an official five-minute break whenever you know the technical department is going to take at least that long to reset or fix something, then the ten-minute break every one and a half hours required for actors should take care of the crew's union requirements as well. Why the musicians' union believes their members' bladders cannot stand up to the same time limitations as an actor's is a mystery, but one you have to deal with or have your rehearsal suddenly interrupted, so always give them five when you can.

Technical Rehearsals

Technical rehearsals are the rehearsals during which the physical production and the actors mesh, and the full show is realized. Often, before actors get on the stage, the crew and stage managers try to "dry tech" as much of the show as possible, setting basic light and sound cues, and getting the scenery and drops moving in the right way. There is more about this subject later in the chapter.

By far the hardest thing about a tech is getting it started. Everyone seems to have last-minute problems. I have found that calling out the time before the tech rehearsal is to start—at half-hour, fifteen minutes, and five minutes before—greatly enhances everyone's belief that the tech will indeed begin. Sometimes, the director will want to address everyone first, and if so, it is a good time to introduce the crew to the cast, something that cannot be done enough in the first few days. The stage manager and assistants, as the liaisons between the actors and crew, should introduce the production's personnel whenever they can. It is important to try to break down the barriers as fast as possible between company members who will work incredibly hard together, under a lot of pressure, in very close quarters, and in the end, will have to depend on each other completely for success.

Dry Techs

In the best of all possible worlds, you will have some time scheduled for a dry tech. This is a purely technical rehearsal that gives the stage managers and the crew a chance to work out scene changes, the movement of set pieces, and light sequences. In the commercial theater, producers rarely want to pay for this extra rehearsal, so you should try to practice some of the more complex scenic moves and changes as soon as everything is loaded-in and set up.

On large, complicated shows it is essential that you run some of the fly and deck moves with the crew members before adding the actors, especially with the complex computer-controlled moves that must be programmed in advance. However, even the simplest show will benefit enormously from a dry tech. It gives the crew and the stage managers a chance to iron out any glitches before the actors and director are running around going crazy.

The First Tech

Armed with schedules, cue sheets, and a cueing script, the stage manager now takes on the challenge of finally pulling it all together. You and your assistants should arrive early and be ready on the first days in the theater to serve as "tour guides," helping the cast find their dressing rooms, the wardrobe and wig rooms, and their quick-change and crossover areas if they need them.

One assistant should be responsible for collecting valuables from dressing rooms for safekeeping in the stage manager's desk. This service should be available and offered every time actors rehearse in the theater. The best tool to accomplish this is the "valuable bag." These can be strong zip-lock bags or fine mesh laundry bags made by the wardrobe department. Each actor should have a bag with their name on it in their dressing room every time they come into the theater. These are collected during the half-hour, or actors can bring them to the stage manager's desk themselves at "places." They are then returned after rehearsal or performance to their rooms, thus being ready for the next use or need.

Each assistant should also have a preliminary cue and checklist, detailing what actors they will be responsible for getting on and offstage, and what technical events and changes they will be checking or supervising. This list will grow rapidly as the technical rehearsals continue. By the opening preview, it should eventually resemble the wonderfully complete tracking description of ASM cues in Appendix 8, prepared by Charles Kindl, one of the best assistants I have ever worked with. You'll notice that he has even diagrammed a desk top so that every prop's position is clearly mapped.

Some shows, particularly those that are very simple technically, lend themselves to going "cue-to-cue," which means taking each cue or technical event and working it before going on to the next one. This means that often large sections of the show are skipped as everyone moves from one cue to another. However, it is my experience that trying to jump ahead by a page or several lines only wastes time as everyone tries to figure out where they are. Unless there is a five- or six-page section in which no new character, prop, set piece, or lighting cue is introduced, it is better to go straight through the play once. This will give everyone time to see the lights, set, costumes, and learn their entrances and exits.

If the show is one where the only real "tech" occurs during scene changes and at the beginning and end of each act, then it may be wise to go cue-to-cue. You can get every cue written and rehearsed once technically before letting the actors and director refocus on the performing as the lighting adjustments continue around them. In any case, be sure everyone knows in advance how you will be proceeding. When I stage managed *Death of a Salesman*, we had a cue-to-cue technical rehearsal for which I drew up an outline (see Appendix 9). The one I drew up for the show is a very good example of a schedule that should answer every department's questions about what is and isn't included in the tech. It also gives all the actors exact information on what lines and scenes will be run, so they don't have to guess whether they will be working through their scenes or skipping them. The schedule, approved by the director, should be given to everyone involved: cast, crew, designers, wardrobe, and stage management personnel, with a copy to the manager or producer's office.

Another problem with cue-to-cue techs is that crew members won't get a sense of how much time they have between cues. Other than starting a technical rehearsal, the most difficult part of techs is persuading the director to let the crew run sections of a play all the way through so that they will get a clear idea of how fast their cues come. Often each element of a sequence is run and discussed and fixed and then, due to time pressure, the director will insist on moving on to the next cue. Therefore, the crew ends up with a bunch of cues written but no idea if they can execute them in "real time." Then along comes the dress rehearsal or first preview, and everyone's timing is way off. The stage manager must use good judgment and rely on the crew to tell him or her when it is and isn't necessary to rerun a section. If it is necessary to repeat a cue, the stage manager must insist on it even if it means temporarily incurring the wrath of the director. It is better than having a fiasco or a dangerous situation occur later, perhaps during a performance.

An example of this problem occurred during the techs of *Accomplice*. There was an electrocution sequence near the end of the play with many elements—sound, light, trap doors opening, smoke, and explosions. This cue was run endlessly to try and perfect its execution. After we ran the sequence, there would always be endless discussion about how to perfect it, and then we would have to skip through to the end of the play. Therefore, no one on the crew ever realized how little time there was between the explosions and the final curtain and sound and light sequences. Sure enough, at the first preview, which was the first time we were ever allowed to go through to the end of the play without being stopped, I cued the final curtain and it didn't come in. I figured it was not going to come in at all, and I started the curtain call music and lights. All of a sudden the curtain flew in, trapping one actor in front of it and the rest of the cast in back.

The problem was that the curtain men never realized that the time between the explosion and the final curtain was so short, and they were only on their way to their position when the cue was given. So they untied and brought the curtain in as fast as possible, but by then I had gone on without them. All this could have been avoided by my insisting the ending be run just once all the way through, from the beginning of the effects sequence through the curtain calls. But in the heat of trying to perfect the cues in the complex special effects section, I had mistakenly decided the final cues were routine and didn't need the same time and work.

Communications Systems and Cueing

Before starting the tech, the stage manager should be sure the communications and cueing systems are functioning perfectly. At the stage manager's desk or console should be a headset/microphone attachment that can talk selectively to every position where cues take place and to every position from which there may be an entrance or exit of actors or scenery.

The current "state-of-the-art" unit is a Clear-Com system that allows up to five channels to be separately or collectively programmed to talk and/or listen to the stage manager. This means that the stage manager can assign one channel to lights, another to the fly floor, another to winches, another to ASMs, and one to the designers and director at the "tech table" in the house. All those stations can hear the stage manager without hearing each other, so if the lighting designer is using one channel to set cues with the light board operator, no one but the stage manager will be able to hear. However, everyone will hear everything the stage manager says unless the stage manager turns them off at the console. This system allows the director to talk to crew members or the stage manager privately and without shouting.

Cue Lights

Because the stage manager must remain at the desk in order to cue the lights and sound effects through the headset, a second mode of cueing has developed. Basically, a cue light is a dark colored light bulb of low wattage that is turned on by a switch at the stage manager's console, serving as a warning to the crew or to a performer that a move or entrance is about to happen. When the stage manager turns off the cue light, the crew person or performer executes the cue. Stated as a mathematical equation, the concept of the cue light is: ON = WARN; OFF = GO. In the case of the fly floor, it is often necessary to have several different colored bulbs, so that several drops or pieces can simultaneously be warned to move, but then cued to move separately a few beats or words apart.

Cue lights are used at all operator positions and entrances and exits; basically, once the show is set, all cues other than lighting (and sometimes sound) cues are given by cue lights. This avoids confusion because the electrician or light board operator will know all verbal cues he hears are for lights and does not have to distinguish all night the light cues from the set cues, and so forth. Cue lights should always have two bulbs at the cueing position, so if one burns out the other is still lit. I've included some cue sheets and examples of the way the cues are written in the stage manager's book in Appendix 10.

At the desk or console, the stage manager should have a cue-light panel with each switch carefully defined and marked. When the light is switched on, an indicator light should light up on that switch. The "name" of each cue light should be the same as the name in the cueing script.

Often actors will tell you they don't want a cue light or don't need one. But the lights are especially necessary if actors cannot see what is happening onstage just before they open a door, or if they can't hear their cue line clearly in the wings. The cue light serves as a safety against their walking in and seeing a piece of action they aren't supposed to see or overhearing dialogue or facts they should only discover later.

The Stage Manager's Console

In addition to the cue-light panel, the stage manager's console should be equipped with two microphones, one to talk to the dressing rooms and one to talk into the stage and house speaker system. During techs, it is important to make all announcements (half-hour calls, breaks, places) on both mikes. The house speaker system is also useful to tell everyone when the tech is ready to resume and what cue line to start from. It is also vital in emergencies, both before and after the show is running. This mike also becomes the "audience announce" microphone—sometimes a stage manager will be required to remind audiences that smoking and the taking of flash photographs is prohibited. The dressing room or paging mike allows the stage manager to call and make announcements to the cast and backstage crew before and during the tech or performance.

It is important that the stage manager be able to turn up the volume of the paging system to the dressing rooms if there is an emergency or an important announcement that will have to cut through the backstage and dressing room din. It is equally important to remember to turn off the show monitor in the dressing rooms when there is no rehearsal or performance in progress. Especially during technical rehearsals, this allows conversations to take place onstage or in the front rows of the audience that are not broadcast to the whole building and prevents any hammering or sawing occurring onstage to go pounding into the ears of everyone backstage.

The stage manager's desk may have to be equipped with sound and video monitors. This is necessary because often the position of the desk does not allow for an unobstructed view of the stage, and the stage manager often will not be able to hear the dialogue clearly enough "live" to call cues.

Calling Cues

There are very few exceptions to the way a stage manager calls cues in the theater. For every cue, a stage manager should give a warning, about thirty seconds in advance, and then a "stand-by" warning, one or two lines in advance. The cue itself is then called by giving the title or number of the cue a few words or beats ahead, before stating the word "GO," one beat in advance of the desired moment of execution. The beat allows the crew member to hear and respond, and it must be consistent and clear. This same beat must be built into the cueing of any production element on a cue light, because the operator or actor must register that the light has gone out before doing their cue.

After you have given a warning, a stand-by, or a cue number, avoid ever saying anything on a headset other than the cue itself. Once during the run of the Broadway musical *The Wiz*, we were having a technical rehearsal for the new actress who was taking over the role of Dorothy. Just as we were getting ready to do the tornado sequence that involved Aunt Em's house twirling across the stage, lightening and thunder, and the entrance of a chorus of dancers, all taken off the "GO" for the lights, a chorus girl asked me if she could be excused early and skip the curtain call. I emphatically responded "NO," and you can imagine what happened next as lights blacked out, sound cues started, and wagons rolled. It was a disaster. If only I had said yes!

During a tech rehearsal, the stage manager initially should verbally give warnings for a lot of the cues that will eventually be done by cue lights. This will ensure that everyone is doing the same cue and understands how and when to execute it. Once the cues have been practiced in techs, the cues can be warned by the cue light.

As the tech begins, the stage manager should make sure that chatter is kept to an absolute minimum on the headsets and that only cues and checks or questions are going back and forth. Make sure *everyone* is ready to perform a cue or sequence before you start it, because the wasted time and energy of running a cue over and over is a serious drain on everyone's nerves and energy. The most frequently used words by the stage manager during tech week are "Thank you" and "Quiet!"

Keep the actors aware of what is going on while setting up for a cue. A simple announcement stating, for example, that you are going back to a certain point to run the lights and sound again, and it will take a couple of minutes, so please relax, will gain much respect and good will. Then give the company a "stand-by" warning and then clearly and loudly request a line of dialogue as a starting point. Choose a line three or four lines before the cue and ask them to please take it from that line when they are ready. The tech continues this way through the end of the day.

Techs can be frustrating and tedious for a lot of people, especially the actors and crew members who are standing around doing nothing for large amounts of time while small technical adjustments are made. But for stage managers techs are the period of time when all their work and preparation pay off. The stage manager must always be alert, anticipating the next step, while clearly communicating to everyone exactly what is going on and who will be needed to do something next.

The tone of the stage manager begins to control the mood of a tech very quickly. Try to be clear and commanding without being officious, frazzled, or rude. It is also the time to employ full understanding of the great rule of theater taught me by my mentor Bob Currie, *"All things are not of equal importance."* Basically, this rule is a constant reminder that as every day in a theater progresses, priorities will emerge that the stage manager must keep straight, even as others maintain that their problem or need should be the number one priority. It is also a gentle reminder that we are not doing brain surgery or nuclear fission experiments but an adult version of "dress up." I print this rule in clear letters and hang it somewhere near the stage manager's console. Sometimes in the heat of trying to keep a tech flowing, with egos colliding and fatigue putting an edge to everyone's work, reflecting on this dictum may help you get through the moment.

Furthermore, the stage manager must fully accept that during the tech week he or she is perceived as being responsible for everything. Actors will complain about the food at a local restaurant as if it was you who ordered them to go there. Every schedule you post will anger at least half the people who read it, and they will think you are responsible for their early call. (It's never the designer who needs them for the fitting or the director who wants to go over a scene once more.) People will tell you to tell other company members things that you must use your common sense and ignore, as in,

"You tell that so-and-so that if he thinks I am coming in at ten to run her scene. . . ."

Think of techs as Tommy Tune describes them, as the chance to reenact our childhood fantasy of "putting on a show" in the garage or living room, and it will make it a lot more fun. Maintain a positive and pleasant tone and keep what you are doing in perspective. Once during a particularly trying technical rehearsal, Glynis Johns was raving on and on at the designer about the costumes and how the jelly madrilene bowls were wrong and how she couldn't be expected to perform a lady of class in this mess. I happened to look over at the headline of the paper, and it said, "Nuclear Disarmament Talks To Start Today." It put things in a healthier perspective.

Remember that all shows do eventually get off the ground. One mental exercise that has always helped me during techs and periods of stress has been to picture myself on the other side of the event happy and feeling that all has gone well, then looking back and seeing what steps it took to get me there. Somehow the journey to completion seems easier from that vantage point than from the beginning.

At every break, go over the tech's progress and priorities with the director and designers. Schedule discussions often occur as people are rushing out the door to dinner; be sure to be available and involved so that there are no surprises later on. Basically, anything is possible as long as there is time to plan and prepare for it. If there are to be any changes, try to update the schedules and get them posted as quickly as possible.

The stage management crew should try to meet and go over notes and problems every chance they get. The assistant stage managers are invaluable sources of information, and often they hear and see things during the course of a tech that can forestall or eliminate problems before they occur: actors not getting along with their dressers, or safety problems that can be fixed with a little additional glow tape or foam padding on a sharp corner. Sometimes, the assistants can give a more realistic appraisal of whether or not a certain costume or set change will get faster or smoother or if additional help is needed. All their input should be discussed and then the stage manager must decide which problems can be dealt with and which ones must be taken to a higher court for a decision.

The running of technical rehearsals is a totally absorbing time for the stage manager. Sometimes, even though I live in New York, I find it better to check into a hotel to block out the demands of family and regular life. In that way I can better focus on the job at hand. No one in the normal world can conceive of how much we achieve in a short period of time by the combination of fierce concentration, creative energy, and a large dose of pre-planning by the stage manager. Keep communication with all departments and creative personnel fluid and constant. Keep an eye on priorities and the clock. And the show will go on. It always does.

6

Previews and Opening Night

O nce you have guided your show through all the technical and dress rehearsals, it is time to add that unknown element—the audience. The first preview or public performance often creeps up suddenly. This is especially true when you've had a dress rehearsal or final tech that afternoon—it is always a shock to come back from dinner and find the house full of strangers.

The stage managers must be a firm and supportive part of the transition between private and public performances because everyone else's nerves will be on edge, and the more the stage managers can treat the event as business as usual, the better. Try to complete all checks and preparations early so you can be ready to deal with last-minute needs of others—a forgotten makeup kit, first-aid needs, wardrobe or prop problems, and a hundred other unforeseen possibilities. The stage manager should try to quell any frenzy produced by actors as they confront what seems to them an insurmountable problem with a calm statement like "Don't worry, we'll take care of it; you just worry about getting ready for the show."

Opening the House

The first preview is also the time to solidify with the house manager the plan for opening the house (allowing the audience into the theater), starting the show, and late seating. Well before the first performance it is a good idea to approach the director and discuss the late seating policy so you can clearly translate the information to the house manager. As the stage manager, try to initiate this discussion by telling them what time you will start the show unless they tell you differently. That solves a lot of guesswork on both sides and gives them the responsibility of getting the audience seated and ready.

If you have a curtain, the best way to signal that you are ready for the house to be opened is to close the curtain. Otherwise, show them the preset (the "pretty lights" as I like to call them) and tell them that as soon as they see those lights up instead of the work lights, they may open the house at their leisure. Then make very sure the electrician knows never to turn the preset on until you call for it.

Late Seating

Seating ticket buyers after a show has started is one policy that often raises animosity between the house management staff and the production personnel. The ushers and house manager are faced with a horde of angry, obnoxious people (only angry, obnoxious people arrive late for the theater), and the staff wants to get them seated as soon as possible. On the other hand, you and the director are trying to protect the rights of the people who have arrived on time. Early in a play, important dialogue must be clearly established and the mood of the evening set. This is made difficult when an audience's suspension of disbelief is suddenly interrupted by the arrival of late-arriving theatergoers led into the theater by flashlight-swinging usherettes.

Everyone tries to find a place where the action is pedestrian—a scene shift or a long procession—but invariably the interruption overlaps into the next scene, and actors get distracted and upset. Try to be the instrument of the policy; let the producer and director argue the concept of timing with the house manager. Stage managers should only have to work out a way to give a clear cue warning the ushers and house manager that the seating interval is imminent. Then go over very clearly what they must see or hear before they start the people down the aisle.

Because there is no controlled late seating after the intermission, it is important to make sure that the audience is back in before starting. Otherwise the first scene or number in the second act may be ruined. At the first preview of *Orpheus Descending,* Sir Peter Hall became so distraught at the way in which the returning hordes of people were destroying the opening moments of Act Two that he shouted from the back of the house, "SIT DOWN!" at which point Tammy Grimes, who was on stage at the time, promptly sat on the stage floor. The best way to handle latecomers after intermission is to make sure that at least the front of the orchestra section is filled.

Musicals often afford the stage managers the luxury of an overture and an entr'acte which greatly alleviates the problem of late seating. Nothing moves audience members to their seats (or actors to places, by the way) faster than the orchestra starting.

The First Preview

The first preview is often a technical nightmare for the stage manager because all those cues that were set without audience reactions now must be executed in and around laughter and applause. Furthermore, the audience responses occur in totally unexpected places.

When the musical *A Day in Hollywood/A Night in the Ukraine* had its last out-of-town tryout, the staid old Baltimore subscribers gave it hardly a chuckle. Certain songs were met with no applause or response at the end. The audience reception was so bad that the producer reportedly was trying to sell the show to the highest bidder before it got to New York, but there were no takers.

Lead by the charismatic and inspirational tone that Tommy Tune creates when he works, the cast stepped onto the stage of the Golden Theater on Broadway undaunted, believing in themselves and the show. The first night of previews the house came down— there were ovations after the musical numbers and show-stopping laughter throughout the second act, which was a Marx Brothers movie put to music. Of course, all the cues had been timed for the type of response we received in Baltimore. During that first performance in New York there were times when at the end of a number the lights would cross-fade into the next cue, while the actors waited in near darkness for the applause to subside. Some numbers ended in poses that became physically difficult to maintain, because the cast had never had to hold them for any length of time in Baltimore. That first night in New York, a couple of performers either fell over or lost their balance trying to remain still long enough for the applause to ebb. It was a thrilling, surprising night. The show became a big hit and ran for two years.

Often, the performers themselves will throw a lot of curves at the stage manager during the first performance in front of an audience. Actors have a tendency to either speed up or go slower, and speak louder or softer than they had in rehearsals. This can wreak havoc with the timing of your cueing between warnings and "GOs," but usually it seems worse to the stage manager than to the audience.

The crew may also have trouble hearing cues because of laughter and applause and may consequently miss cues. The stage manager must be especially alert the first performance and check everything and everybody more than at any other time.

During the preview period, a show is often still rehearsing and making changes. The stage managers are the central clearing house of information, ascertaining what the desired changes are, advising the director on how much time will be needed to achieve the changes, and then scheduling the work and rehearsals to implement these changes. At the same time, the stage managers must protect the company's ability to do a clean and safe show for the public, and there is a delicate balance between the pressure and desire to look at fixes and changes and the cast and crew's ability to perform them.

I always try to explain that it is sometimes better to wait one more day before inserting revised material or a new effect than to rush it into the show and see the result half realized. Often the creators don't care, and the result is that the show is really doing rehearsal work in front of an audience, a practice that often generates the dreaded bad word of mouth that can sink a show. Mainly, the stage manager must remember he or she is in a service position at this time. Try to give the creators, who may be embroiled in a fight for their professional lives, as much support as is humanly possible.

I have had no better experience of this creative process than on *A Day in Hollywood/A Night in Ukraine*, thanks to director Tommy Tune's ability to understand the show's problems, and work them out, while sharing his creative impulses with everyone involved. Although the show had developed well in rehearsal, major changes were clearly called for. However, because the opening in Baltimore was so close, it was decided to freeze the show until after the first performance so the company could get through technical rehearsals without simultaneously dealing with new material. After the opening weekend, the schedule called for two full days and nights off and the day off before that evening's performance. All changes would be implemented during this period.

For two days the whole creative staff gathered in Tommy's hotel room and slowly worked through the show making revisions. Each time there was a change, we would collectively go back through the show with the musical director, singing through the music, while I called the cues. We discovered where there were problems, and where new music or dialogue or scenic or lighting cues had to be created. The writers then were called in and given their assignments, and slowly over the two days a new first act emerged.

The ensuing rehearsals to implement the changes were exciting and fruitful, because everyone had shared the experience of creating the new material and nothing was being tried that was impossible or irrational. As I said, this kind of experience is a rare one in the theater; I have never been so closely involved in the evolution of a successful show. Stage managers are often looked upon as mere minions who execute the dictums of the creative people. However, while working with Tommy Tune I could feel and see my own input having a direct effect on the total outcome, and that is a thrill like no other in theater.

Opening Night

Opening night is similar to the first performance of a preview period, except that the show has hopefully become a little more routine. Stage managers should arrive long before curtain time on opening night to handle any last-minute emergencies and also to help deal with flowers and telegrams. At the opening of *Sugar*

Babies, we discovered early in the afternoon that if we didn't do something with Ann Miller's flowers, the halls would become impassable, and we would be unable to do the show. We had to order a van to come and cart the flowers back to where she was staying.

The advent of computer-operated light boards has done much to add to the sophistication and art of stage lighting, but in my experience they have seemed as jittery as any human performer on an opening night. On the opening nights of both *A Day in Hollywood/A Night in the Ukraine* and *Sugar Babies* there were problems with the light board. On *Hollywood/Ukraine* everything was calm—everyone expected the best after the tumultuous response during previews—and while there was excitement backstage, there was no panic. The audience was arriving, and I made one last check of the stage before calling the actors to places. As I stepped on stage, every light in the theater suddenly came up to its fullest reading. I thought maybe the electrician was playing a trick on me or maybe making one last full check of his lights before returning to the preset. Basically, I didn't really think anything of it until I walked off the stage and into the alley outside the stage door and saw the electrician standing there. "How come all the lights are full?" I asked. "[Expletives deleted]," he replied and ran back into the theater. After a few worrisome minutes, he brought all the lights down manually, reprogrammed the board with a second computer disc, the proper preset came up, and the show ran smoothly. We guessed that there may have been a surge on the power lines that affected the light board's sensitive computer controls. Perhaps the reason for the surge was that our early opening night starting time coincided with the approximate time that the other Broadway theater electricians came in and turned on their power. Since then, surge regulators have been developed to prevent such an occurrence.

On *Sugar Babies,* the reverse happened. About half-way through the show, Mickey Rooney was doing a long monologue in a spotlight with very dim blue light washing the remainder of the stage. I was enjoying Mickey's routine and the audience response when I noticed the blue lights very slowly fading out. Since we had no cues for about five minutes during this monologue, the electrician was off headset relaxing. I flashed him by flicking his cue light on and off. (Even though the light cues are given verbally, it is a good idea to have a cue light run into the light booth in case the headset system goes dead or an emergency like this one occurs.) He got on the headset, and I asked him if there was a reason that all the stage lights had just gone out. For a second he thought I was joking, then he realized it was absolutely true. After considering various options, he decided that the only possibility was to turn off the board, turn it back on and re-program it with a fresh disc, then punch in the cue that was supposed to be up and see what happened. By now there were a lot of people on the headset asking where the pretty blue lights had gone. We all held our breaths and, as if he was an astronaut and we were in Houston control, the electrician talked us through each step: "I am now turning off the board, removing the old disc, putting in the new disc, turning on the board, calling up the cue. . . ." His litany progressed, and we all watched the blue lights as they came back to a nice low glow. I'm sure the collective sigh of relief made the audience think the air conditioning had come on. Fortunately, the show continued without a hitch. No one ever really knew why it happened, just that it did. The board may have had a power surge or drop. Luckily, the new line voltage regulators seem to have stopped these problems from happening.

Backstage Superstitions

Opening nights intensify many of the superstitions and traditions that most theater cast and crew members believe very strongly. Among the more universal are:

1. Never wish an actor or singer "good luck." Instead, the accepted backstage version of good wishes is "Break a leg." Singers use the expression *"voco lupe"* (Italian for "voice of the wolf") to wish good luck to each other. French perform-ers offer each other the expletive *"merde,"* politely trans-lated as "crap."
2. Never whistle backstage or in dressing rooms. This has a very practical origin: cues for the fly floor used to be given by whistles, so an inadvertent whistle could result in scenery falling on someone's head.
3. Never mention the character or play *Macbeth* in the theater.
4. Never say the last line of a play except during performance.

7

Maintaining and Running a Show

After opening night, there is an exodus of the creative personnel. The director and designers move on to their next project, and when the dust settles, it is the stage manager who is responsible for maintaining the artistic quality of the show.

Obviously, in a community or university theater situation where the show only runs a weekend or two, the stage manager's responsibility for maintaining the show's quality will be slight compared to a run of several weeks in a regional theater or a commercial run or tour that may last months or years. Here are some steps that are taken as a matter of course when settling in for a long run; they will be valuable to understand and follow to whatever extent they are applicable to your particular situation.

Training Stage Managers

As soon as possible after opening night, all assistant stage managers should learn to call the show and run each other's deck cues. This means the stage-right assistant should learn what the stage-left assistant does, and all assistants should be trained by the stage manager to call cues for the show. The PSM should know everyone's position and then be free to go out front and watch a performance. As soon as it's practical, every assistant stage manager should watch the show from the front, especially before calling the show so that he or she has a concept of what happens when a cue is called.

Training an assistant stage manager to call a show progresses at a different pace with everyone. There are several steps involved, and depending on the complexity of the show, they will take varying amounts of time. First, the person learning the show should see it from the front, so he or she will understand each cue better as it is taught. I like to go over the cueing and how all the cues are written and what all my symbols mean before having someone watch with me as I call the show. This is best done at the desk or console, so they become familiar with the cue-light positions, the TV monitors, the paging system, and so on.

During the show, I try to talk through each sequence before it is run, then execute it while the assistant watches, and answer any follow-up questions. It is often very helpful to make an audio-cassette at the desk with the show's dialogue and music recorded from the monitors. This results in a tape of the show with the lyrics, music, and words in the background and the stage manager's spoken cues louder on top of it. It provides the stage-manager-in-training with an audio record of the exact placement of the cues, along with any instructions or questions that might have arisen while the assistant was watching with me.

Actors' Equity has very strong rules about taping the performance of any of its members, whether on video or audio. The union is attempting to protect against pirate tapes that can be reproduced and sold without any compensation to the performers. Clearly no one is going to be interested in paying for a cassette tape of a show with the poor audio quality one gets from the stage manager's monitors, and with two stage managers reciting cues and talking over most of the show. However, in any situation that may be at odds with the union, it is best to tell the Equity deputy and the stage hands what it is you're doing to avoid any problems.

The new stage manager can then take the tape and work on getting the exact timing of the cues. These tapes are invaluable tools for learning to accurately and safely call the cues for a show. Obviously, a videotape of the show that the training stage manager could take home to study would make this process even easier and far safer for the performers, whose lives sometimes depend on the accurate movement of set pieces or firing of effects. However, the unions continue to refuse to allow videotape as a rehearsal tool. Perhaps, the time has come for the union to understand how videotape can be used to enhance the creativity of the rehearsal period and promote the safety and quality of the performances after opening night.

Most often, it is the Actors' Equity members themselves who suffer most from not being able to use videotape. For instance, if a choreographer creating a piece could go home at night and review his work for the day, he could then eliminate the tedium of starting each new rehearsal reviewing the work of the day before, most of which he will cut or change anyway. How much more exciting and enjoyable it would be for the performers to start each day with new material instead of rehashing the old. In the Tony Award-winning musical *City of Angels* there is a magnificent fight sequence that is a spoof on old Hollywood movies. Each punch is accompanied by a sound effect—a "Biff" or a "Bam"—and there are crashes, glass tinkling, and so on. The sound operator had to learn this sequence by heart so he could time his sound effects perfectly. In order to do this, he told the company that he either had to have the actors come in and run the sequence over and over again, or they would have to provide him with a simple three-minute videotape of the sequence. The union insisted the actors be called.

The learning stage manager should make a number of "dry runs" at the desk or console, simulating the cueing, and training their fingers and speech to coordinate and execute the written cues successfully before trying them in performance. It is often helpful for the person learning the show to write their own book, so the cues are in their handwriting, and the little notes or reminders are in symbols or phrases they understand. The PSM must be sure to go over the rewritten book to make sure no warning or cue has been left out. The placement of the warnings and pause between the time the number of a cue is spoken and the "go" should always remain the same. For instance, if the lighting man is accustomed to hearing "Lights 25," a pause that lasts a measure of a song, and then the word "go," and someone new only waits a single beat before the "go," the board operator will be late until he or she adjusts to the new stage manager. The rhythm of calling a show should remain constant, both from night to night, and from stage manager to stage manager as new people take over the responsibility.

As soon as possible I try to let the training stage manager call uncomplicated segments of the show (internal light cues in a scene, for example), which allows the crew to get used to the stage manager, and the stage manager to grow comfortable with the task. The faster, more difficult sections take longer, and often I try to have each new assistant stand with me and tap my shoulder at the point when he or she would give the cues, until the taps and my cues are simultaneous. I then turn the headset and cueing over to the assistant, remaining by his or her side for two or three shows as a safety net, until there are no mistakes and the stage manager is comfortable with the entire show.

Understudies and Replacements

If your production looks like it is going to run for awhile, hopefully there were understudies who were hired during the rehearsal process and have watched and learned the show along with the cast. Understudies should have attended every rehearsal that involved the actors that they are covering, taking down blocking and interpretive notes from the director. If this is the case, the stage manager's job is simplified greatly. If not, the stage manager must start from scratch.

Read through all your notes on the discussions of character that took place during auditions, rehearsals, and previews, and explain them as best as you can to the understudy. Then sit somewhere with your blocking/rehearsal script and have him or her take down all the blocking and stage business notes. Afterwards, the real work of getting a performance ready can be developed. It is very important to remember that the primary responsibility of the stage manager's work with an understudy is to get the actor ready to go on in a moment's notice. In order to reach this emergency state of readiness, many of the niceties of the creative process have to be sacrificed.

At first, understudies should watch every performance, and once they know their roles, they should return once or twice a week to keep up with the little changes and nuances that both the persons they cover and the people they will be playing with develop.

The stage manager's task is to help each understudy develop a performance that can be fit into the show, often without the benefit of rehearsal with the whole cast, as seamlessly as possible.

Of course, the actor and the stage manager may be tempted to "improve" the role and make it fit better on the understudy. But that is not the job. It is a far more difficult and creative challenge to develop a viable and truthful performance within the boundaries of another actor's interpretation than to start with no bounds and give free reign to interpretation and character development.

Understudy performances are always charged with excitement the first time they happen. Often the infusion of a new performer creates a different direction or pace that is a needed contrast to the uniformity of a long-running production's performance. The rest of the company usually rallies and is very supportive for an understudy's first show.

The subsequent performances are more difficult, because the other actors will give the stage manager, or worse, the understudy a lot of notes, usually only from their own acting point of view. It is a delicate and diplomatic time for the stage manager who must try to keep the cast happy while not undermining the understudy's ability to give a decent performance. Once understudies become paranoid or lose the confidence of the rest of the cast, their performances fade into some obscure realm of "defensive acting," as though they are performing in order to avoid getting a note. To prevent this situation, try to get the understudy to work onstage, before the curtain, with the regular cast member on whatever moments are giving them trouble. It is often the only time the understudy gets to rehearse with the actor with whom they are playing. This small amount of rehearsal often boosts the confidence of both actors and helps eliminate any negative feelings.

Once during the run of *Hollywood/Ukraine*, the actor playing Groucho was on vacation, and the understudy who was supposed to play for the week did not show up at the theater for the matinee. We called his home, tried his agent, friends, family, and so on. No one knew where he was. I remembered, however, that David Garrison, who had been nominated for a Tony Award when he originated the role, was rehearsing a new play nearby. I called his rehearsal hall and got him on the phone; after a moment of disbelief, he agreed to do the show, even though he had been out of the cast for about six months. We held the curtain fifteen minutes, but the audience didn't mind when I switched the microphone to "public address" and told them the reason for the delay. They were delighted that they were going to see the original instead of the replacement's understudy.

David was unbelievably good. I have never seen a performer pull off anything like he did that afternoon; it was an inspired performance. And of course the audience and the rest of the cast were 100 percent behind him. When he did falter or forget for a moment, it just made the performance better. Fortunately, as Groucho, he was able to get away with a lot of wild ad libbing and improvisation. It was by far the most successful emergency I have ever been through.

Normally, understudy rehearsals are held once or twice a week. As soon as the actors know their parts, it is best to run the show straight through and not spend a lot of time working on scenes, because understudies must keep up their stamina, honing their ability to play their role from beginning to end. This process is much like keeping an athlete in shape. Occasionally, if an understudy is going to be on for an extended period of time, the regular cast will join the rehearsals and run scenes and work out any special business or fights. Furthermore, a tech/dress is usually scheduled the afternoon the substitute goes in.

Replacements

Cast replacements are usually handled in a slightly different manner than understudies. Often the director is more involved with the replacement process and will mold the new actor's performance to fit within the original interpretation. The director may work with the full cast to help them play certain moments or scenes with a new attack.

It is a fascinating process to watch a show evolve with different actors playing the same roles and yet bringing whole new meanings and emotions to scenes and moments. The play *I'm Not Rappaport* was particularly affected by the replacement casts. Over the course of a two-and-a-half-year run the two male leads changed from Judd Hirsch and Cleavon Little to Hal Linden and Ossie Davis to Jack Klugman and Ossie Davis and then back to Judd and Cleavon. The running time of the show changed by over twenty minutes during the course of this run, with different casts taking it faster and slower. The balance of strength between the characters changed totally from one cast to the other, and yet the play remained the same. It was the emotional content of the evening that was in constant flux.

Technical Maintenance

It is the responsibility of the stage manager to see that the physical quality of the show remains at a high level. This requires a watchful eye from the front for any technical problems: fading color quality in the lights, worn out set pieces, costumes that are fraying.

It is important to balance the cost and effect of the fixes. A costume that might cost thousands of dollars to replace may appear on its last legs backstage, but because it is only worn for one dance number or during a fleeting crossover it may not need to be replaced. On the other hand, a suit that looks all right in the dim backstage light may show threadbare and worn under the stage lights, and a new one should be ordered.

Always try to coordinate any maintenance work calls so that the crews come in all at once, and the cost is held down and more work can be done. Often, only the lights need attention, and the stage manager must make a separate call to change gel colors and fix the focus.

Every technical element that involves the safety of the cast or crew should have a regular maintenance schedule. Do not wait until these items show wear or tear to fix them. Every moving and working piece should be tested before every performance for function and safety. Because almost all special effects must be rigged and/or charged before every show, this attention serves as a constant check. Railings, ropes, and steps should be inspected constantly for sturdiness and wear.

The crew and stage managers should usually get to the theater at least an hour before curtain time for these checks. Sometimes with more complicated productions or shows without a curtain, this call could be extended to an hour and a half before curtain. This must all be worked out carefully as it may involve overtime payment to crew members.

Of course, no matter how well a stage manager maintains and inspects a show, there will always be mishaps. Every stage manager will collect a number of anecdotes about unforeseen emergencies that occurred during a performance. One of the most frightening experiences I've had was the time I had to put out a fire onstage. Some wigs were stored behind a piece of scenery, and they blazed up when hit by sparks from a flash-pot effect. I had my assistant hold back the entering cast members, while I leapt up on the piece of scenery with a blanket to smother the flames and was met by one of the electricians with a fire extinguisher. In less time than it has taken you to read this, the fire was out, and the show was continuing, interrupted only by the audience's applause.

During the run of *Othello*, I was watching from the back of the house as the transition into the climactic bedroom scene began, where Desdemona (Dianne Weist) is murdered by the jealous and enraged Othello (James Earl Jones). As blocked, Desdemona would cross the stage to her bedroom in dim light, accompanied by a hauntingly beautiful piece of viola music, and her maid would enter to help her prepare for sleep just as the bed, driven on by a motorized winch, would appear. I was always bothered by the noise that the winch made during this transition and had been working with the carpenter to muffle its sound. Simultaneously, I had been working with the sound man to find a level for the viola music that would drown out the winch's hum but not be so loud as to alter the mood of the scene.

At this particular performance, I thought we had finally found the perfect sound level, but then to my horror I realized no bed was appearing. The music drew to its final measures, and now a constant strained whining hum could be heard. I ran as fast as I could backstage and saw the crew trying to fix the winch but having no success. I grabbed the ASM, who also played a servant in this scene, and together we pulled the mattress off the bed and dragged it as ceremoniously as we could on to the stage and dumped it in front of a startled and slightly terrified Dianne Weist, indicating to her to get into it as if she was in an early Venetian hippie pad. We exited, the lights came up, and we all breathed a sigh of relief . . . until we realized that the dagger James Earl Jones used in the scene was preset on the headboard of the bed that lay worthlessly in the wings. James also realized this and spent a great deal of one of Shakespeare's most famous soliloquies making eye contact with us backstage while maneuvering himself to a doorway where he could stand with his back in the arch and grab the dagger which we had waiting for him.

Unfortunately, there is no way to teach someone "successful reactions to stage emergencies." You'll find that most theater workers have a built-in instinct for quick reactions to such situations, and as in the examples from my experience demonstrate, everyone works together to ensure that the show goes on. Don't be overzealous about continuing a performance however. The safety of the performers and audience is the top priority. If someone is seriously injured onstage or a fire breaks out that can't simply be smothered by a blanket or doused by a fire extinguisher, don't be afraid to stop the show completely in order to deal with the situation.

Performance Logs

It is vital to keep accurate logs of every performance, just as it was necessary to keep reports of rehearsals. The performance logs are a resource that possibly may be used to arbitrate all payroll and insurance disputes. They also serve as a way for the stage manager to air grievances to the producer, manager, and often, the director. Any artistic feelings or needs voiced by the cast should be written down in the log. These daily report forms are also useful as a place to note any growing technical, artistic, or temperament problems that may eventually affect the ongoing operation of the show. Figure 7–1 is an example of a form that I use for my daily performance logs. All the boxes for notes should be self-explanatory, but I have included an example of a filled-in form in Appendix 12.

Giving Actors Notes

Giving actors notes on their performance and calling and running brush-up rehearsals are perhaps the most delicate and important part of the stage manager's maintenance work on a show. Very few performers are of the mind-set of Dustin Hoffman. After a performance, he would take me by the arm and plead, "Give me some notes," and mean it. However, few actors have Dustin Hoffman's ongoing dedication to perfecting the craft of acting. Most often, a

```
┌─────────────────────────────────────────────────────────────┐
│              T H E   M E R C H A N T   O F   V E N I C E      │
│  STAGE MANAGER REPORT                    46TH STREET THEATER  │
├─────────────────────────────────────────────────────────────┤
│  DAY:                    DATE:            PERFORMANCE #       │
├──────────────────────────────┬──────────────────────────────┤
│  ACT I  Up          :        │    WEATHER/AUDIENCE/FOH       │
│                              │                              │
│  ACT I  Down        :        │                              │
│                              │                              │
│    Running Time:  Hr.  Mins. │                              │
│                              │                              │
│  Intermission:    Mins.      │                              │
│                              ├──────────────────────────────┤
│  ACT II  Up         :        │                              │
│                              │    ABSENT, ILL, ACCIDENT     │
│  ACT II  Down       :        │                              │
│                              │                              │
│    Running Time:  Hr.  Mins. │                              │
│                              │                              │
│  Total Running Time:    :    │                              │
│                              │                              │
│  Total Elapsed Time:    :    │                              │
├──────────────────────────────┬──────────────────────────────┤
│  REHEARSAL, WORK CALLS, P.R. │   NOTICES, OFFICE NOTES       │
│                              │                              │
│                              │                              │
│                              │                              │
├──────────────────────────────┴──────────────────────────────┤
│           PERFORMANCE & TECHNICAL NOTES                      │
│                                                              │
│                                                              │
│                                                              │
│                                                              │
│                                                              │
│                                                              │
│                         STAGE MANAGER:  Tom Kelly            │
└─────────────────────────────────────────────────────────────┘
```

Figure 7-1 A Sample Performance Report Form

stage manager's acting notes are met with a hostile and negative response. Don't let this stop you.

Confronted by a stage manager giving them a note, most actors will give notes back, usually concerning someone else's performance. (It is amazing how few problems are ever solved by one note.) If possible, therefore, get everyone together for a note session that will allow small sections and problems to be worked out on their feet. With the whole cast present, no one feels cornered or attacked or singled out, and much more can be achieved.

There are ways to go about offering notes as a stage manager that are different than that of the director. I will often enlist the help and advice of one or two of the actors in a scene, asking them how we can get back to the original pace, intensity of emotion, or whatever. Share the problem with the cast, asking them how, as a company, everyone can get the show back to the level at which it was originally performed. Don't demand the result you want or give notes in a punitive fashion.

Giving acting notes to performers is the most delicate and hard-to-teach function of stage managing. The best way to learn is by doing it. If you are enrolled in a university theater program, be sure to take acting and directing classes. They will help make you aware of the complexity of the task. However, the main thing a stage manager must remember is that he or she is a maintenance director, not an interpretive director. The role of the stage manager is to fulfill the director's vision and keep the level of performance as close to the original as possible. There are a number of acting problems that a stage manager must watch for carefully.

Pacing

As actors get to know a play by performing it over and over, they often start to speed up the pace of the show. Actors' tongues start to move faster than the thought behind the lines, because they no longer have to remember the words or consider their meaning. This results in a mechanical, one-level performance. Getting actors out of this habit can be achieved by gentle reminders or requests to go back to the text, and reacquaint themselves with the subtext and the meaning of their lines.

An occasional brush-up rehearsal may be necessary when a scene or section has become rushed or superficial. In this manner, the play can be broken down again and worked on without an audience. During these rehearsals strive to get the performers' creative juices flowing again.

The opposite pacing problem also occurs. Usually, a slower pace is caused by actors falling in love with certain lines or sections and becoming indulgent with them, basking in the laughter or emotional response of the audience, milking every moment. Eventually, especially in a dramatic play, an actor's emotional indulgence can numb and stupefy an audience and distort the meaning by giving a moment or a scene portentous weight. Tactful notes and some brush-up rehearsal are necessary, as well as the cooperation of all the actors in a scene. It doesn't help if the actor portraying Hamlet, for instance, is cooking along, putting energy and pace back into the performance, only to have Gertrude, Ophelia, or Claudius drain the energy from every moment they have with Hamlet.

Stage Business

Some actors employed in a long-running show get bored. This usually leads to the creation or expansion of "stage business." Simple actions, discovered by an actor at one performance, may get a big reaction from that audience. Thereafter, the business will find its way into the play. If a fly appeared onstage during one performance, and the actors' attempts to swat it away drew loud laughs, soon the shooing of the fly will become a permanent bit. The folding of a handkerchief or the balancing of a coffee cup on a tray may become whole one-act plays in themselves. The stage manager must be ruthless in holding this down, or the play will become overrun with such "bits."

The danger is that stage managers are also human and become bored watching the same show, and sometimes the business or bit seems so inspired it is tempting to let it stay in. Remember that all such stage business is only the director's prerogative. As directors are fond of reminding stage managers, it is their name out front and in the program following the phrase "Directed by." They are not interested in having the cast and stage managers become associates.

Ad Libbing and Audibility

A big tendency in a long run is for ad libs to become part of the play. If actors have trouble with a certain line or phrase they will often find a suitable (to them) alternative that conveys the same meaning or emotion. However, the rhythms and word choices are the playwright's and must be changed only by him or her.

Some actors have a habit that is annoying to other actors and drives playwrights to distraction: they add little "uh-huhs" or "rights" or "phews" to the dialogue. Sometimes this gets to the point where there are literally hundreds of additional words in a play. These insertions interrupt the play's rhythms and get in the way of the flow of dialogue as envisioned by the writer; they must be policed by the stage manager.

A constant audience complaint in the theater is "I can't hear." This is partially caused by the amplification of electronic media; because they bombard our ears and supply handy volume controls, movies and television have reduced listening skills to lost attributes. However, the actor and stage manager must also remember the audience is hearing the play for the first time, and although the performers know it by heart, certain key phrases or meanings must be underscored vocally and with pace. Otherwise, it is difficult for an audience to stay with the narrative flow and understand what is happening on the stage.

Morale and Company Spirit

There is a certain talent to stage managing a long-running show that is hard to describe and that all stage managers should possess in their own fashion: promoting company get-togethers that help engender a positive working atmosphere. Sometimes there are company members who take on this responsibility, but often it is the stage manager.

Almost everyone will respond to softball games, a trip to a bowling alley, or other sporting activities. In New York there are show business leagues in both these sports, and if the show has a team it can be fun to attend or play in the games. Birthdays are another excuse to get together for cake and a small celebration after the show. Don't feel shy about going around to the company members and asking for their birth dates.

On matinee days sometimes it is fun to do "pot luck" dinners in the theater between the two shows. Once in a while on Broadway, companies will take turns hosting each other; you might have two or three shows taking turns being the pot luck host.

Contests are another company morale booster. All sorts of pos-sibilities exist, from the standard betting pools on sporting events such as the Super Bowl, the World Series, and so on, to pastimes such as baby-picture contests where everyone brings in their own baby picture, posts them on a board, and then everyone tries to guess who is who. Other contests include postcard contests (with categories for the prettiest, funniest, and tackiest) or holiday deco-ration contests with similar categories. All these are simple to or-ganize and they bring the company together for something other than the doing the "job."

Holidays shouldn't go uncelebrated either. A "Secret Santa" party at Christmas, where everyone gets one other person a gift, is fun. Easter egg hunts in the theater, Halloween pumpkin carving contests—it all makes for a happier and more involved company.

As important as special days and events are, it is also important to keep a generally positive, genial side to the day-to-day operation of stage management. Try to make the theater a pleasant place for people to come to work. This can have many dividends, including people staying with the show longer, which will hold down on those extra replacement rehearsals.

Accidents and Medical Emergencies

No matter how careful people are, there will be emergencies. In-juries and accidents happen, and the stage manager should be well-prepared. All stage managers should take a first-aid or CPR course so that they know the basics of emergency treatment.

There should be a clear system of handling emergencies worked out among the stage management personnel as well. The system must designate who keeps the show running, who calls for the ambulance, and who helps the person with whatever first-aid is required.

The backstage first-aid kit should be equipped with adequate bandages for major cuts, smelling salts, peroxide, ice packs, and a small oxygen tank and mask. These are basic requirements, and the well-equipped first-aid kit should go well beyond. There should be treatment for every part of the body—from a headache to a corn on the little toe—so anything that might prevent a performer from going on doesn't. (Check the list of first-aid supplies in Chapter 3.)

Maintaining a show is a little like caring for a family. Everyone's health and happiness is of direct consequence to the successful operation of the whole, and it is the stage manager who must constantly remind people of the importance of rest and good health as well as keep tabs on the performance of their job. As the stage manager of a running show, it is important to set up a schedule so that you watch the show and call it on a regular basis, because if left to chance, the quality of the show, in some way, will slide with your lack of attention.

8

Closing a Show and Touring

T he end of a show is a time when most of the cast involved with a production is getting ready for a break and some rest, while the stage managers and crew have to get it together one more time to cleanly close the show, strike the scenery, take inventory, and move out of the theater. Sometimes a show will tour after closing, which creates separate problems. (Sometimes the financial situation is so bad that the producers cannot even afford to get the show *out* of the theater, but these are rare occurrences.) It is important for a stage manager to know the basic responsibilities involved with striking a closing show, as well as striking a production that will then tour.

When the general manager and producer have decided to close a show, they notify the stage manager and crew to start planning. In regional and stock theater, this date is usually pre-established by the season schedule, but the same planning and care must be taken.

Immediately following the final performance of a show, in the midst of all the emotion and farewells, the stage manager must secure the production's property and pack his or her own supplies and equipment. I always try to do as much of this in advance as possible, moving any of the producers' equipment or supplies to their offices, and letting the first-aid kit and other supplies run down to the bare necessities. To further ease the work load on a closing night, I try to make sure any extraneous personal possessions of mine have been brought home before that final curtain.

All shows and theaters are different. On tour the show usually loads out directly after the last performance; in New York or a regional theater, the load-out might wait until the next day. If it is immediate, the stage managers should pack up their things as quickly as possible to be out of the crew's way and be available for emergencies and to supervise the proceedings. Always save packing the first-aid kit as long as possible; many accidents happen during load-outs, because everyone is moving fast, and a lot is happening at once.

Load-Out

The first step to a successful and smooth load-out is to have an advance production meeting with the heads of all departments to discuss their time and manpower requirements. Prior to this meeting the stage manager will have had to find out certain key facts from the producer:

1. Will the show tour, and if so, will the same set be used?
2. What belongs to the producer or theater in the way of props and set pieces, and what is borrowed or rented?
3. Which set, costume, and prop pieces will be saved and which will be destroyed?
4. What kind of arrangements or truck rentals will you have to make in order to return or donate props and costumes? Many theaters and some active commercial producers keep warehouse space for storing set pieces, costumes, and props for future shows. Other theaters and producers prefer to try and sell their stock or donate it to schools or not-for-profit theater organizations for a tax deduction.

Once the above questions are answered, the crew and stage managers can carefully schedule the load-out in terms of necessary manpower and trucking. As with the load-in, the process will be simplified by advance planning that will ensure that no one is impeding anyone's progress because the stage is full of their equipment or scenery at the same time another department needs to have space. Careful ordering of trucks combined with timing of each department's work will keep the process flowing. In Appendix 14 there is a fairly detailed schedule outlining the move of *I'm Not Rappaport* from the American Place Theater, a small Off-Broadway venue, three blocks west to the Booth Theater, a Broadway house. It should give a clear example of the complexity of moving what was a pretty simple show.

The Last Performance

At the final performance, it is very important for the stage manager to stay calm amid the emotion and general craziness that sometimes surrounds the event. For instance, actors often have a brilliantly funny joke they want to play on someone in the cast during the performance. These brilliantly funny jokes are usually funny only to the jokesters who do them, and they invariably go over horribly on stage. Discourage any change from the normal performance of the show; try to maintain the integrity of the production as fully as possible.

Also, in conjunction with the department heads, it is the stage manager's responsibility to ensure a minimal amount of "souvenir procurement" by the cast. Clearly you have the right to give away items that are otherwise going be thrown out, but you must help protect those costumes and props that certain cast members may have been eyeing for months but that have been sold, given away elsewhere, or that the producer expects to see in his office or home.

The first area of responsibility for the stage manager should be the dressing rooms. If the strike is not going to immediately follow the final curtain, try to remain at the theater on closing night until all the actors have left. Go through the dressing rooms after they have gone and check on what may have been left behind. Remove immediately any company property—phones, fans, heaters, or refrigerators, for example—and lock them all up in the stage manager's office so they are not laying around when the load-out crew arrives to strike. Speaking of the crew, the last performance can be ruined by excessive backstage noise as some of the workers begin packing and the extra stagehands start arriving during the show. This is especially true on tour. Try to have a word about last-night noise with everyone backstage before the show. A stage manager's loyalties are torn, because you want the crew to get as much done as possible, but not at the expense of the show.

During the actual load-out, keep a close eye on the progress, and be available for any questions of "to save or not to save." Sometimes on a try-out tour, you must decide if you can leave behind any scenery or furniture that has been cut from a scene or that was in a scene that was cut. Be wary of leaving anything behind, because the director may want the scene back or the designer might find use for the set piece in some new and different scene. Only leave behind something that itself was cut, not something that was part of a scene or song that was cut.

Touring

On tours, the stage manager sometimes "calls the load" or tells the loading crew what goes on the truck and in what order. This is vital because often there is only one way the entire physical production will fit into the truck or trucks allotted to it. You don't want to let others start loading and then end up with a bunch of full trucks and part of the show still sitting on the loading dock. This will usually be worked out with your carpenter and prop man, but on tour they sometimes prefer the stage manager to be at the truck, so they can be on stage moving the local crew along.

One terrible night in Chicago, Leo Herbert, the prop man of *Sugar Babies*, a legendary and brilliant man with over a hundred Broadway shows to his credit, came to me enraged and demanded I come look at the truck. Previously, the wardrobe cartons had successfully fit into the front third of a 45-foot truck. Now they had filled half the truck and were still coming. It seems a new wardrobe mistress had gotten the brilliant notion of packing every cast member's costume in a separate box, thinking this would facilitate unpacking on the other end while cutting down on the wrinkling due to packing many costumes tightly in one box. Needless to say this had doubled the number of costume boxes and, therefore, the space that wardrobe had taken on the truck. A stage manager should be constantly on the lookout for this kind of incident.

On tour, it is vital that the stage manager know in advance what the next theater is like. Before you arrive in the next town or city, contact that theater's house crew and go over all the needs and requirements of your show and try to iron out any potential problems with load-in. For example, some theaters have raised load-in docks that require forklifts. Often these must be ordered to get the show off the truck and into the theater. This is an example of something you must take care of in advance.

Be sure you have a clear picture of the dressing room layout and the rooms available for wigs and wardrobe. Then once you arrive, go through the dressing rooms and make sure the assignments you've made in advance make sense. Sometimes a dressing room described on the phone will bear little resemblance to reality, so be prepared to change and adapt your company's room assignments real fast.

On tour you are moving quickly, and so much changes for the performers from week to week that anything the stage managers can do to keep things similar the better. If it is possible, try to keep actors on the same side of the theater in terms of dressing rooms so their traffic patterns stay the same. Carry the same name cards or signs for their dressing room doors, and make the callboard as uniform as possible from city to city.

Backstage in the wings, things should be exactly the same to the greatest possible extent. This means that prop tables and dressing booths should travel with you and be in the same place whenever possible. All signs and tape marks on the steps and floor offstage should be exactly the same.

On the road, the theater becomes the "family home" for a large group of people, so try to let the environment reflect that. Try to always have a "green room" area where the company can gather, have coffee, and read or play games.

During the load-in on tour, the stage manager is often responsible for focusing lights and must be totally familiar with the light plot and design concept. In this way, during the hanging of the lights, you can make decisions about light positions and instruments that can or can't be cut if there is not ample space. The lighting designer should arm the stage manager with lots of paperwork, including all the information on the basic focus. This is basically a written description of where the stage manager should stand so that the "hot spot" or brightest part of the light may be focused on him or her. Then the designer indicates how the light should be cut off, or shuttered off of certain pieces of scenery or furniture, or how high up the back drop or wall the light is to play. The stage manager should be with the lighting designer the first time the lights are focused to learn all the intricacies of the plot, and then he or she must translate that from theater to theater.

One constantly changing element in theaters is the distance from the stage to the front of the balcony where lights are hung. It is sometimes necessary to carry two sets of lights for that position. Then you can change instruments depending on the length of the throw required.

Another fascinating and terrifying wrinkle to touring is the constantly changing crew. In New York or at a regional or stock theater, the crew with whom you train and learn the show is the crew you basically have every night, but on the road, you are constantly training and teaching the show to new crews. Depending on the size and complexity of the production, various numbers of stagehands will travel with the show. For instance, there is always a "road" carpenter and usually an electrician and prop man. Increasingly, producers will attempt to hold down on the number of road men because of the cost of their travel and housing. Always try to convince the producers to err on the side of paying for too many at first and then cutting back if they're not necessary, rather than going out on the road shorthanded with their promise that skilled crew members will be added later (read: it will never happen).

If you have good road men, they will train and watch the local crew, and you are free to supervise and run the cues in the more difficult sections. Make sure the local crew is clear about the terminology and cueing system that you are using. The crew probably deals with a lot of different shows and all manner of stage managers, and they are not always seasoned stagehands used to any one style of cueing. There are theater crews that may not automatically know to wait for the stage manager's "Go" or that may read a cue light turning on as the signal to execute the cue instead of taking it as a warning.

Never take anything for granted. House lights are often operated on a strange system that requires you to call on an intercom or paging device; be sure to check out how they are run. Also check the ventilation system. If you have drops and curtains, be sure to run them with whatever blowers or air conditioning systems will be circulating during performance. Frequently, if left untested, curtains or drops may billow or blow back on the stage, which is distracting at best, and at worst, may knock over furniture or people.

Always try to have a sound check and some rehearsal with the cast on stage before the first show in a new theater (although you and the cast should realize this sometimes may be impossible). A sound check is vital because the acoustics vary tremendously from theater to theater. Every microphone and speaker needs to be adjusted and balanced differently, and the cast has to understand that their audibility will vary from house to house. In one theater the cast may feel like they are shouting to be heard in the balcony, and the next week they hardly will have to project. But if the sound man is going to help with the audibility of the show, he must have a chance to hear the cast on stage.

Unfortunately, sometimes schedules are so tight that there is no time for sound checks with the cast. Once with *Sugar Babies* in Detroit, the load-in was so far behind schedule that we had half of the set outside at the start of the show and had to keep bringing in pieces as we needed them during the performance. Occasionally this would mean that a backstage crossover passage that had been clear for dancers before their number was blocked by the time they finished. With a few hair-breadth arrivals and costume changes we made it through, but it was harrowing for the performers.

Throughout the trials and tribulations of that pre-Broadway tour, the spirit and good humor of Mickey Rooney was a godsend and a great example to all of us. Once, the computer light board was going haywire, running cues on its own, and bringing up strange combinations of lights for other cues. (Early computer boards were a lot like the early days of the space program, well-meaning but often a total disaster.) Mickey stepped to the edge of the stage and proceeded to give an impromptu lecture on the evils of modern technology and compared working with these computer-board-operated lights to being inside a pinball machine gone wild. He was always willing to cover when we had problems, even working some of the glitches into the show permanently.

There was a scene with a telephone in it that I once accidentally rang at the wrong time, and from that night on, Mickey and I had a scene together where I would purposely ring a phone at the wrong time or fail to ring it at all. He would get exasperated by its ringing or not ringing at the proper time and then build and build his reaction to hilarious proportions. He also had a fake fight with Ann Miller during one performance in which his wig got knocked off, and he replaced it backwards on his head. This one-time mistake also grew into a major comedic moment in the show. His comic instincts were incredible; he always knew just how far to go with those moments so that they remained funny and didn't become stupid or mean-spirited. Most importantly, it was a great lesson in making the best out of a bad situation. Unfortunately, it is a lesson stage managers must learn well.

Basically, a touring stage manager is always on his or her toes, adapting, dealing with a lot of different situations and personalities, but somehow making the show work every night. It is never boring, and it can be a lot of fun. It is vital to keep the cast active and together on tour, and the stage manager and company manager can work together to arrange sightseeing jaunts, parties, and tours, anything to keep people together and into the show.

Maintaining the artistic quality of a show on the road is quite a challenge, not only in terms of finding time for rehearsals and accomplishing all the technical tasks, but due to the vast difference in audience reactions from one section of the country to another. What may play well and get huge laughs in one city will die in the next, and a local reference or inside joke can cast a whole new light on a scene.

The stage manager must keep accurate contact sheets on the road. Convince everyone that it is essential that they report any change in their hotel or living accommodations immediately to the stage manager.

Travel days are far from a day off for stage managers. Stage managers should help move the company by: assisting in baggage pickup and handling, organizing and scheduling bus pickups, signing people in, and in general, shepherding the company from one city to the other.

A tour stage manager must use the same skills and attributes necessary for successfully stage managing a stationary production: a combination of a lot of detail and organizational work with hands-on caring and attention to the well-being and spirit of the company and crew.

9

Career Information

Most frequently, stage managers find jobs through word-of-mouth. The more a stage manager works, the more his or her work will be known, and the more he or she will be recommended to friends and associates.

It is vital to remember one thing: every hour a stage manager spends in a theater is valuable, no matter what the job. Stage managers must feel completely at ease and at home in the theater and backstage environment so that they can in turn make their production's company feel relaxed. The more time you spend working on any facet of theater the better.

Any backstage technical work is valuable for two main reasons. First, the contacts you make may lead to jobs in the future. For example, the lighting designer that you help hang lights one day may remember you are really a stage manager the next time he or she is asked for a recommendation. But perhaps more importantly, every technical job you take will add to your understanding of your role as stage manager, a position that requires a working knowledge of many theater skills and their impact on a theater production.

As a young stage manager combing trade papers or advertisements for job listings, look out for notices seeking production assistants. These are often non-Equity assistant stage manager positions that involve running errands, buying rehearsal props, sweeping the rehearsal room, and so on, but they are a great way to meet working stage managers and directors. Or try to get on a show as a director's assistant, taking notes and facilitating his or her instructions. In any such position, you will learn a lot about the theater, and will meet people who will get to know your talents in a working environment rather than hear you talk about them in an interview situation.

There are many organizations and publications that will aid you in your search for work as a stage manager. Don't forget, however, that in the end, your contacts and previous employers are your most important source of theater jobs. But to start out, here are some of the more useful publications and organizations for a budding (or an experienced but unemployed) stage manager.

ArtSearch

ArtSearch is subtitled the "National Employment Service Bulletin for the Arts" and is published by Theatre Communications Group, a not-for-profit organization serving the country's theaters. *ArtSearch* is a bulletin that is issued twice a month, listing information about stage management, design, teaching, and other theater-related job opportunities in many nonprofit resident and university institutions around the country. TCG publishes 23 issues a year at a cost of $48. To subscribe, write *ArtSearch,* c/o TCG, 355 Lexington Ave., New York, NY 10017, or call (212) 697-5230 for more information.

TCG also prints many other useful publications, including *American Theatre* magazine, annual and biennial theater directories, plays, and other theater-related books. They will keep you better informed of what is going on in theater in this country, which will help you know where to look to find work. You can write or call TCG and ask for a publications catalog.

The Alliance of Resident Theatres/New York

The Alliance (ART/New York for short) is a trade and service organization for more than 130 not-for-profit theaters in New York City. Their office maintains two "books" that may be of interest to an unemployed young stage manager, especially one new to the town. The "Job Book" is a collection of job descriptions of employment opportunities at ART/New York's member theaters. The "Resume Book" is a file that the organization maintains, consisting of resumes from stage managers and other technical personnel. A prospective stage manager coming to New York should write the Alliance for more information: The Alliance of Resident Theatres/New York, 131 Varick St., Room 904, New York, NY 10013, or call (212) 989-5257.

Theatrical Index

Published weekly by Price Berkley, *Theatrical Index* lists the staffing information for almost every show currently running in New York theater, both on Broadway and off. The names of all production stage managers are listed, and it is an excellent way to get their names and the theater address to which you can send a letter and resume seeking an interview as an assistant or future replacement.

Also, every week *Theatrical Index* has a section describing shows that are planned for the future. This allows you to send letters and resumes in advance to those managers and producers with whom you think you would like to work. It can be subscribed to weekly, twice monthly, or monthly by writing *Theatrical Index*, 888 Eighth Ave., New York, NY 10019, or calling (212) 586-6343.

The Stage Manager's Association

This organization was started in 1982 as a professional organization founded by and for stage managers. It seeks to create and develop an ongoing network through which stage managers can share their problems, exchange ideas and information, and educate themselves and those for whom they work about stage management issues. The organization has meetings regularly in New York and around the country. They sponsor insightful forums on many topics relating to stage management as well. They publish a newsletter and have a program called "Operation Observation," which allows members to join stage managers as they run their shows, observing the workings of a Broadway or regional theater firsthand. For information on membership or publications write The Stage Manager's Association, P.O. Box 2234, Times Square Station, New York, NY 10108, or call (212) 691-5633.

Back Stage, Show Business, and Variety

There are three trade weeklies that stage managers can peruse in New York for listings of job opportunities and theater news: *Back Stage*, *Show Business*, and *Variety*. All three publications also feature informational articles and up-to-date news items concerning theater production.

Resource and Research Suggestions

There are many ways to go about gaining additional information about a career in stage managing and there are many resource publications that help the stage manager begin to amass the information needed to start feeling truly qualified to take on the responsibility of a major production.

Theatre Crafts/Lighting Dimensions

Published ten times a year, *Theatre Crafts* has articles about every facet of theater technology and design written by many of the best people doing it. There are also many advertisements in the magazine for a myriad of technical devices, aids, and shops. Writing these companies for brochures and information is the best way to keep up with advances in light and sound technology, as well as new scenic, prop, and costume techniques and materials. Once a year, *Theatre Crafts* publishes a directory that is the most complete listing I have ever found of theatrical supply shops and services, many of which you may have an opportunity to work with during your stage managing career.

   Lighting Dimensions is published nine times a year, and as its title suggests, is geared toward lighting designers and electricians. Nevertheless, it couldn't hurt to acquaint yourself with the different instruments and new technological innovations with which you will work in the theater. You can subscribe to either *Theatre Crafts* or *Lighting Dimensions* by writing to them at 135 Fifth Ave., New York, NY 10010, or you can order subscriptions to either magazine—at a cost of $22.95 for one year—by calling 1-800-435-0715.

The New York Theatrical Sourcebook

The Association of Theatrical Artists and Crafts People compile and edit an annual directory called *The New York Theatrical Source Book.* It is a spiral-bound specialty guide (sort of a theatrical Yellow Pages) to everything you need to know about companies that provide theatrical products and services; organizations that set safety and health standards; firms that sell and manufacture personal protective equipment; organizations that offer support services to theaters and the arts; and a listing of New York theater and dance rehearsal spaces, sound shops, and stages. Whether you need fake blood or bleached-blond wigs, it is a wonderful resource for the working stage manager. It also serves as an eye-opening learning experience for anyone wanting to know more about how technical theater crafts people find the basic (and often exotic) materials that go into most theater productions. This sourcebook may be ordered from Broadway Press, 12 West Thomas St., Box 1037, Shelter Island, NY 11964. The 1991 edition costs $30. For more information, call (516) 749-3266.

Conclusion

Writing this book has been a revelation to me. At the beginning I thought it would be a relatively simple task, because actually doing the job seems easy after all these years, especially compared to say, raising a teenage daughter, or understanding the ins and outs of the budget deficit. However, trying to explain endless details and responsibilities without losing sight of stage management's more lofty purpose in the general scheme of creative collaboration, from which all successful theater grows, has proven a difficult and complex task.

When I started writing this book I resolved to attempt to make it more fun to read than a straightforward textbook. But as you've undoubtedly noticed, there is an overwhelming amount of information and basic knowledge that a young stage manager must absorb in order to perform well in the position. I believe that this book should simplify the process of stage managing a show for those who are trying it for the first time, while offering useful alternative methods and suggestions to those who have already begun their career.

Throughout the book, I have tried to stress the human aspects of the position over the increasingly overwhelming technical side of today's theater, because I believe that the working relationships one must establish and maintain are the top priority. What makes live theater one of the most exciting arts is the joint collaboration of so many artists and craftspeople, all working together to make a show happen on a nightly basis. As theater begins to rely more and more heavily on the computer chip and synthesized sound, theater may overwhelm and amaze audiences with the spectacle of technological innovation, but it runs the risk of not involving an audience emotionally, of not making them care. Even as this book is being written, the push towards over-mechanized theater has resulted in actors being hit over the head by falling scenery that no one could stop, shows closing or not being able to open due to "technical difficulties," and a helicopter being loaded into a theater to appear nightly in the newest Broadway extravaganza, *Miss Saigon.*

When I first became involved in the theater, it was a very different world backstage, one that involved a lot of human beings and not so many different machines and motors and computers. I used to get a thrill every night during the runs of *The Wiz* and *Sugar Babies* because in order to make these shows successful over a hundred people were required to work together in whatever harmony and structure the stage managers provided. Now, all too often, the show is completely programmed and the only excitement backstage is overcoming a "glitch" in the system. Fortunately, in many arenas— community theater, some college and university programs, and in smaller theater companies everywhere—the theater remains a live, vibrant, and very human art. It is to the people who want to learn, practice, and experience that art that this book has been addressed.

Obviously, these ideas are an indication of how *I* feel about stage managing, and my own approach to stage management is reflected throughout the book. However, I hasten to remind any budding stage managers that there is no one way of doing this job, any more than there is one method of acting or directing. And as actors must in the end perform, stage mangers must in the end support and facilitate that performance to the utmost of their ability. While there are many ways of accomplishing this, every stage manager should have the same goal: a smooth-running show and a happy, satisfied company.

I believe experience is the best teacher. Hopefully, some of my experiences described in this book will help the learning stage manager. However, one's own experiences, in any endeavor, serve as the ultimate graduate course.

Stage managing is not a dull profession; often it is *too* exciting. The stress and pressures that befall stage managers can often be the job's greatest drawback. The position offers little glamor, but then for many of us, that is part of its appeal.

Many things that help make stage managing easier or more successful are also invaluable in life, and that has been one of its joys for me. As I matured and learned to take life one day at a time, I saw immediately the value of doing so in my work. Conversely, stage managing has taught me the ability to prioritize, and that talent has made a big difference in my personal life.

Most of all, in both my life and work, I have learned the value of fully knowing and appreciating that *all things are not of equal importance.* And so I will end with that thought and the hope that however you translate it in your work, it will prove as valuable a tool as the eraser and the three-hole punch.

Appendixes

1. Definitions of a Stage Manager
2. Sample Production Schedules
3. Sample Contact Sheets
4. Production Meeting Notes
5. Rehearsal Schedules and Scene Breakdowns
6. Rehearsal Report Form
7. Sample Cue Sheets
8. Tracking Sheet and Prop List
9. Technical Rehearsal Schedules
10. Cue Lights
11. Actors' Equity Association Work Rules
12. Performance Report Forms
13. Production Schedules for Touring/Closing a Show

1. Definitions of a Stage Manager

AEA Production Contract

The following June, 1984 revision of stage managerial duties is contained in all Actors' Equity Association Production contracts (the contract most commonly used for all commercial Broadway productions).

**Definition of the Duties and Obligations of a
Stage Manager**

A Stage Manager under Actors' Equity Contract is, or shall be obligated to perform at least the following duties for the Production to which he is engaged, and by performing them is hereby defined as the Stage Manager:

1. He shall be responsible for the calling of all rehearsals, whether before or after opening.

2. He shall assemble and maintain the Prompt Book, which is defined as the accurate playing text and stage business, together with such cue sheets, plots, daily records, etc. as are necessary for the actual technical and artistic operation of the production.

3. He shall work with the Director and the heads of all other departments, during re-hearsal and after opening, schedule rehearsal and outside calls in accordance with Equity's regulations.

4. Assume active responsibility for the form and discipline of rehearsal and performance, and be the executive instrument in the technical running of each performance.

5. Maintain the artistic intentions of the Director and the Producer after opening, to the best of his ability, including calling correctional rehearsals of the company when necessary, and preparation of the Understudies, Replacements, Extras and Supers, when and if the Director and/or the Producer declines this prerogative. Therefore, if an Actor finds him/herself unable to satisfactorily work out an artistic difference of opinion with the Stage Manager regarding the intentions of the Director and Producer, the Actor has the option of seeking clarification from the Director or Producer.

6. Keep such records as are necessary to advise the Producer on matters of attendance, time, welfare benefits, or other matters relating to the rights of Equity members. The Stage Manager and Assistant Stage Managers are prohibited from the making of pay-rolls or any distribution of salaries.

7. Maintain discipline, as provided in the Equity Constitution, By-Laws and Rules where required, appealable in every case to Equity.

8. Stage Manager duties do not include shifting scenery, running lights, operating the box office, etc.

9. The Council shall have the power from time to time to define the meaning of the words "Stage Manager" and may alter, change or modify the meaning of Stage Manager as hereinabove defined.

10. The Stage Manager and Assistant Stage Managers are prohibited from handling contracts, having riders signed or initialed, or any other function which normally comes under the duties of the General Manager or Company Manager.

11. The Stage Manager and Assistant Stage Managers are prohibited from participating in the ordering of food for the company.

12. The Stage Manager and Assistant Stage Managers are prohibited from signing the closing notice of the company or the individual notice of any Actor's termination.

Excerpts from Various Other AEA Contracts

The following excerpts define additional duties and obligations—and the limits of those obligations—of a professional stage manager. They are extracted from the Actors' Equity Association COST (Council of Stock Theaters), Dinner Theater, Industrial, LORT (League of Resident Theaters), and Off-Broadway contracts.

Definition of the Duties and Obligations of the Producer and a Stage Manager

- Because of the responsibilities of the Stage Manager for the success of the production and safety of the Actors, the Producer agrees that Producer will use Producer's best efforts to employ a person who is experienced in theatrical stage management. (Industrial) (Dinner Theatre)

- In every company in which an Equity member is employed, all Stage Managers, Assistant Stage Managers and Advance Stage Managers shall be and continue to be members of Equity in good standing, and shall be signed to the appropriate contract. Because the duties of the Advance and Resident Stage Manager include a comprehension of the technical and artistic aspects of a production, these positions should not be considered entry-level positions, but should be filled by individuals with stage managerial experience. The Stage Manager has the right to consult with the Producer in the selection of an Assistant Stage Manager(s). (COST)

- Whenever a Stage Manager or Assistant Stage Manager does work related to the production, which shall include but not be limited to attending meetings, doing administrative work, scheduling and contracting cast, crew and liaisons, said work shall be regarded as part of the permitted work week. (Industrial)

- It is agreed that it is the duty of the Stage Manager to assemble and maintain the production script required for the actual technical and artistic operation of the production and that production script remains the property of the Theatre. (LORT)

- The Stage Manager or the Assistant Stage Manager must be present in the rehearsal area and during all performances and must keep a prompt book which includes technical cues, blocking, business, direction, plots and daily records. No Stage Manager's or Assistant Stage Manager's duties shall be performed by anyone other than a Stage Manager or Assistant Stage Manager respectfully under an Equity contract. (Dinner Theatre)

- No member of the Stage Managerial staff will be required to prepare any additional production script or book for publication or archival purposes or for use in any other production of the play or musical. (LORT)

- A member of the Stage Managerial staff shall be present in the rehearsal area and during all performances except in an emergency. The Stage Manager's or Assistant Stage Manager's duties shall not be performed by anyone other than a Stage Manager or Assistant Stage Manager respectively, under an Equity contract. (Off-Broadway)

- A Stage Manager or Assistant Stage Manager must be present on the deck or in communication from the booth with all backstage areas during all performances, run-throughs, technical rehearsals, and dress rehearsals. Under no circumstances shall anyone other than the Equity Stage Manager or Assistant Stage Manager be on book calling the cues of a production. (LORT)

STAGE MANAGER'S DUTIES *DO NOT* INCLUDE THE FOLLOWING:

- [The Stage Managerial staff shall not be required to] arrange for living accommodations for the company, but may act as the means of communication between the Actor and the Producer. (COST)

- Members of the Stage Managerial staff are prohibited from doing janitorial, custodial or building maintenance work as part of their Stage Managerial duties. (COST)

- Members of the Stage Managerial staff are not required to design, build, hang, shop for lights, sound, scenery, props, wardrobe, etc. as part of their Stage Managerial duties; and they are prohibited from doing janitorial, custodial, building maintenance or restaurant work as part of their Stage Managerial duties. (Dinner Theatre)

- It is agreed that the Stage Manager will not be assigned responsibility for the preparation of payroll, reservation of accommodations (except prior to commencement of rehearsal), preparation of contracts, provision of transportation (except in an emergency on the road), procurement of food, and that the Stage Manager shall not function as Director or Choreographer. It is further agreed the personnel assigned duties of a Stage Manager or Assistant Stage Manager shall be signed to an Equity contract. (Industrial)

- The Stage Manager or Assistant Stage Manager shall not be required to design, build, shop for, or hang scenery, props, lights, or costumes. Further, the operation of lights and the design and operation of sound is not a basic Stage Managerial duty but may be agreed to on an individual basis. (LORT)

- It is not the function of the Stage Manager or the Assistant Stage Manager to transport any employees of the Theatre, including, but not limited to, Actors, Directors, and Designers, to appointments, performances, or rehearsals. (LORT)

A General Manager's Definition of an Ideal Stage Manager

Jose Vega is a general manager on Broadway (*The Wiz*, *Ain't Misbehavin'*) and shared his ideas on the duties of a stage manager at a roundtable discussion sponsored by the Stage Managers' Association in 1985.

Could You Describe the Ideal Stage Manager?

"That's simple . . . someone with a good working knowledge of all technical aspects. Someone who can act as a director but who doesn't want to be one, who just likes maintaining the show. Someone who, on the road, can be a parent figure for all the actors, keep them together, keep them as happy as you can possibly keep actors.

"So when a general manager looks around for a stage manager, what does he get? If you have a show that is not technically difficult, you look for someone who can direct and maintain shows. It it's technically difficult, you look for one person who can do the technical part and one who can work with actors. One thing you don't want is any personality problem with the stage manager *whatsoever*. [A GM] has enough other problems without the one person you've got to keep problems away from you creating personality problems of his or her own."

How Do You Define the Duties of a Stage Manager?

"I think the stage manager should know everything that goes on on that stage. One thing stage managers [forego] a lot of the time is working with the crew. No matter how good a crew you have, they all have their departments, and *their* departments are the most important. You, hopefully, are objective. If you see the carpenter's set is going to get up but the lights are not going to get hung, you should be able to go to the carpenter and say 'Look, he's way behind, let him on the stage,' or, 'You start with your back pipe, and let the property man (who never gets a chance to do anything) come onstage now.' I see that happening less and less. Without a lot of experience you can get your head knocked in because they [the crew] are not going to take it unless you know what you're doing."

Describe the Division of Duties Between a Stage Manager and a Company Manager.

"I think a SM, from the curtain line back, is responsible for everything that happens. The company manager is there for the day-to-day business, to make decisions the SM can't, from the apron out. It differs—some company managers have 'their' crews. I'm against that. I think the crew should go to the SM. You are not co-managers, which is something you have to live with and use as productively as possible. Yes, there are CMs who interfere with everything back there and they shouldn't. But your job is to please the people you work for, and if your CM thinks it's his job to come backstage, well, that's the person you're working for, and there's nothing you can do. If there is a decision to be made, the CM is going to make it and the SM is going to have to live with it."

A Resident Theater's Definition of a Production Stage Manager

The following duties and responsibilities were part of a job description for a production stage manager at Seattle Repertory Theatre in 1983.

1. Stage manage two shows.
2. Organize and maintain stage management office.
3. Oversee and advise stage management staff.
4. Authority to make additional assignments to stage management staff.
5. Daily scheduling of rehearsals and fittings in conjunction with Stage Manager of each production.

6. Daily scheduling of space (rehearsal rooms).

7. Responsible for maintenance of Equity rules and standards.

8. Dealing with welfare of acting company in matters directly connected with production.

9. Supervising and monitoring of all technical rehearsals and previews.

10. To be present at staff meetings representing stage management and company.

11. Organize and monitor production meeting with stage manager of production running the meeting.

12. To take part in building of tech schedules.

13. Dealings with P.R. Department with regard to photo calls, interviews, special events.

14. Reviewing and submitting of petty cash flow.

15. Understudying of stage manager position on all occasions.

16. Overseeing New Play productions.

17. Maintaining production records and info.

18. Organization of understudy meeting and general responsibility for overseeing their work.

19. To work with Production Manager on any projects regarding productions, personnel, or stage management department.

20. Responsible for making any new member of the company feel right at home.

2. Sample Production Schedules

The production schedules that follow are all structured basically the same. There are three columns: the left column is for the day and month; the middle column is for the exact time, or as exact as possible when the schedule is drawn up; and the right column, for which the most room should be left is for the description of what happens during each time slot.

Some reminders when preparing a production schedule:

1. When work is happening simultaneously at shops, in rehearsal rooms, and/or at the theater, note location of each call or event.

2. Always date each revision because production schedules change frequently.

3. Remember that these schedules, as opposed to rehearsal schedules, should focus on the technical aspects of the show.

4. Don't be afraid to use the acronym TBA (to be announced) if a date is open or subject to change.

5. Don't be rigid about the form of the schedule; circumstances will dictate whether changes or improvements are advisable.

One-Man Show/West End Transfer: *Kipling*

This schedule is for the Broadway production of *Kipling,* Alec McCowen's one-man show, an acclaimed portrayal of the well-known English poet. Written by Brian Clark and directed by Patrick Garland, the show had performed in London prior to the New York engagement. This is why the first preview is a few days after McCowen's arrival in town. The following production schedule makes clear how many details must be taken care of and how many meetings must be arranged, even on a relatively simple show. (Note that this schedule uses the words "take-in" and "take-out," alternatives to load-in and load-out.)

<u>KIPLING</u>

<u>PRODUCTION SCHEDULE</u>

<u>AS OF AUGUST 30, 1984</u>

TUES SEPT 4th		PATRICK GARLAND ARRIVES BA FLIGHT #175 AT 1:30 pm - KENNEDY AIRPORT. TO BE MET BY TOM KELLY TO BEGIN PRE- PRODUCTION MEETINGS
WED SEPT 5th	10:00 am	STAGE DOORMAN ON CALL MEETING AT ROYALE THEATRE, 242 WEST 45th STREET - PATRICK GARLAND, NEIL PETER JAMPOLIS [designer], TOM KELLY
	12:00 pm	VALERIE SPRADLING [sound opera- tor] JOINS ABOVE
THURS SEPT 6th	10:00 am	MASQUE SOUND - 331 WEST 51st STREET PATRICK GARLAND, TOM KELLY & VALERIE SPRADLING - SOUND TAPE RECORDING
	PM	ADDITIONAL MEETINGS TBA
FRI SEPT 7th		PATRICK GARLAND MEETINGS TBA
		PATRICK GARLAND RETURNS TO LONDON VIA BA FLIGHT #176 DEPARTING KENNEDY AIRPORT AT 9:00 pm
MON SEPT 17th		SHOP WORK BEGINS AT FOUR STAR - JIM SPRADLING [electrician]
SAT SEPT 22nd		PHYSICAL PRODUCTION SHIPPED BY THEATOURS SHIPPING & FORWARDING VIA AIR FROM LONDON TO KENNEDY AIRPORT
MON SEPT 24th	10:00 am	ROYALE THEATRE BOX OFFICE OPENS
		SHOP WORK BEGINS AT MASQUE SOUND - VALERIE SPRADLING

"KIPLING" - PRODUCTION SCHEDULE - PAGE 2 - AS OF AUGUST 30, 1984

TUES SEPT 25th	8:00 am to 12:00 pm 1:00 pm to 5:00 pm	SPOT CALL - ROYALE THEATRE - 242 WEST 45th STREET - HOUSE CARPENTER, FLYMAN, PLUS 4 MEN ARTIE SICCARDI [production supervisor]
WED SEPT 26th	TBA	ERIE TRUCK TO PICK UP PHYSICAL PRODUCTION FROM RADIX CUSTOMS AT KENNEDY AIRPORT AND RETURN TO BARN OVERNIGHT
	TBA	ERIE TRUCK TO PICK UP PLATFORMS AND FLATS FROM METRO SCENERY AND RETURN TO BARN OVERNIGHT
THURS SEPT 27th	8:00 am	ERIE TRUCK PICK UP AT FOUR STAR AND DELIVER TO ROYALE THEATRE AND PICK UP AT MASQUE SOUND FOR DELIVERY TO ROYALE THEATRE
	9:00 am to 12:00 pm	BEGIN TAKE-IN AT ROYALE THEATRE - (ELECTRICS - 11 MEN; CARPENTRY - 10 MEN; PROPS - 3 MEN)
		ERIE TRUCK WITH PHYSICAL PRO- DUCTION TO ARRIVE AT THEATRE AT 9:00 am
	1:00 pm to 6:00 pm	CONTINUE TAKE-IN BLACKS AND TREES DELIVERED TO THEATRE FIREPROOFING OF LONDON SCENIC ELEMENTS
FRI SEPT 28th	8:00 am to 12:00 pm	TAKE-IN CONTINUES AT ROYALE THEATRE FOCUS LIGHTS, PROGRAM SLIDES
	1:00 pm to 5:00 pm	CONCLUDE TAKE-IN BREAK TAKE-IN CREW

SAT SEPT 29th		DAY OFF
		ALEC McCOWEN ARRIVES BA FLIGHT #175 AT 1:30 pm - KENNEDY AIRPORT
		PATRICK GARLAND, NATHAN JOSEPH AND BRIAN CLARK ARRIVALS FROM LONDON TBA
SUN SEPT 30th		DAY OFF
MON OCT 1st	8:00 am to 12:00 pm	WORKING CREW ONLY AT ROYALE THEATRE
	1:00 pm to 5:00 pm	LIGHT, SOUND AND SLIDE CUES SET WITH PATRICK GARLAND
	PM	PAINT CALL - DECK
TUES OCT 2nd	8:00 am to 12:00 pm	RUN ALL LIGHTS, SOUND, PROJECTION DRY TECH WITH PATRICK GARLAND
	1:00 pm to 5:00 pm	TECH WITH ALEC McCOWEN
	5:00 pm to 6:00 pm	FIXES, PRESENT, NOTES BREAK
	7:00 pm to 10:00 pm	COMPLETE DRESS
WED OCT 3rd	8:00 am to 12:00 pm	
	1:00 pm to 5:00 pm	AVAILABLE FOR FIXES, IF NECESSARY
	7:00 pm	1 HOUR PRESET
	7:30 pm	HALF HOUR
	8:00 pm	PREVIEW NUMBER ONE

"KIPLING" - PRODUCTION SCHEDULE - PAGE 4 - AS OF AUGUST 30, 1984

THURS OCT 4th		PERFORMANCES EVENINGS AT
thru		8:00 pm
SUN OCT 7th		
		SUNDAY MATINEE AT 3:00 pm
MON OCT 8th		COMPANY DAY OFF
TUES OCT 9th		FINAL PREVIEW PERFORMANCE
WED OCT 10th	6:45 pm	OFFICIAL OPENING

Pre-Broadway Tour: *Peccadillo*

Garson Kanin's drawing room comedy *Peccadillo* starred Christopher Plummer, Glynnis Johns, and Kelly McGillis. Unfortunately, the show never did make it *to* Broadway, although Florida audiences responded enthusiasticly. The following production schedule is a good example of the complexities of rehearsing a play in a different city than that in which it will open. Notice, for instance, that as production stage manager, I was required to be in Florida before the rest of the company to supervise the focus.

Rev. January 28, 1985

PECCADILLO PRODUCTION SCHEDULE

Important phone numbers for any emergencies regarding schedule:
Tom Kelly	XXX-XXXX
Chuck Kindl	XXX-XXXX
Production Office	XXX-XXXX
Garson Office	XXX-XXXX

Mon. Jan. 28	2:00 - 10:00	First Rehearsal	MANHATTAN CENTER XXX West XXth St. (XXX) XXX-XXXX 7th Floor Stage XXX-XXXX
Tues. Jan. 29	12:30 - 8:30	Rehearsal	
			Interviews set-up with St. Petersburg Critic,
Wed. Jan. 30	12:30 - 8:30	Rehearsal	Tom Sibullus NYC Cinnamon

1) By end of week, finalize all costume/hair designs & complete first fittings

Thurs. Jan. 31   12:30 - 8:30   Rehearsal

2) Light plot complete & bid in shop

Fri. Feb. 1   12:30 - 8:30   Rehearsal

3) Sound plot complete & set recording session for week ending Feb 9 - Set who & how to record "Fledermouse" audition song

Sat. Feb. 2   12:30 - 8:30   Rehearsal

Sun. Feb. 3   DAY OFF

DURING WEEK

Mon. Feb. 4   11:30   Production Meeting

1) Record session CP, GJ, CK and AUDITION SONG

Tues. Feb. 5   12:30 - 8:30   Rehearsal

2) Finalize all props, furniture, etc. Begin delivery of any actual props, furniture, etc. to 311 W. 34 for use in reh.

Wed. Feb. 6   12:30 - 8:30   Rehearsal

Thurs. Feb. 7   12:30 - 8:30   Rehearsal

3) Finish show tape for use in reh.

Fri. Feb. 8   12:30 - 8:30   Rehearsal

4) Costume & wig fittings

Sat. Feb. 9   12:30 - 8:30   Rehearsal

5) Finalize all travel & hotel plans for Florida

Sun. Feb. 10   DAY OFF

6) Order all trucks for Florida

Rev. January 28, 1985   2.

PECCADILLO PRODUCTION SCHEDULE

Mon. Feb. 11	11:30	Production Meeting	**DURING WEEK**
	12:30 – 8:30	Rehearsal	1) Confirm Fla. baby grand piano
Tues. Feb. 12	12:30 – 8:30	Rehearsal	2) Final fittings MON & TUES
Wed. Feb. 13	12:30 – 8:30	Rehearsal	1) Local truck pick up props from reh. hall, etc. & deliver to scenery shop – also work boxes etc.
Thurs. Feb. 14	12:30 – 8:30	Rehearsal	2) Load-out props, set, cost, sound, elec.
Fri. Feb. 15	12:30 – 8:30	Rehearsal	
Sat. Feb. 16	12:30 – 8:30	Rehearsal	3) Pre-hang elex in St. Petersburg
Sun. Feb. 17	DAY OFF		4) T. Kelly & Crew to St. Petersburg
Mon. Feb. 18	12:30 – 8:30	Rehearsal	FLA. 8:00-Midnight load-in, hang, etc. focus in St. Pete

Tues. Feb. 19   12:30 TRAVEL CALL at 311 W. 34th Street

                3:00 (Approx) Co. Flight to Fla.

In Fla.   8:00 – 12:00 (Midnite) Continue load-in, hang, focus & set cues in Fla.

Wed. Feb. 20	8:00 – 12 Noon	1) Piano tuned
		2) Finish cue setting, clean-up & pre-set props & costumes & quick-change rooms
		3) Dry tech all scene changes w/out actors
	1:00 – 6:00	Begin TECH/DRESS with actors
	7:30 – 12:00	Continue TECH/DRESS with actors
Thurs. Feb. 21	8:00 – 12 Noon	TECH work as needed
	1:00 – 6:00	Finish TECH/DRESS with actors
	7:30	Half Hour
	8:00	FULL DRESS REHEARSAL
Fri. Feb. 22	8:00 – 12 Noon	Tech work as necessary
	1:00	Full Company, Notes & Scene work
	2:30	Half Hour
	3:00	DRESS REHEARSAL

Rev. January 28, 1985   3.

PECCADILLO PRODUCTION SCHEDULE

Fri. Feb. 22	6:00	D i n n e r	
	7:30	Half Hour	
	8:00	**PERFORMANCE**	
Sat. Feb. 23	12:30 Noon	Notes	
	1:30	Half Hour	
	2:00	**MATINEE**	
	7:30	Half Hour	
	8:00	**EVENING PERFORMANCE**	
Sun. Feb. 24	1:30	Half Hour	1) Pre-hang Elex in Palm Beach
	2:00	**MATINEE**	
	6:30	Half Hour	
	7:00	**EVENING PERFORMANCE**	2) Load-out & truck to PB

Mon. Feb. 25   COMPANY DAY OFF - COMPANY TRAVEL TO PALM BEACH
                8:00 a.m. - Midnight Load-in, hang & focus Palm Beach

Tues. Feb. 26	8:00 - 12 Noon	Finish hang, focus, etc.
	1:00	Pre-set & dry tech
	3:00	TECH with Actors
	6:00	Break
	8:00	Half Hour
	8:30	**OPEN PALM BEACH**

REMAINDER PALM BEACH PLAYING SCHEDULE

Week ending March 3	WED - SAT	EVE at 8:00
	WED - SAT - SUN	Mat at 2:00
Week ending March 10	TUES - SUN	EVE at 8:00
	WED - SAT	MAT at 2:00

Mon. Mar. 11   COMPANY DAY OFF - COMPANY TRAVEL TO FT. LAUDERDALE
                8:00 a.m. - 12 Midnight Load-in, hang & focus Ft. Lauderdale

Tues. Mar. 12	8:00 - 12 Noon	Finish hang, focus, etc.
	1:00	Pre-set & dry tech
	3:00	TECH with Actors
	6:00	Break
	8:00	**OPEN IN FT. LAUDERDALE**

FT. LAUDERDALE PLAYING SCHEDULE

Week ending Mar. 17	TUES - SAT	EVE at 8:00
	WED - SAT - SUN	MAT at 2:00

3. Sample Contact Sheets

Contact sheets are crucial to the smooth operation of any theater production. Two different contact sheets from the same show are included here. The first is a "long form," listing every person connected with the production of the 1990 Broadway revival of Shakespeare's *The Merchant of Venice*, directed by Sir Peter Hall and starring Dustin Hoffman as Shylock. It includes the addresses and phone numbers of every member of the production, creative, and departmental staffs, including assistants. At the top, the words "Strictly Confidential" indicate that this contact sheet should only be distributed to those who have permission to receive it. The "short form" (what I call a refrigerator list) is a compressed version of the longer contact sheet.

Whatever form is used, remember to separate the creative staff from the technical and production crews because often a stage manager will need to contact one group or the other, but not both. Therefore, a strict alphabetical list, for instance, would make contacting the cast for a rehearsal change more difficult because the stage manager would have to sift through the names, looking for the actors.

Contact Sheet—Long Form

THE MERCHANT OF VENICE CONTACT SHEET

Strictly Confidential   March 1, 1990

PRODUCERS

Jerome Minskoff	XXXX Xth Avenue	XXX XXX-XXXX
	New York, N.Y. XXXXX	XXX XXX-XXXX fax
Duncan Weldon	Triumph Theatre	XXX XXX XXX-XXXX
	Productions	XXX XXX XXX-XXXX fax
	XXXXXXX XXXXXXXX	
	Suite X	
	XX XXX XXXXXX	
	London XXXX XXX	
Punch Productions	XX XXXXXXXXXXX XXXXX	XXX XXX-XXXX
Lee Gottsegen	Suite XXXX	
Timothy Meyers	NYC XXXXX	
Marianne Ruffano		

EXECUTIVE PRODUCER

Thelma Holt	Peter Hall Co.	XXX XXX XXX-XXXX
	XX XXXXXX Street	
	London XXX England	
Assistant		XXX XXX XXX-XXXX
Malcolm Taylor		XXX XXX XXX-XXXX fax
		XXX XXX XXX-XXXX fax

DIRECTOR

Peter Hall	Peter Hall Co.	XXX XXX XXX-XXXX fax
	XX XXXXXX Street	
	London XXX England	
Associate Director		
Giles Block	XX, XXXXXX Road	XXX XXX XXX-XXXX
	London XXXX XXX	
	England	

GENERAL MANAGER

Joseph P. Harris, Sr.	XXXX Broadway	XXX XXX-XXXX
Peter T. Kulok	Suite XXX	XXX XXX-XXXX fax
	NYC XXXXX	
Assistants		
Nancy Simmons	X XXXXX XXXX	XXX XXX-XXXX home
	Apt. #XXX NYC XXXXX	
Geraldine Higgins	XX XXXXXXXXX Avenue	XXX XXX-XXXX
	Livingston, NJ	
Kathleen Griffin	XX West XXrd #XX	XXX XXX-XXXX
	NYC XXXXX	

THE MERCHANT OF VENICE CONTACT SHEET

Strictly Confidential   March 1, 1990   2.

PRESS REPRESENTATIVE
Josh Ellis   XXX West XXth Street   XXX XXX-XXXX Office
  Adrian Bryan Brown   NYC XXXXX   XXX XXX-XXXX Home
  Jackie Green   XXX XXX-XXXX Home
                                                  XXX XXX-XXXX Home

STAGE MANAGEMENT
Thomas A. Kelly   XX XXXXXXXXXXX Drive   XXX XXX-XXXX
                        Croton-on-Hudson
                        NYC XXXXX

Charles Kindl   XXX West XXth Street   XXX XXX-XXXX
                        #XX-X
                        NYC XXXXX

James Dawson   XX West XXth Street   XXX XXX-XXXX
                        #X
                        NYC XXXXX

Donna A. Drake   XXXX XXXXXXX Avenue   XXX XXX-XXXX
                        Jersey City, NJ XXXXX

Stage Manager - UK
  Sarah Parkin   XX XXX XXXXX Crescent   XXX XXX XXX-XXXX
                        London XXX England

DESIGNER
Chris Dyer   XX XXXXX XXXXXX Road   XXX XXX XXX-XXXX
                        London XX XXX
                        Stratford   XXXX-XXXXXX

ASSOCIATE SET DESIGNER - NY
Duke Durfee   XXX XXXXXXXXX Street   XXX XXX-XXXX Home
                        Brooklyn, NY XXXXX

ASSOCIATE COSTUME DESIGNER - NY
Barbara Forbes   XXX XXXXX Avenue   XXX XXX-XXXX
                        Teaneck, N.J. XXXXX

LIGHTING DESIGNERS
Mark Henderson   Agent: Peter Bennet   XXX XXX XXX-XXXX
                        Jones   XXX XXX XXX-XXXX

Neil Peter Jampolis   XXX West XXth Street   XXX XXX-XXXX Home
                        #XX   XXX-XXXX Office
                        NYC XXXXX
                        Office: XXX W XXth St
                                Rm XX
                                NYC XXXXX

THE MERCHANT OF VENICE CONTACT SHEET

Strictly Confidential   March 1, 1990   3.

ASSOCIATE LIGHTING DESIGNER
William D. Anderson   XXX West XXth St   XXX XXX-XXXX Office
                       Room XX
                       NYC XXXXX

MUSIC BY
Robert Lockhart   XX XXXXXXXXX Road   XXX XXX XXX-XXXX
                       London XXX

SOUND DESIGNER
Paul Arditti   First Floor Flat   XXX XXX XXX-XXXX
                       XX XXXXXXX Road
                       London XXX XXX

CASTING
Johnson/Liff   XXXX XXXXXXXX   XXX XXX-XXXX
                       Suite XXXX   XXX XXX-XXXX
                       NYC XXXXX

VOICE COACH - UK
Julia Wilson-Dickson   X XXXXXX Road   XXX XXX XXX-XXXX
                       London XXX XXX

TEXT ADVISOR
Chris Newell   XXX XXXXXXXXX Road   XXX XXX XXX-XXXX
                       London XX XXX

PRODUCTION MANAGER
Michael Cass Jones   Unit 1 Production   XXX XXX XXX-XXXX
                       Services Ltd   XXX XXX XXX-XXXX fax
                       X XXXXXXXX Road   XXX XXX XXXXXXXXXX
                       XXXXXXXXX, Middlesex   Mobil

                       XX XXXXXX XXXXX   XXX XXX XXX-XXXX
                       Putney - London XXXX   Home
                       XXX

CREATIVE ARTISTS
CAST

William Beckwith   XXX East XXst Street   XXX XXX-XXXX
  (Innkeeper etc)   #XX
                       NYC XXXXX

Neal Ben-Ari   XX XXXXXXXXXX Street   XXX XXX-XXXX
  (Balthasar)   Brooklyn, NY XXXXX

THE MERCHANT OF VENICE CONTACT SHEET

Strictly Confidential   March 1, 1990   4.

Ben Browder   XXXX XXXXXX Trail   XXX XXX-XXXX
  (Leonardo)   XXXXXXXXX, NC XXXXX
                      USA
                      In England:
                        % Maggie Parker
                        Al Parker Agency   London XXX XXXX
                        XX XXXX Lane
                        London XX

Francesca Buller   Same as above for
  (Jessica)   Browder

Donald Burton   XXX East XXth Street   XXX XXX-XXXX
  (Salerio)   NYC XXXXX

Michael Carter   XX XXXXXX Street
                      East Dulwich
                      London XXXX England

Margery Daley   XX XXXXXXXXX Avenue   XXX XXX-XXXX
  (Soprano)   #X-X
                      NYC XXXXX

Peter-Hugo Daly   XX XXXXXXX XXXXX
  (Lancelot)   Tressel Close
                      XXXXXXXXX London XX
                      XXX
                      England

Dale Dickey   XXX West XXth Street   XXX XXX-XXXX
  (Casket Bearer etc) #XXX
                      NYC XXXXX

Herb Downer   XXX XXXXXXX XXXX XXXX   XXX XXX-XXXX
  (Prince of Morocco) NYC XXXXX   Svc XXX XXX-XXXX

Elisabeth Engan   XXX XXXX Avenue   XXX XXX-XXXX
  (Soprano)   XXXXXXXX, CA XXXXX

Richard Garnett   XXX XXXXXXXX XXXX   XX XXX XXXX
  (Lorenzo)   London XX XXX England

Gordon Gould   XXX XXXXXXX XXXX XXXX   XXX XXX-XXXX
  (Solanio)   NYC XXXXX   Svc XXX XXX-XXXX

Peter Jay Fernandez   XXX XXXXXXXXX Drive   XXX XXX-XXXX
  (Courtier etc)   NYC XXXXX

Basil Henson   XX, The Drive
  (Duke of Venice)   XXXXXXXXX
                      XXXX XXX XXX England

THE MERCHANT OF VENICE CONTACT SHEET

Strictly Confidential   March 1, 1990   5.

Dustin Hoffman   % Punch Productions   XXX XXX-XXXX
(Shylock)   XX XXXXXXXXXXX XXXXX
                        #XXXX
                        NYC XXXXX

Denis Holmes   XX XXX XXXXX Road   XXX XXX-XXXX
(Beggar etc)   XXXXXXXX, N.J. XXXXX

Geraldine James   XX, XXXXXXXXX XXXXXXX   XX XXX XXXX
(Portia)   London XXXX XXX
                        England

Leigh Lawson   X XXX XXXXXXX XXXXX
(Antonio)   XX, XXXXXXX XXXXXX
                        London XX England

Leo Leyden   XXX East XXth Street   XXX XXX-XXXX
(Old Gobbo)   XX-X
                        NYC XXXXX

Leon Lissek   Mindle Cottage   XXXXXXXX XXXXX
(Tubal)   X, Copthall Corner   (0753)
                        XXXXXXXX XXX XXXXX   XXXXXX
                        XXXXX XXX XXX England

Nathaniel Parker   XX, XXXXXX XXXXX
(Bassanio)   London XXX XXX
                        England

Wilbur Pauley   XX XXXXXXXXXX Avenue   XXX XXX-XXXX
(Bass)   NYC XXXXX

Margaret Poyner   X XXXXXXX Drive   XXX XXX-XXXX
(Casket Bearer etc)   XXXXXXXXXX, NJ XXXXX

Gray Rayppy   XXX West XXst Street   XXX XXX-XXXX
(Courtier etc)   #X-X
                        NYC XXXXX

Michael Siberry   Third Floor
(Graziano)   4, XXXXXXX Road
                        XXXX XXXXXXXXXX
                        London XXX XXX
                        England

Christina Sunnerstam   XXX West XXth Street   XXX XXX-XXXX
(Violinist)   #X-X
                        NYC XXXXX

Julia Swift   XX, XXXXXXXX Road
(Nerrisa)   London XX XXX England

THE MERCHANT OF VENICE CONTACT SHEET

Strictly Confidential   March 1, 1990   6.

John Norman Thomas   XXX XXXXXX Street   XXX XXX-XXXX
  (Courtier etc)   #X-X
                          XXXXXXXXX, NJ XXXXX

Isiah Whitlock   XXX West XXth Street   XXX XXX-XXXX
  (Courtier etc)   NYC XXXXX

John Wojda   XX-XX XXXXX Street   XXX XXX-XXXX
  (Stephano etc)   XXXXXXXXX, NY XXXXX

Taylor Young   XX XXXXX XXXXXXXX   XXX XXX-XXXX
  (Portia U/S)   Avenue
                          Brooklyn, NY XXXXX

TECHNICAL SUPERVISOR
Jeremiah J. Harris   Mobil phone -
                          XXXXXXXXXX + XXXXXXXXXX

Jeremiah J. Harris   XXXX XXXXXXXX   XXX XXX-XXXX
  Assoc   Suite XXX   XXX XXX-XXXX fax
                          NYC XXXXX

Partners
  Roy Sears   XXX XXX-XXXX Home
  John Wolf   XXX XXX-XXXX Home
  Fred Gallo   XXX XXX-XXXX Home

Assistants
  Lenora S. Seckinger   XX XXXXXX Avenue   XXX XXX-XXXX Home
                          NYC XXXXX

  Alexandra Von   XXX East XXth Street   XXX XXX-XXXX Home
    Othegraven   NYC XXXXX

CARPENTER
Danny Champ   XX-XX XXXth Street   XXX XXX-XXXX
                          Flushing, NY XXXXX

ELECTRICIAN
Scott Schilk   XXX West XXXrd Street   XXX XXX-XXXX
                          #X-X
                          NYC XXXXX

PROPERTIES SUPERVISOR
Joseph P. Harris, Jr.   XXXX XXXX XXXX Drive   XXX XXX-XXXX
                          Teaneck, NJ XXXXX   XXX XXX-XXXX beeper

SOUND SUPERVISOR
Scott Anderson   XXX XXXXXXXXXX Avenue   XXX XXX-XXXX
                          XXXXXXXXXX, NJ XXXXX

THE MERCHANT OF VENICE CONTACT SHEET

Strictly Confidential   March 1, 1990   7.

SOUND OPERATOR
Cathey Chaffee   XXX XXXXXXX Place   XXX XXX-XXXX
                        Brooklyn, N.Y. XXXXX

ASSOCIATE to MS FORBES
Robert Bevinger   XXX XXXX XXXXXX XXXXX   XXX XXX-XXXX
                        #XX
                        NYC XXXXX

WARDROBE MISTRESS
Kathleen Gallagher   XX West XXth Street   XXX XXX-XXXX
                        #XX   XXX XXX-XXXX
                        NYC XXXXX   Temporary

COSTUMES SUPERVISOR - UK
Allan Watkins   XXX XXXXXXXXX Road   XXX XXX XXX-XXXX
                        London XX

DUSTIN'S DRESSER/ASSISTANT
Barbara Toye   X, XXXXXX XXXXX
                       XXXXXX Street
                       London XXX XXX

WARDROBE MISTRESS - UK
Nicola Beveridge   X XXXXXXXXXX Road   XXX XXX XXX-XXXX
                        XXXXXX XXX, London XX

HAIR SUPERVISOR - UK
Jonhenry Gordon   Les Forge De   XX-XX-XXXXXX
                        Montgaillard
                        XXXXX XXXXXXXXXX
                        XXXX
                        France

WIGS
Jeffrey Frank   Elsen Associates   XXX XXX-XXXX
                        XXX XXXXXXXXX Drive
                        NYC XXXXX

HAIR
Shontae Olivia   PO Box XXXX   XXX XXX-XXXX
  Johnson   Midtown Sta
                        NYC XXXXX

DRESSERS
Michael DiFonzo   XXX XXXXX Street #X-X   XXX XXX-XXXX
                        NYC XXXXX

THE MERCHANT OF VENICE CONTACT SHEET

Strictly Confidential   March 1, 1990   8.

Marcia McIntosh	XXX West XXth Street #X-X NYC XXXXX	XXX XXX-XXXX
Ursula Ingrid Nachum	XXX XXXXXXXX Terrace Forest Hills, NY	XXX XXX-XXXX
James Dursi		XXX XXX-XXXX
Lorraine Spencer	XXX East XXXth Street Bronx, NY XXXXX	XXX XXX-XXXX
Hilda Garcia-Suli	XXX West XXth Street NYC XXXXX	XXX XXX-XXXX Svc XXX-XXXX
Ralph (Rafe) Warshaw	XXX XXXXXXXX Ave Apt XX-X NYC XXXXX	XXX XXX-XXXX
Joan Weiss	XXX West XXst Street NYC XXXXX	XXX XXX-XXXX

THEATRE

XXth Street Theatre	XXX West XXth Street NYC XXXXX	XXX XXX-XXXX Backstage XXX XXX-XXXX Box Office
STAGE MANAGER'S OFFICE	XXX West XXth Street	XXX XXX-XXXX
Nederlander Org. Arthur Rubin Peter Russell	XXX XXXXXXX Avenue NYC XXXXX	XXX XXX-XXXX

THEATRE STAFF

Electrics	George Balin	XXX XXX-XXXX
Props	Dennis Larkin	XXX XXX-XXXX
House Mgr	Neil Howard	XXX XXX-XXXX
Doorman	Joe Cartagena	XXX XXX-XXXX
Doorman	Frank Lazarto	

SHOPS & SERVICE SECURITY

Excel	24-hour service	XXX XXX-XXXX
Tony Mascia		XXX XXX-XXXX Home
Joe Del Gado		XXX XXX-XXXX Home

SCENIC SHOP

East Coast Theatre Supply, Inc.	Shore Road Cornwall, NY	XXX XXX-XXXX XXX XXX-XXXX fax

THE MERCHANT OF VENICE CONTACT SHEET

Strictly Confidential   March 1, 1990   9.

LIGHTING SHOP

Bash	XXXX Dell Avenue	XXX XXX-XXXX
	North Bergen, NJ	XXX XXX-XXXX
	XXXXX	
	24-hour service	XXX XXX-XXXX

SOUND SHOP

Sound Associates	XXX West XXth Street	XXX XXX-XXXX
Peter Fitzgerald	NYC XXXXX	XXX XXX-XXXX
Richard Fitzgerald		

COSTUME SHOP

Donna Langman	XX West XXth Street	XXX XXX-XXXX
	Xth Floor	
	NYC XXXXX (Between	
	Xth & Xth Ave)	
London Town Car		XXX XXX-XXXX

SHOPPERS

Nancy Palmatier		XXX XXX-XXXX
Murrey Nelson	XXX West XXth Street	XXX XXX-XXXX
	NYC XXXXX	

MILLINER SHOP

Lynne Mackey	XXX XXXXXXXX Terrace	XXX XXX-XXXX
	#XXX	
	NYC XXXXX	
Deborah Trout	XX XXXXXX Avenue	XXX XXX-XXXX Home
	NYC XXXXX	
WELLINGTON HOTEL	XXX XXXXXXX Avenue	XXX XXX-XXXX
	NYC XXXXX	
MAYFLOWER HOTEL	CPW & XXst Street NYC	XXX XXX-XXXX
	XXXXX	
ESPLANDE HOTEL	XXX West End Avenue	XXX XXX-XXXX
	NYC XXXXX	

UNIONS

Actor's Equity	XXX West XXth Street	XXX XXX-XXXX
	NYC XXXXX	
Musician's Union	Local XXX XXX	XXX-XXXX
	W XXnd St	
	NYC XXXXX	
IATSE Local One	XXX West XXth Street	XXX-XXXX
	NYC XXXXX	

Contact Sheet—Short Form

THE MERCHANT OF VENICE - CAST CONTACT SHEET

November 13, 1989

CAST

William Beckwith (Innkeeper etc) XXX East XXst St. #XX   XXX XXX-XXXX
Neal Ben-Ari (Balthasar) XX XXXXXXXXXX St. Bklyn XXXXX   XXX XXX-XXXX
Ben Browder (Leonardo)   Temp   XXX XXX-XXXX
Francesca Buller (Jessica)   Temp   XXX XXX-XXXX
Donald Burton (Salerio) XXX East XXth St. NYC XXXXX   XXX XXX-XXXX
    Agent: Byran Drew XXX XXX XXX-XXXX
Michael Carter (Aragon) XXX West XXth St. #X-X   XXX XXX-XXXX
Margery Daley (Soprano) XXX West XXth St. #XXX NYC XXXXX   XXX XXX-XXXX
Peter-Hugo Daly (Lancelot) XXX XXXXX Ave   XXX XXX-XXXX
Dale Dickey (Nerissa/Jessica U/S) XXX West XXth St.   XXX XXX-XXXX
Herb Downer (Morocco) XXX XXX Agent-Sames XXX-XXXX   Svc: XXX-XXXX XXX-XXXX
Elisabeth Engan (Soprano) XXX West XXth St. #X NYC XXXXX   XXX XXX-XXXX
Richard Garnett (Lorenzo) XXX XXXX Place Bklyn XXXXX   XXX XXX-XXXX
Gordon Gould (Solanio) XXX XXX NYC XXXXX   Svc: XXX-XXXX   XXX-XXXX
Basil Henson (Duke of Venice) XXXXXXXX Hotel XXX XXXX XXX Ave   XXX-XXXX
Dustin Hoffman (Shylock) % Punch Prod.   XXX XXX-XXXX
Denis Holmes (Beggar etc) XXX E. XX. XXXXXXXX Ave. NJ   XXX XXX-XXXX
Geraldine James (Portia) XXX E XXth St. #XX-X NYC XXXXX   XXX XXX-XXXX
Leigh Lawson (Antonio) XX West XXth St. NYC XXXXX   XXX-XXXX or XXX-XXXX
Leo Leyden (Old Gobbo)   XXX XXX-XXXX
Leon Lissek (Tubal) XXX XXXXXXXXXX Place   XXX XXX-XXXX
Nathaniel Parker (Bassanio) XXX W XXXth St. #XX NYC XXXXX   XXX XXX-XXXX
Wilbur Pauley (Bass) XX XXXXXXXXXX Ave. NYC XXXXX   XXX XXX-XXXX
Margaret Poyner (Casket Bearer etc)   XXX XXX-XXXX
Gary Rayppy (Courtier etc) XXX West XXst St. NYC XXXXX   XXX XXX-XXXX
Michael Siberry (Graziano) XX W XXnd St. #3 NYC XXXXX   XXX XXX-XXXX
Christina Sunnerstam (Violinist) XXX W XXth St. #X-X NYC XXXXX   XXX XXX-XXXX
Julia Swift (Nerissa) XX West XXth St. #X-X NYC XXXXX   XXX XXX-XXXX
John Norman Thomas (Courtier etc) XXX XXXXXX St. #X-X NJ XXXXX   XXX XXX-XXXX
Isiah Whitlock (Courtier etc) XXX West XXth St. NYC XXXXX   XXX XXX-XXXX
John Wojda (Stephano etc) XX-XX XXXXX St. Sunnyside, NY XXXXX   XXX XXX-XXXX
Taylor Young (U/S Portia) XX X. XXXXXXXX Ave. Bklyn XXXXX   XXX XXX-XXXX
Alex Hardy (U/S Parker) XXXXXXXXXX Hotel XXX Xth Ave   XXX XXX-XXXX

Josh Ellis (Press) XXX West XXth St. Adrian & Jackie   XXX-XXXX
Johnson-Liff (Casting) XXXX B'way #XXXX   XXX-XXXX
Wellington Hotel XXX XXXXXXX Ave.   XXX-XXXX
Mayflower Hotel   XXX-XXXX
Omni Park Central XXX Xth Ave.   XXX-XXXX
Esplande Hotel XXX XXXX XXX Ave. NYC XXXXX   XXX-XXXX
Actor's Equity XXX West XXth St. NYC XXXXX   XXX-XXXX
Musician's Union Local XXX   XXX-XXXX
IATSE Local One XXX West XXth St.   XXX-XXXX

46TH STREET THEATRE
    XXX West XXth St. NYC XXXXX   Box Off   XXX-XXXX
                                     Backstage   XXX-XXXX
Stage Manager's Office   XXX-XXXX
Nederlander Org. XXX XXXXXXX Ave.   XXX-XXXX
    Arthur Rubin
    Peter Russell

THEATRE STAFF

George Balin (Elex)   XXX XXX-XXXX
Dennis Larkin (Props)   XXX-XXXX
Kevin Camus (Curtain)

THE MERCHANT OF VENICE - CAST CONTACT SHEET

November 13, 1989

Neil Howard (House Mgr)   XXX-XXXX
Joe Cartagena (Door Man)   XXX-XXXX
Frank Lazarto (Door Man)

CREATIVE STAFF

Sir Peter Hall (Dir) Wyndham Hotel XX West XXth St.   XXX XXX-XXXX
Nicki Frei (Asst) Wyndham Hotel XX West XXth St.   XXX XXX-XXXX
Giles Block (Associate Dir) XXX West NYC XXXXX   XXX XXX-XXXX
Chris Dyer (Set & Costume Design) Wellington Hotel   XXX XXX-XXXX
Mark Henderson (Original Lighting)
Neil Peter Jampolis (Lighting) XXX WXX #XX   XXX-XXXX
    Office XXX West XXth St. #XX   Off   XXX-XXXX
William D. Anderson (Assoc Lite Des) Office XXX W XXth St. #XX   XXX-XXXX
Robert Lockhart (Music) Wellington Hotel   XXX-XXXX
Paul Arditti (Sound) Wellington Hotel   XXX-XXXX

PRODUCTION

Jerome Minskoff (Prod) XXXX Xth Ave NYC XXXXX   XXX-XXXX
Duncan C. Weldon (Prod) Triumph Theatrical Prod. London   XXX XXX XXX-XXXX
Thelma Holt (Exec Prod) % Jos Harris Assoc XXXX B'way #XXX   XXX XXX-XXXX
Punch Productions (Prod) XX XXXXXXXXXXX XXXXX #XXXX NYC XXXXX   XXX-XXXX
Joseph P. Harris (Gen Mgr) XXXX B'way Suite XXX NYC XXXXX   XXX-XXXX
Peter Kulok (Joseph Harris Assoc - Gen Mgr) XXXX B'way #XXX   XXX-XXXX
Thomas A. Kelly (Prod Stg Mgr) XX XXXXXXXXXXXX Dr., Croton   XXX XXX-XXXX
Charles Kindl (ASM) XXX West XXth St. NYC XXXXX   XXX-XXXX
James Dawson (ASM) XX West XXth St. NYC XXXXX   XXX-XXXX
Donna A. Drake (ASM) XXXX XXXXXXX Ave. XXXXXX XXXX, NJ XXXXX XXX XXX-XXXX
Sarah Parkin (Stg Mgr-UK) X XXXXXX St. #X-X NYC XXXXX   XXX XXX-XXXX
Michael Cass Jones (Prod Mgr) Wellington Hotel   XXX-XXXX
Jeremiah Harris (Tech Adv)   Off XXX-XXXX   Mobile XXXXXXXXXX + XXXXXXXXXX
East Coast Theatre (Scenic Shop) Shore Road, Cornwall, NY   XXX XXX-XXXX
                                           fax XXX XXX-XXXX
Danny Champ (Prod Carp) XX-XX XXXth St., Flushing, NY XXXXX   XXX XXX-XXXX
Joe Harris (Prod Props) XXXX East Lawn Dr. XXXXXXX, NJ   XXX XXX-XXXX
                                     beeper XXX XXX-XXXX
Scott Schilk (Prod Elex) XXX W XXXrd St. #X-X NYC XXXXX   XXX-XXXX
Allan Watkins (Costume Supervisor-UK) XXX St. XXXXXXXX Ave. #X-X XXX-XXXX
Barbara Forbes (Costume Supervisor)   XXX XXX-XXXX fax XXX XXX-XXXX
Robert Bevinger (Asst/Forbes)   XXX XXX-XXXX fax XXX XXX-XXXX
Kathleen Gallagher (Wardrobe Mistress)   Temp XXX XXX-XXXX XXX-XXXX
Barbara Toye (Personal Asst to Mr. Hoffman) Esplande Hotel   XXX-XXXX
                                     Dresser
Bash (Lite Shop) XXXX Dell Ave. XX. XXXXXX, NJ XXXXX   XXX XXX-XXXX
                      XXX XXX-XXXX 24 Hour Svc #   XXX-XXXX
Scott Anderson (Sound Supervisor)   XXX XXX-XXXX
Cathey Chaffee (Prod Sound) XXX XXXXXXX Pl. Bklyn XXXXX   XXX XXX-XXXX
Sound Associates (Sound Shop) XXX West XXth St.   XXX-XXXX
    Peter/Richard Fitzgerald   XXX XXX-XXXX
Donna Langman (Costume Shop) XX W XXth St. Xth Fl   XXX XXX-XXXX
Lynne Mackey (Milliner Shop) XXX Overlook Terr. #XXX   XXX XXX-XXXX
Deborah Trout XX XXXXXX Ave. NYC XXXXX   XXX XXX-XXXX
Jonhenry Gordon (Hair Supervisor) Esplande Hotel   XXX XXX-XXXX
Jeffrey Frank (Wigs) Elsen Associates XXX XXXXXXXXX Dr. NYC XXXXX XXX-XXXX
Jonathan Miller (Music Contractor)   XXX-XXXX
John Haynes (Photographer) Wellington Hotel   XXX-XXXX
Excel Security Tony XXX XXX-XXXX Joe XXX XXX-XXXX 24 Hr Svc XXX XXX-XXXX
London Town Car XXXX B'way   XXX-XXXX

4. Production Meeting Notes

The following are minutes (or notes) of a preproduction meeting for *The Merchant of Venice*. Stage managers should take careful notes during all such meetings, and at the first opportunity, type them up and distribute them to all participants. The most important features to include when typing minutes are (1) the date; (2) the names of all attendees; and (3) the major headings that were discussed, which can be taken right from the agenda.

```
THE MERCHANT OF VENICE

Notes of Production Meeting 10/11/89

In attendance: Tom Kelly
               Barbara Forbes
               Kathleen Gallagher
               Scott Anderson
               Joe Harris, Jr.
               Duke Durfee
               Jeremiah Harris
               Donna Drake
               Chuck Kindl
               Peter Kulok
               Kathleen Griffin

Truss
1. A request has been made from the designers for both a
   lighting truss and a sound truss. There is however not
   enough steel in the ceiling for a truss to be hung. Due to
   the fact that the theatre is landmarked we would have to go
   through the ceiling and tie to the steel in the roof. This
   is a very costly operation and is being considered by the
   powers that be. More later.

Sound
1. Scott Anderson has just received the shop order from Paul
   and will now proceed to amend and flesh out the list before
   it goes to Sound Associates. He will also be adding
   communication equipment for the Stage Managers.
2. Scott has requested that the portals which are being built
   to match the existing house portals be made at least
   partially of acoustic cloth so that speakers can be placed
   at strategic points.

   This is a potentially expensive proposition since the cloth
   will have to be died to match the existing theatre color.
```

page 2

The position of these speakers will be dependent upon the
possible installation of a sound truss.

3. Sound position will eliminate eight seats at house left.
   Four seats will be pulled from the last two rows.
4. The three "musicians" will be wearing body mics. This should
   not necessarily force us to hire a backstage sound op since
   they wear the mics throughout, and wardrobe is used to
   dealing with them.
5. For teching the show, the communication and cueing system
   will be duplicated in front of house and backstage so Tom
   can initially cue and run techs and first dress from house.

Lights
1. We are waiting on additional information from Mark Henderson
   and Cass so that the final shop order can be put together.
   It is becoming increasingly important that Neil receive this
   information as soon as possible.
2. The preliminary bids have been returned and Jeremiah is
   going over them. More later.

Schedule
1. The containers are due to arrive at the dock on October 18.
   They will be transported from there to East Coast Theatre
   Supply by the 23rd where they will be broken down, customs
   inspected, and the necessary work undertaken.
2. Load-in will begin at the theatre on the 30th to be
   completed by the 4th. Once the focus is finished we will
   break to minimum crew until the beginning of Tech rehearsals
   or need.
3. The schedule needs to be finalized to reflect the proper
   playing schedule for Christmas week.
4. Everyone seems to be comfortable with the progress to this
   point. Although there is some concern that the new costume
   designs and remainder of the light order arrive very soon.

Pyro
1. There are kerosene torches carried in the show which will
   have to be cleared with the fire marshall here. A licensed
   pyro tech may also have to be on staff. Jeremiah and Joe
   Jr. will be dealing with this.
2. It is possible some fireproofing may need to be done to
   costumes worn by torch carriers. Also, wardrobe voiced their
   concern over the blackening of hands and costumes due to
   dripping of kerosene.

Wardrobe
1. Barbara is going to discuss budget with Peter so that she
   can begin the process of finding a shop or shops which can
   handle the necessary work.
2. Once the costumes are broken out of the containers at East
   Coast they will be sent to the 46th Street Theatre for a

page 3

> wardrobe call. Barbara and Kathleen will then start fittings and determine what work needs to be done.

3. Are the costumes in wooden crates, cardboard boxes, or loose racks?

4. It is very important that Barbara have the new costume designs as soon as possible as all shops are very busy at this point and the longer we wait the more expensive this will become.

5. Barbara also voiced her concern over the lateness of the final casting and how this may affect the cost and readiness of costumes.

Seats

1. There is a possibility that we will gain a few seats on the pit. This will be known once the deck is installed.

5. Rehearsal Schedules and Scene Breakdowns

Rehearsal schedules come in many forms and may change frequently. At the beginning of a production, it is possible to create a rough schedule for the entire rehearsal period. This can be done in a linear fashion, like the production schedules. However, it may be better to provide the company with a calendar-style schedule, an example of which is included here.

As the rehearsal period progresses, it will be possible to draw up weekly schedules that detail what scenes and acts will be rehearsed at a given time. Using the rehearsal scene breakdown that can easily be created from the stage manager's initial production analysis, he or she can list every actor needed for each scene. However, in a large-cast play or musical, the stage manager can save him- or herself work by providing the company with a rehearsal scene breakdown that details what actors are necessary for each section of the play. Then the stage manager can simply write a schedule listing the scenes to be worked on each day.

The sample scene breakdowns here, in conjunction with the weekly schedules that follow, gave all company members a clear idea when they were or were not needed at rehearsal. Breakdowns are also helpful to other members of the production team—costume designers or press representatives, for instance—because they can determine which actors might be available for outside appointments.

All schedules, as well as a copy of the scene breakdown, should be posted on the callboard.

Calendar-Style Rehearsal Schedule

November 1989

THE MERCHANT OF VENICE

SUN	MON	TUE	WED	THU	FRI	SAT
	October	**1** 8:00am Load-In 12:00pm Lunch 1:00pm Load-In 6:00pm BREAK Giles Bloch Casting Calls- American Actors	**2** 8:00am Load-In 12:00pm Lunch 1:00pm Load-In 6:00pm BREAK Giles Bloch Casting Calls- American Actors	**3** 8:00am Load-In 12:00pm Lunch 1:00pm Load-In 6:00pm BREAK	**4** 8:00am Load-In 12:00pm Lunch 1:00pm Load-In 6:00pm BREAK	
5 DAY OFF	**6** 2:00pm Final Casting w\ Mr. Hall English cast arrive Hardy to NYC	**7** 10:00am American cast rehearsal 6:00pm BREAK American Costume Fittings	**8** 10:00am Full Cast, Intro, Equity, Etc. 1:00pm Lunch 2:00pm Rehearsal as called 6:00pm BREAK Finish Amer Cast Fittings	**9** 10:00am Reh. 1:00pm Lunch 2:00pm Reh. 6:00pm BREAK Siberry 1st Day	**10** 10:00am Reh. 1:00pm Lunch 2:00pm Reh. 6:00pm BREAK Garnett 1st Day	**11** 10:00am Rehearsal 1:00pm Lunch 2:00pm Rehearsal 6:00pm BREAK
12 DAY OFF Lockhart & Arditti - Arrive	**13** 10:00am Reh. 1:00pm Lunch 2:00pm Reh. 6:00pm BREAK D. Hoffman 1st Day Lissek 1st Day	**14** 10:00am Reh. 1:00pm Lunch 2:00pm Reh. 6:00pm BREAK Parker to NYC Hardy to UK	**15** 10:00am Rehearsal 1:00pm Lunch 2:00pm Rehearsal 6:00pm BREAK	**16** 10:00am Rehearsal 1:00pm Lunch 2:00pm Rehearsal 6:00pm BREAK	**17** 10:00am Rehearsal 1:00pm Lunch 2:00pm Rehearsal 6:00pm BREAK	**18** 10:00am Rehearsal 1:00pm Lunch 2:00pm Rehearsal 6:00pm BREAK
19 DAY OFF	**20** 10:00am Rehearsal 1:00pm Lunch 2:00pm Rehearsal 6:00pm BREAK	**21** 10:00am Rehearsal 1:00pm Lunch 2:00pm Rehearsal 6:00pm BREAK	**22** 10:00am Rehearsal 1:00pm Lunch 2:00pm Rehearsal 6:00pm BREAK Haynes to NYC	**23** DAY OFF THANKSGIVING	**24** 10:00am Rehearsal 1:00pm Lunch 2:00pm Rehearsal 6:00pm BREAK	**25** 10:00am Rehearsal 1:00pm Lunch 2:00pm Rehearsal 6:00pm BREAK
26 10:00am Rehearsal 1:00pm Lunch 2:00pm Rehearsal 6:00pm BREAK	**27** 8 - 12 Crew 12:30 1/2 Actors 1:00 TECH 5:30 Break Actors 6 Crew Break 7 1/2 Hr Actors 7:30 TECH 12:00 BREAK	**28** 9 - 10 CREW 10:00 1/2 Hr ACTORS 10:30 Continue Tech I 1:00 All BREAK 2:00 Continue Tech/Finish I 6:00 BREAK 7:00 1/2 Hr Dress/Tech I 10:00 BREAK	**29** 8-12 CREW 12:30 1/2 Hr Actors 1:00 Act II Tech 5:30 Actors Break 6:00 Crew Break 7 1/2 Hr Actors 7:30 TECH 12:00 BREAK	**30** 9-10 Crew 10 1/2 Hr Actors 10:30 TECH II 1:00 ALL BREAK 2 1/2 Hr Dr II 5:30 Actors Break 6 Crew Break 6:30 1/2 Hr Actors 7 Dress II 10:00 BREAK	December	

October:
S	M	T	W	T	F	S
1	2	3	4	5	6	7
8	9	10	11	12	13	14
15	16	17	18	19	20	21
22	23	24	25	26	27	28
29	30	31				

December:
S	M	T	W	T	F	S
					1	2
3	4	5	6	7	8	9
10	11	12	13	14	15	16
17	18	19	20	21	22	23
24	25	26	27	28	29	30
31						

Preliminary Schedule   10/14/1989

Sample Rehearsal Scene Breakdown 1

THE MERCHANT OF VENICE

SCENE BREAKDOWN

November 21, 1989

ACT/SCENE	CHARACTER	NAME	UNDERSTUDY
I-1	ANTONIO	Lawson	Carter
	BASSANIO	Parker	Wojda
	GRAZIANO	Siberry	Rayppy
	SALERIO	Burton	Beckwith
	SOLANIO	Gould	Rayppy
	LORENZO	Garnett	Browder
	BEGGAR	Holmes	Dawson
	INNKEEPER	Beckwith	Dawson
I-2	PORTIA	James	Young
	NERISSA	Swift	Dickey
	BALTHASAR	Ben-Ari	Beckwith
I-3	ANTONIO	Lawson	Carter
	BASSANIO	Parker	Wojda
	SHYLOCK	Hoffman	Ben-Ari
II-1	PORTIA	James	Young
	NERISSA	Swift	Dickey
	MOROCCO	Downer	Whitlock
	BALTHASAR	Ben-Ari	Beckwith
	CASKET BEARER	Dickey	Drake
	" "	Young	Drake
	" "	Poyner	Drake
	MOROCCO'S TRAIN	Wojda	Dawson
	" "	Whitlock	Dawson
	" "	Rayppy	Dawson
	" "	Thomas	Dawson
	BASS	Pauley	Thomas
	SOPRANO	Engan	Poyner
	SOPRANO	Daley	Poyner
II-2	BASSANIO	Parker	Wojda
	LEONARDO	Browder	Whitlock
	GRAZIANO	Siberry	Rayppy
	LANCELOT	Daly	Thomas
	OLD GOBBO	Leyden	Holmes
	ANTONIO'S MAN	Beckwith	Whitlock
II-3	JESSICA	Buller	Dickey
	LANCELOT	Daly	Thomas
	OLD GOBBO	Leyden	Holmes

1

Sample Rehearsal Scene Breakdown 1 (cont.)

<u>THE MERCHANT OF VENICE</u>

<u>SCENE BREAKDOWN</u>

November 21, 1989

ACT/SCENE	CHARACTER	NAME	UNDERSTUDY
II-4	LORENZO	Garnett	Browder
	GRAZIANO	Siberry	Rayppy
	SALERIO	Burton	Beckwith
	LANCELOT	Daly	Thomas
	SOLANIO	Gould	Rayppy
II-5	SHYLOCK	Hoffman	Ben-Ari
	JESSICA	Buller	Dickey
	LANCELOT	Daly	Thomas
II-6	ANTONIO	Lawson	Carter
	LEONARDO	Browder	Whitlock
	LORENZO	Garnett	Browder
	GRAZIANO	Siberry	Rayppy
	SALERIO	Burton	Beckwith
	JESSICA	Buller	Dickey
	ANTONIO´S MAN/TORCH BEARER	Beckwith	Whitlock
	VIOLINIST (Masquer)	Sunnerstam	
II-7	PORTIA	James	Young
	NERISSA	Swift	Dickey
	MOROCCO	Downer	Whitlock
	BALTHASAR	Ben-Ari	Beckwith
	CASKET BEARER	Dickey	Drake
	" "	Poyner	Drake
	" "	Young	Drake
	MOROCCO´S TRAIN	Thomas	Dawson
	" "	Wojda	Dawson
	" "	Whitlock	Dawson
	" "	Rayppy	Dawson
	BASS	Pauley	Thomas
	SOPRANO	Engan	Poyner
	SOPRANO	Daley	Poyner
II-8	SALERIO	Burton	Beckwith
	SOLANIO	Gould	Rayppy

2

THE MERCHANT OF VENICE

SCENE BREAKDOWN   November 21, 1989

ACT/SCENE	CHARACTERS	NAME	UNDERSTUDY
II-9	PORTIA	James	Young
	NERISSA	Swift	Dickey
	ARAGON	Carter	Ben-Ari
	BALTHASAR	Ben-Ari	Beckwith
	CASKET BEARERS	Dickey	Drake
	" "	Young	Drake
	" "	Poyner	Drake
	MESSENGER	Wojda	Browder
	ARAGON'S TRAIN	Holmes	Dawson
	" "	Browder	Dawson
	" "	Whitlock	Dawson
	" "	Rayppy	Dawson
	" (CONQUISTADOR)	Thomas	Dawson
	BASS	Pauley	Thomas
	SOPRANO	Engan	Poyner
	SOPRANO	Daley	Poyner
III-1	SALERIO	Burton	Beckwith
	SOLANIO	Gould	Rayppy
	SHYLOCK	Hoffman	Ben-Ari
	TUBAL	Lissek	Holmes
	ANTONIO'S MAN	Beckwith	Whitlock
III-2	BASSANIO	Parker	Wojda
	LEONARDO	Browder	Whitlock
	LORENZO	Garnett	Browder
	GRAZIANO	Siberry	Rayppy
	SALERIO	Burton	Beckwith
	JESSICA	Buller	Dickey
	LANCELOT	Daly	Thomas
	STEPHANO	Wojda	Browder
	PORTIA	James	Young
	NERISSA	Swift	Dickey
	BALTHASAR	Ben-Ari	Beckwith
	BASSANIO'S TRAIN	Beckwith	Dawson
	" "	Holmes	Dawson
	" "	Whitlock	Dawson
	" "	Rayppy	Dawson
	" "	Thomas	Dawson
	CASKET BEARERS	Dickey	Drake
	" "	Young	Drake
	" "	Poyner.	Drake
	SOPRANO	Engan	Poyner
	SOPRANO	Daley	Poyner
	BASS	Pauley	Thomas
	VIOLINIST	Sunnerstam	

3

Sample Rehearsal Scene Breakdown 1 (cont.)

<u>THE **MERCHANT OF VENICE**</u>
SCENE BREAKDOWN   November 21, 1989

ACT/SCENE	CHARACTER	NAME	UNDERSTUDY
III-3	ANTONIO	Lawson	Carter
	SOLANIO	Gould	Rayppy
	SHYLOCK	Hoffman	Ben-Ari
	JAILER	Carter	Dawson
	COURTIERS	Wojda	Dawson
	"	Whitlock	Dawson
	"	Rayppy	Dawson
	"	Thomas	Dawson
	"	Beckwith	Dawson
	"	Poyner	Drake
	"	Pauley	
	"	Engan	Poyner
	"	Daley	Poyner
III-4	LORENZO	Garnett	Browder
	JESSICA	Buller	Dickey
	PORTIA	James	Young
	NERISSA	Swift	Dickey
	BALTHASAR	Ben-Ari	Beckwith
	MAID	Dickey	Drake
	MAID	Young	Drake
	MAID	Poyner	Drake
III-5	LORENZO	Garnett	Browder
	JESSICA	Buller	Dickey
	LANCELOT	Daly	Thomas
IV-1	ANTONIO	Lawson	Carter
	BASSANIO	Parker	Wojda
	GRAZIANO	Siberry	Rayppy
	LEONARDO	Browder	Whitlock
	SALERIO	Burton	Beckwith
	SOLANIO	Gould	Rayppy
	SHYLOCK	Hoffman	Ben-Ari
	PORTIA	James	Young
	NERISSA	Swift	Dickey
	DUKE	Henson	Holmes
	JAILER	Carter	Dawson
	MAGNIFICO	Pauley	Dawson
	"	Ben-Ari	Dawson
	"	Holmes	Dawson
	"	Leyden	Dawson
	CLERK	Thomas	Dawson
	PEOPLE OF VENICE	Rayppy	Dawson
	" "	Beckwith	Dawson
	" "	Wojda	Dawson
	" "	Whitlock	Dawson

4

THE MERCHANT OF VENICE

SCENE BREAKDOWN   November 21, 1989

ACT/SCENE	CHARACTER	NAME	UNDERSTUDY
IV-2	PORTIA	James	Young
	NERISSA	Swift	Dickey
	GRAZIANO	Siberry	Rayppy
V-1	ANTONIO	Lawson	Carter
	BASSANIO	Parker	Wojda
	LORENZO	Garnett	Browder
	GRAZIANO	Siberry	Rayppy
	JESSICA	Buller	Dickey
	LANCELOT	Daly	Thomas
	PORTIA	James	Young
	NERISSA	Swift	Dickey
	STEPHANO	Wojda	Browder
	SOPRANO (Citizen)	Engan	Poyner
	SOPRANO (Citizen)	Daley	Poyner
	BASS	Pauley	Thomas
	VIOLINIST (Citizen)	Sunnerstam	
	LEONARDO	Browder	Whitlock

5

Sample Weekly Schedule 1

THE MERCHANT OF VENICE

REHEARSAL SCHEDULE

FRIDAY 11/17

10:00	Act II-2
11:30	Act I-1, Act II-8, and top of Act III-1 to Shylock's entrance.
1:00	LUNCH
2:00	Act IV-1 from after Duke's exit to end of play.
6:00	Conclude

SATURDAY 11/18

10:00	Act I-2
11:00	Act II-1 and Act II-7 Morocco's Scenes
12:30	Act II-2 and Act II-3
1:00	Act II-4
1:30	Act II-6
2:00	Act II-8
3:00	Conclude

SUNDAY 11/19 DAY OFF

MONDAY 11/20

10:00	Understudy rehearsal
1:00	LUNCH
2:00	Act II-9
3:00	Act III-2
4:30	Act III-4
5:00	Act III-5
6:00	Conclude

TUESDAY 11/21

10:00	Act IV-1
1:00	LUNCH
2:00	Act IV-1 from after Duke's exit to end of the play.
6:00	Conclude

WEDNESDAY 11/22

10:00	Understudy rehearsal
11:30	Scenes to be announced
1:00	LUNCH
2:00	FULL RUN-THRU with all cast and tech

THURSDAY 11/23 DAY OFF

REMAINDER OF SCHEDULE TO BE ANNOUNCED.

Sample Rehearsal Scene Breakdown 2

Here's an alternative version of a rehearsal scene breakdown. Every time a new configuration of actors appears, whether through an entrance, exit, or the beginning of a new scene, number that section and continue numbering consecutively through the end of the play. Doing this for *Death of a Salesman*, I came up with 44 scenes.

DEATH OF A SALESMAN

Rehearsal Scene Breakdown

ACT I

Page	Scene	
1- 8	# 1	Willy & Linda
8-18	2	Biff & Happy
18-24	3	Biff, Happy & Willy
24-26	4	Biff, Happy, Willy & Bernard
26-30	5	Biff, Happy, Willy & Linda
30-32	6	Willy & Woman from Boston
32-34	7	Linda, Willy, Bernard (Woman—Off Stage)
34-38	8	Happy, Willy & Charley
38-41	9	Uncle Ben, Willy & Charley
41-46	10	Uncle Ben, Willy, Linda, Biff & Happy
46-48	11	Charley, Linda, Willy, Ben, Bernard
48-49	12	Linda & Willy
49-58	13	Biff, Linda & Happy
58-63	14	Willy, Biff, Linda & Happy
63-64	15	Linda, Biff & Happy
65-68	16	Linda, Willy, Happy & Biff

DEATH OF A SALESMAN

Rehearsal Scene Breakdown

ACT II

Page	Scene	
1- 5	17	Willy & Linda
6	18	Linda
6-15	19	Willy & Howard
16-20	20	Willy, Ben, Linda, Bernard, Happy & Biff
20-22	21	Charley, Willy, Linda & Biff
22-23	22	Willy, Bernard & Jenny
23-27	23	Willy & Bernard
28-29	24	Bernard, Willy & Charley
29-32	25	Charley & Willy
32-34	26	Stanley & Happy
34-36	27	Stanley, Happy & Miss Forsythe
36-38	28	Biff, Happy & Miss Forsythe
38-40	29	Biff & Happy
40-45	30	Willy, Biff, Happy & Stanley
45-47	#31	Bernard, Happy, Biff, Willy & Linda
47-50	32	Biff, Willy, Happy, Operator, Page & Woman
51-52	33	Happy, Miss Forsythe, Letta, Woman, Biff, Willy
52-54	34	Letta, Miss Forsythe, Biff & Happy
54-58	35	Willy, Woman & Biff
58-60	36	Willy & Biff
60-61	37	Willy, Stanley & Waiter
62-65	38	Happy, Linda, Biff & Willy
65-68	39	Willy & Ben
68-69	40	Biff & Willy
69-75	41	Willy, Biff, Linda & Happy
75-78	42	Ben, Linda, Willy & Happy
78-79	43	Willy, Linda, Biff & Happy, Charley & Bernard
R-1- 3	44	Linda, Biff, Charley, Happy & Bernard

Sample Weekly Schedule 2

Once the rehearsal scene breakdown is complete, it is much easier
to draw up a more specific schedule. Further, when a partial run-
through is scheduled (see Tuesday, 3:30 pm, for example), the stage
manager doesn't have to list every actor included in that chunk of
the script.

```
                        DEATH OF A SALESMAN

                        Rehearsal Schedule

MINSKOFF REHEARSAL STUDIO #1
1515 Broadway—3rd Floor
212-575-0725

Monday, December 12—11:00 Full Company Assemble
    12:30    Scene  #1    Willy & Linda
     2:00           2     Biff & Happy
     2:30    LUNCH
     4:00    Scene  #3    Biff, Happy & Willy
     4:30           4     Biff, Happy, Willy & Bernard
     5:30           5     Biff, Happy, Willy & Linda

Tuesday, December 13
    10:00    Scene  #6    Willy, and Woman from Boston
    10:45           7     Linda, Willy, Bernard (Woman—Off Stage)
    11:30           8     Happy, Willy & Charley
    12:15           9     Uncle Ben, Willy & Charley
     1:00    LUNCH
     2:30    Scene #10    Uncle Ben, Willy, Linda, Biff & Happy
     3:00          11     Charley, Linda, Willy, Ben & Bernard
     3:30    RUN-Scene #1-11
     4:30    Scene #12    Linda & Willy
     5:00          13     Biff, Linda & Happy

Wednesday, December 14
    10:00    Scene #13    Biff, Linda & Happy
    10:30          14     Willy, Biff, Linda & Happy
    11:30          15     Linda, Biff & Happy
    12:00          16     Linda, Willy, Happy & Biff
     1:00    LUNCH
     2:30    Scene # 17   Willy & Linda
     3:15           FULL COMPANY—Equity Business
     3:30    RUN-Scene #11-17
     4:30    Scene #18    Linda
     5:00          19     Willy & Howard
```

DEATH OF A SALESMAN

Rehearsal Schedule Continued

Thursday, December 15

Time	Scene	Characters
10:00	Scene #19	Willy & Howard
11:00	20	Willy, Ben, Linda, Bernard, Happy & Biff
12:15	21	Charley, Willy, Linda & Biff
1:00	LUNCH	
2:30	Scene #22	Willy, Bernard & Jenny
3:00	23	Willy & Bernard
3:45	24	Bernard, Willy & Charley
4:15	25	Charley & Willy
5:30	26	Stanley & Happy

Friday, December 16

Time	Scene	Characters
10:00	Scene #26	Stanley & Happy
10:30	27	Stanley, Happy & Miss Forsythe
11:00	28	Biff, Happy & Miss Forsythe
11:30	29	Biff & Happy
12:15	30	Willy, Biff, Happy & Stanley
1:00	LUNCH	
2:30	Scene #30	Willy, Biff, Happy & Stanley
3:00	31	Bernard, Happy, Biff, Willy & Linda
3:30	32	Biff, Willy, Happy, Operator, Page & Woman
4:30	33	Happy, Miss Forsythe, Letta, Woman, Biff & Willy
5:00	34	Letta, Miss Forsythe, Biff & Happy

Saturday, December 17

10:00	RUN-Scene #19-34	
11:30	Scene #35	Willy, Woman & Biff
12:00	36	Willy & Biff
12:30	37	Willy, Stanley & Waiter
1:00	LUNCH	
2:30	Scene #38	Happy, Linda, Biff & Willy
3:30	39	Willy & Ben
4:15	40	Biff & Willy
4:45	41	Willy, Biff, Linda & Happy

Sunday, December 18   D A Y   O F F

PLEASE NOTE:

This schedule is clearly subject to change, and you will also
be called individually for costumes, hair and make-up. So
PLEASE make no commitments you cannot easily break during
rehearsal hours. We will endeavor to schedule as far in advance
as possible, but last minute flexibility is essential.

                                        Thank you.

Tom Kelly   Chuck Kindl
xxx-xxxx   xxx-xxxx

Sample Daily Schedule

Stage managers should try to post a daily schedule on the callboard or in some other prominent place so everyone in the theater
or rehearsal room knows what is happening and when. The following schedule from *The Merchant of Venice* is a good example.

```
                    THE MERCHANT OF VENICE

                  SCHEDULE/ MON. NOV. 13

NEDERLANDER THEATRE              46TH STREET THEATRE
XXX West XXst St.                XXX W. XXth Street
XXX-XXXX                         XXX-XXXX
10:00   Act III-1                 8:00 a.m.  FULL CREW
        Salerio, Solanio,                    Work call & Hang &
        Shylock                              Focus & Truss
        Tubal, Antonio's Man      6:00 p.m.  Conclude
12:00   Act III-3
        Antonio, Solanio,
        Shylock
        Jailer, Courtiers        CARROLL MUSIC
12:00   Julia Swift to           XXX W. XXst St.
        Wigs @ 46th St.          XXX-XXXX
 1:00   LUNCH                     10:00  Robert Lockhart
 1:00   Dustin Hoffman to                w/ Wilbur Pauley
        Wigs @ 46th St.                     Margery Daley
 2:00   Act I-2                             Elisabeth Engan
        Portia, Nerissa,                    Christina Sunnerstam
        Balthasar                 3:00  Conclude
 2:00   Francesca Buller to
        Wigs
 3:00   Act II-8
        Salerio, Solanio
 3:00   Geraldine James to
        Wigs
 3:30   Act I-1
        Antonio, Bassanio,
        Graziano
        Salerio, Solanio,
        Lorenzo
        Beggar, Innkeeper
 4:00   Verse with Sir Peter
        Hall
        All new company
        members and any
        old company who care
        to renew.
 6:00   Conclude
```

6. Rehearsal Report Form

The following rehearsal report form is one that I completed during work on *The Merchant of Venice*. A blank form was included earlier in Chapter 4, accompanying the discussion detailing its importance. This "used" form is included to give examples of what kind of notes should be written in the rehearsal log.

THE MERCHANT OF VENICE	
REHEARSAL REPORT 46TH STREET THEATRE	
DAY: Wed.	DATE: Nov. 8, 1989	4, 10

SCHEDULE	FITTINGS OR APPOINTMENTS

10:00 - 1st Reh.
Beckwith, Ben-Ari, Browder,
Buller, Karter, Hugo-Daly,
Dickey, Holmes, James, Lawson,
Rayppy, Swift, Thomas,
Whitlock, Wojda
11:30-1 — Portia & Nerissa
2-6 — Portia & Nerissa scenes
   with all others
Excellent work !
	11:30 — Thomas
	1:00 — Ben-Ari
	2:30 — Wojda
	4:00 — Dickey
	        Pauley

	ABSENT, LATE OR OFFICE NOTES
	① Late/Denis Holmes Confusion about call ② Discuss Alex Hardy capacity ③ Browder now to understudy Lorenzo & Stephano not Graziano

PROP NOTES	SET
① Prop crew standing by and very helpful - drew raves from Thelma, Sara & PH. ② Thelma & PH would like front row out ASAP!	DRY TECH for Thelma to be run Tues. AM Truss to be hung Mon. - Reh. at Brooks if habitable

COSTUME NOTES	LIGHTS & SOUND
① Wig man: Jeff Franks to meet Frida tomorrow ② B. Forbes mtg. w/Dustin Fri. at 9:45 re costumes	① Carroll Music Small room booked for reh. Mon., Wed., Th., Fri. 10-3 / hold on Sat. 10-6

COMMENTS & NOTES:

① Set-up TV shoot for Dustin w/Thomas TV- in front of
stage / Fri. @ 9:00.
ⓐ Barbara Toye & Joe Harris Jr. met about DH dressing rm.
② Great day - getting going - company coming together easily - Sara
a big help with blocking, etc.
③ Peter Hall seems pleased - But:
  ① NOISE (fans, blowers, etc.) ⎱ Big   **Stage Manager:** Tom Kelly
  ② LATECOMERS - LATE CURTAIN ⎰ things with him

7. Sample Cue Sheets

The following pair of sample cue sheets were created for *Death of a Salesman:* one for the winch operator, who was responsible for moving the entire unit set both up and downstage; and one for the turntable operator, who would revolve the turntable that was built into the main unit set. Therefore, the set moved downstage while the turntable on the set revolved simultaneously. As you'll notice, the turntable was only moved in Act Two.

These cue (or "Q") sheets are examples of a fairly standard three-column format. The type of cue sheet and the act in which the cue occurs should be clearly marked at the top. The left column lists each "Q" number and the approximate time at which the cue occurs (all cues were taken from cue lights); the center column describes the "move," or what is to occur during each cue; and the right column is for notes describing how the cue is to be executed (speed, direction, etc.).

For more examples of cue sheets and how to set them up with cue lights, check Appendix 10.

Winch Operator's Q Sheets

Q	MOVE	SPEED
WINCH Q'S—SALESMAN ACT I		
PRESET	US OF CURT.	
-TOP OF SHOW- Q1 ↓	DS to [Colored tape mark to be determined, i.e., to blue tape]	MED. (w/curtain rising)
APPROX. 20 MIN. Q2 ↓	US to	MED/SLOW
APPROX. 10 MIN. Q3	DS to	MED.
APPROX. 5 MIN. Q4	US to	MED/SLOW
APPROX. 5 MIN. Q5	DS to	MED.
APPROX. 20 MIN. Q6	US to PRESET	MED. (w/curtain falling)

WINCH Q'S—SALESMAN   2

ACT II

Q	MOVE	SPEED
PRESET	US OF CURTAIN	
- TOP OF ACT Q7	DS to (PLAY DS THRU TTQ1)	MED/FAST w/curtain
(15 MINUTES) Q8	US to (turntable revolves at same time)₀	MED/FAST
4 MINUTES Q9	DS to (turntable revolves at same. time)	MED/
10 MINUTES Q10	US to (turntable revolves at same. time)	MED/SLOW
20 MINUTES Q11	DS to (turntable revolves at same time)	MED/
3 MINUTES Q12	US to	MED

Turntable Operator's Q Sheets

	TURNTABLE Q'S—SALESMAN	
	ACT II	
Q	MOVE	DIRECTION/SPEED
PRESET ACTS I & II	KITCHEN DS HOWARD'S US	PRESET
(5 MINUTES INTO ACT) Q1	REVOLVE TO HOWARD DS KITCHEN US (UNIT STAYS DS	COUNTER CLOCK / MED.-FAST
10 MINUTES Q2	REV. TO KITCHEN DS HOWARD US (UNIT MOVES US DURING REVOLVE) (HOWARD CHANGE TO CHARLEY US)	COUNTER CLOCK / MED.-FAST
4 MINUTES Q3	REV. TO CHARLEY DS KITCHEN US (UNIT MOVES DS DURING REVOLVE) (CHARLEY CHANGE TO RESTAURANT US)	COUNTER CLOCK / MED.
10 MINUTES Q4	REV. TO RESTAURANT DS CHARLEY US (UNIT MOVES US DURING REVOLVE) (CHARLEY CHANGE TO KITCHEN US)	CLOCKWISE/MED.

	TURNTABLE Q'S—SALESMAN	2
	ACT II	
Q	MOVE	DIRECTION/SPEED
- 20 MINUTES - Q5	REV. TO KITCHEN DS RESTAURANT US (UNIT MOVES <u>DS</u> DURING REVOLVE) <u>END</u> <u>OF</u> <u>TURNTABLE</u>	CLOCKWISE / MED.

8. Tracking Sheet and Prop List

As a show becomes set, it is vital that all assistant stage managers prepare a tracking sheet, detailing what each of them does during the running of a performance. This is one of an ASM's more important responsibilities. The sample tracking sheet included here was prepared in meticulous detail by Chuck Kindl for the Broadway replacement cast of *Speed-the-Plow*. (Bob, David, and Flicka refer to Bob Balaban, David Rasche, and Felicity Huffman, the actors playing Fox, Gould, and Karen.) If every ASM prepares such a tracking sheet, an unexpected absence shouldn't cause any undue trauma backstage.

Tracking Sheet

```
                        SPEED-THE-PLOW II

                        C.K. TRACKING

ACT ONE:
              Make hot water for Postum
Make coffee - Clean up THE THROWN BOOK using cleanser, then take BOOK
              to Big Gray Box stage right for Act II desk set-up

Open Stg Mgr Desk - Remove 2 Silver cigarette boxes, cigarette lighter,
                    and Mont Blanc pen - replenish cigarettes - To Desk

                Refill water pitcher & David's Joggers jug
                Place Jogger's jug on Stg Mgr Desk by phone

Check props.

Collect valuables at half hour - David's wallet
                                 Flicka's gold neck chain & wallet

Five minutes before places - Bob's cup of water Stage Left

PLACES - 2 Prop men & House Elex & Bob on deck
         Flash for prop men exit 2nd wing
         As lights come up page curtain for Bob 1st wing

            Place Bob's water cup out of harm's way
            Stand by Stage Door to open when Coffee tray comes to
            Left Prop Table. Close door on Props exit.
            Check the coffee tray placement.
```

```
                                        1. Flick's note pad &
                                           pen
                                        2. Flicka's letters in
                                           leather folder
                                        3. Bob's Filofax
                                        4. Coffee Tray

WARNING FOR FLICKA'S ENTRANCE - "Why not try the coffee machine"
            Stand by to page curtain - Bob's reading of BOOK "The wind against
                    the Plains, cut not a wind of change...."
            Page curtain on "Decide, decide, decide"

WARNING FOR FLICKA'S STAGE EXIT - "Young America at Work & Play"
            Page curtain on "Call the Coventry. Table for two, at one.
                    Thank you."
            Drop curtain & open Stage Door for Prop Man to exit with the
            coffee tray.

WARNING FOR BOB CURTAIN PAGE & FLICKA'S ENTRANCE - "No joking apart, Babe.
                    My perceptions...Say I'm nuts. I don't think so - she
            likes me, and she'd go out with me."
            Cathy (Flicka's dresser) will page the curtain for Bob & Flicka.
                    On "My, my, my" open the stage door and let the
                    Prop man bring in the coffee tray (for Act II) & puts
                    it on the prop table & exits - hold door open for Bob
                    to exit & extend hand out to receive his prop (black
                    file-o-fax & close door as Bob exits. Check the file-o-
                    fax for the film treatment & place on prop table.
                    However, Cathy's sub does not know this page cue so
                    Plan B is to prop open the stage door with sand bag
                    and execute the paging of the curtain & getting
                    Bob's prop on his exit & close stage door on Bob's exit
```

Tracking Sheet (cont.)

WARNING FOR SCENE CHANGE - "Give me a platform to do good, and I'll do good"
   Cue for change - "and tell him that he owes me $500 bucks."
   Follow 2 prop men to curtain man - curtain comes in head-high.
   When Props start to pull carpet with coffee table upstage tap
   the curtain man's shoulder which cues him to bring in the
   curtain.

   Enter stage and work lights will come on - put LS end of carpet
   up on coffee table - place chair upstage (sofa high) out of way
   Then put RS end of carpet on coffee table.

   As Coffee table is being taken to stage right indicate with toe
   SL mark, then cross in front of sofa giving it a look as ·to
   neatness & Book - give SR sofa end carpet a sweep away from
   front of sofa. Take 2 glasses from bar and cross behind sofa.
   Give Flicka empty glass & David glass with water and as you
   exit Stage Right 2, give the drape a flip so it swags properly.

Ready desk for Act II
   Prop men remove all scripts.
   Strike the Flicka leather letter folder to gray box.
   Strike leather pad holder & pen to gray box.
   PLACE - THE BOOK (II) on desk from gray box.
   Set cigarette box, opened appointment book & lighter
   Pick out 3 throwable scripts & 3 scripts for coffee table
      3 throwable scripts with THE BOOK on top - Chair area
      3 coffee table scripts - desk end

   Take leather pad holder & pen to Stg Mgr desk & relieve Tom
   from script - Tear out written sheet from Leather pad & throw
   out & take the Jogger's cup to gray box. Clip pen to closing
   tab. Neaten up the phone messages trying to keep out any
   creases and paper clip to left-hand flap.

   Keep track of book for Light cue #8.5

END OF ACT ONE - Tom relieves you from book - Clean out ash tray with a
   kleenex and put in a couple of drops of water.

   Flash off Flicka & David.

When curtain comes in for intermissin change - retrieve Flicka's shoes
   and 2 glasses. Glasses to green bar - shoes to dresser. Carpet biz.

Check props - Give a look in bar for brandy & 2 glasses
   Place arm chair. Check desk top. As props places coffee cup,
   saucer & spoon, give him the 3 coffee table scripts. Desk chair
   should be turned downstage. (8 items)

ON COFFEE TABLE	1. Ash tray
3 scripts	2. Coffee cup
Cig. box	3. 3 scripts
Cig. lighter	BOOK on top
Tray with coffee etc.	4. Cigarettes
Ash tray	5. Lighter
	6. Appt book
	7. Telephone

SPEED-THE-PLOW II - C.K. TRACKING
END OF ACT ONE (Continued)
   Coffee table - Add: Coffee tray with 1 cup & pot, creamer etc.
         3 scripts
       Cigarette box, lighter, ash tray & phone

   Take Leather correspondence folder from gray box to Prod Office

   Give Bob fresh water
   Go to Quick change table for THE BOOK (Act I) & Flicka's note pad
   Note pad with pen on SL Prop table with Bob's filofax
   Take THE BOOK (Act I) to Prod. Office

   C.K. unplugs hot water & empties. Throws out both coffee grinds.
   Unplugs Decaf.

ACT ·II· PLACES - Standby to page Curtain for Bob's entrance at top of Act.

   Put Bob's water out of harm's way.
   Take THE BOOK (Act I) & diet soda to Stage Right.
   T. Kelly gets soda & THE BOOK placed on gray box with phone
   messages inside.

   Relieve Tom from the script.

   When Bob reads from THE BOOK after David's "wait" turn on the
   phone buzzer.

   Tom takes over script, then go to Stage Left. Tuck up the
   door blacks and wait for the thrown BOOK. Put BOOK in Prod.
   office and go stage right for curtain calls.

   Return the valuables.

   Turn off the phone buzzer.

   When Tom takes out the pre-set - Take Flicka's note pad & pen
   and Bob's Filofax to Production Office sand bagging the SL
   door open so props can return coffee tray to Prod. office.
   Then get 2 silver cigarette boxes, lighter & Mont Blanc pen
   and place in Stage Manager's desk drawer to be locked.
   Look for any buttons on stage.

   Pull plugs on coffee etc.

   Put phone away. Secure stage managers desk.

   Reports.

   Go home.

Prop List

Another important duty for an ASM is the maintenance of an accurate and thorough prop preset list, used by the ASM to carefully check the preset positions of all props. The following sample list from the same production of *Speed-the-Plow* as the preceding tracking list, is a good example of such a prop checklist.

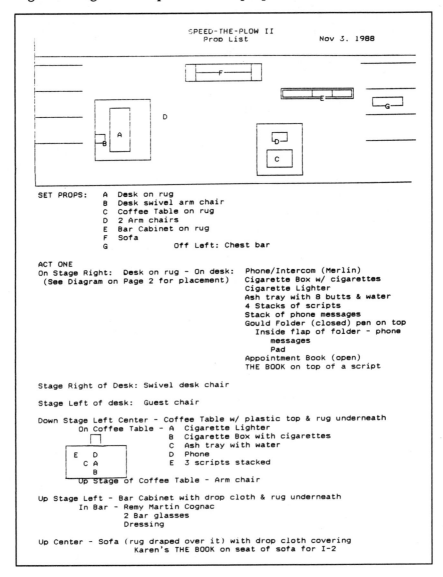

SPEED-THE-PLOW II PROP LIST   Nov 3, 1988
                                        Page 2
OFF STAGE RIGHT: Script (Gould brings on top of Act I)

OFF STAGE LEFT: Silver tray with silver coffee pot of Postum
                2 China cups & saucers
                2 Silver spoons
                1 Silver creamer with fake milk
                1 Silver sugar bowl with sugar & small
                    silver spoon
                Leather folder of mail - Karen
                Small pad with pen - Karen

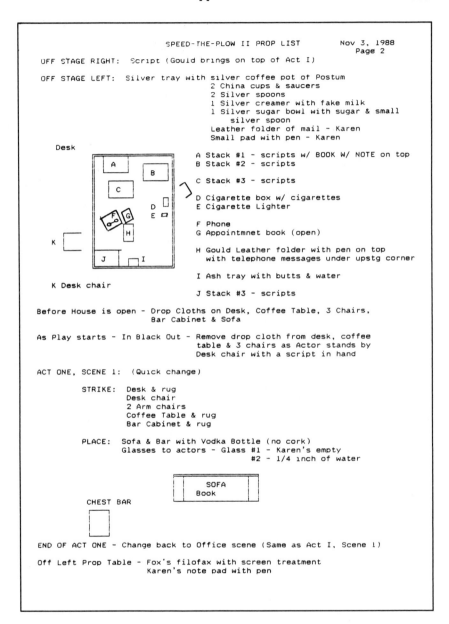

Desk

A Stack #1 - scripts w/ BOOK W/ NOTE on top
B Stack #2 - scripts

C Stack #3 - scripts

D Cigarette box w/ cigarettes
E Cigarette Lighter

F Phone
G Appointmnet book (open)

H Gould Leather folder with pen on top
  with telephone messages under upstg corner

I Ash tray with butts & water

K Desk chair

J Stack #3 - scripts

Before House is open - Drop Cloths on Desk, Coffee Table, 3 Chairs,
                       Bar Cabinet & Sofa

As Play starts - In Black Out - Remove drop cloth from desk, coffee
                       table & 3 chairs as Actor stands by
                       Desk chair with a script in hand

ACT ONE, SCENE 1: (Quick change)

        STRIKE: Desk & rug
                 Desk chair
                 2 Arm chairs
                 Coffee Table & rug
                 Bar Cabinet & rug

        PLACE: Sofa & Bar with Vodka Bottle (no cork)
                 Glasses to actors - Glass #1 - Karen's empty
                                            #2 - 1/4 inch of water

```
                    ┌─────────────┐
                    │   SOFA      │
                    │   Book      │
        CHEST BAR   └─────────────┘
        ┌───┐
        │   │
        │   │
        └───┘
```

END OF ACT ONE - Change back to Office scene (Same as Act I, Scene 1)

Off Left Prop Table - Fox's filofax with screen treatment
                      Karen's note pad with pen

Prop List (cont.)

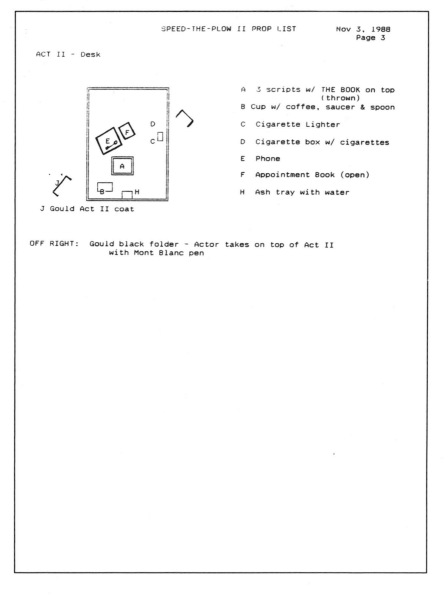

SPEED-THE-PLOW II PROP LIST   Nov 3, 1988
                                       Page 3

ACT II - Desk

A   3 scripts w/ THE BOOK on top
        (thrown)
B   Cup w/ coffee, saucer & spoon

C   Cigarette Lighter

D   Cigarette box w/ cigarettes

E   Phone

F   Appointment Book (open)

H   Ash tray with water

J Gould Act II coat

OFF RIGHT: Gould black folder - Actor takes on top of Act II
             with Mont Blanc pen

9. Technical Rehearsal Schedules

Technical rehearsals can take many forms, as discussed in Chapter 5, and include a wide variety of information. Two schedules are presented here as examples. The first tech schedule is very specific, detailing the work planned for one day; the other is a general overview, much like the production schedules in Appendix 2.

Cue-to-Cue Schedule

The following schedule was created for one technical rehearsal for *Death of a Salesman* in order to keep the cast and crew apprised of the sections that would be worked on that day. It begins by offering general technical guidelines for the actors before listing the sections of the script that will be rehearsed, specifying all costume changes or technical cues that are to be worked through.

DEATH OF A SALESMAN   1.

WEDNESDAY REHEARSAL OUTLINE

1. No wigs necessary.
2. Costumes for Linda, Biff, Happy, Bernard & Charley only
   (Fast changes only)

ACT I

Run - stopping as necessary

From 1-1 Opening
Stop 1-4 LINDA: Take an aspirin.

Cut to 1-8 WILLY: How can they whip cheese?
Stop 1-14 BIFF: Hap, I've had 20 or 30 different jobs

                  (Linda can make her change even with cuts.
                  Should be plenty of time for change)

Cut to 1-17 BIFF: Remember, Bill Oliver.

                  Run with costume change, set change
                          light & sound cues

          Includes: Bernard's entrance
                     Linda's wash entrance
                     Hap has time to change to PJ's
Stop at 1-28 LINDA: It's got the biggest ads.

Cut to 1-30 WILLY: I'm small.
                  Includes: Woman from Boston & Bernard & Linda
Stop at 1-35 Charley's entrance

Cut to 1-38 WILLY: Did you see the ceiling I put up in the living room.

          Includes: Hap has time to change to young boy
                     Ben's entrance
                     Linda & boys sword fight
                     Boys quick change to PJ's
                     Charley's change
Stop at 1-49 BIFF: What is he doing out there?

          Walk thru moves to 1-57 - Linda & Boys - Attention must be paid

---

Start 1-57 LINDA: Biff, I swear to God[Biff, his life is in your hands.
Stop at 1-59 WILLY: Go to Filene's.....

          Walk thru moves to 1-63 - WILLY: Don't be so modest.

Start 1-63 WILLY: Don't be so modest.
Thru end of Act One 1-68.

2.

DEATH OF A SALESMAN - WEDNESDAY REHEARSAL OUTLINE

ACT II

From II-1 Top of Act

                Includes: Coffee scene
                           Linda's phone call
                           Revolve into Howard's Office
                           Linda's change - Set Charley's Office
Stop II-9   End of tape in Howard scene
            Howard: That was my wife.

___

Cut to II-13 Howard: YOu'll have to excuse me, Willy, I gotta see some
                                                                    people.

                Includes: Ben - Linda thru Ebbetts Field
                           Bernard & Charley
                           Bernard's quick change
                           Revolve into Charley's Office
                           Charley's quick change
                           Set Cafe juke box

Stop II-27 Charley's entrance - Charley: Hey, you're goin' miss that train.

___

Cut to II-31 Charley: You been jealous of me all your life, you damned fool.

                Includes: Revolve into cafe
                           Set kitchen
                           Stanley & Happy & Miss Forsythe
Stop II-36 Biff entrance - Biff: Hello, kid, sorry I'm late.

___

Cut to II-40 Willy's entrance - Happy: You leave the house tomorrow......

Stop II-41 Willy: Well, what happened, boy?

___

CUT TO II-45 Willy: Famous for the way he listens.

                Includes: Mrs. Loman, Mrs. Loman - Bernard & Linda
                           Standish arms
                           Woman from Boston
                           Miss Forsythe
                           Letta

Stop II-55 Biff enter in Boston - Biff: Why didn't you answer.

___

                Walk moves thru Woman exit

___

Cue-to-Cue Schedule (cont.)

```
                                                                    3.
              DEATH OF A SALESMAN - WEDNESDAY REHEARSAL OUTLINE

                            ACT II (Continued)

   Start II-60  Biff exit - Biff:  You fake.

                    Includes:  Biff quick change
                               Revolve into kitchen
                               Linda, Happy & Biff roses

   Stop II-62  Linda knocks flowers to floor
   ─────────────────────────────────────────────────────────────

   Cut to II-65  Biff:  Scum of the earth and you're looking at him.

   Stop II-69  Biff:  People ask where I am ...........

                    Includes:  Willy seeds
                               Ben
   ─────────────────────────────────────────────────────────────

              Walk thru moves for lights to II-75  Biff:  I'll go in the
                                                                morning.
   ─────────────────────────────────────────────────────────────

   Start II-75  Biff:  I'll go in the morning.  Put him - put him to bed
                    Includes:
                               Linda's quick change

   Stop  R-1  All in place for the Requiem
   ─────────────────────────────────────────────────────────────

   Cut to R-3  Happy:  All right, boy.

                    Thru the end of the Requiem
   ─────────────────────────────────────────────────────────────
```

Technical Week Schedule

The following schedule, prepared for *Accomplice,* focuses on the tech week. It attempts to give the actors an idea of what section of the script will be teched (Act One or Two) and what level of technical readiness they should expect (full dress or props only). If a show is technically complex, it may not be possible to schedule accurately (*see* Thurs. April 5).

```
2/22/90                ACCOMPLICE SCHEDULE


MON. MARCH 19-FRI. MARCH 30:  Load-in, Hang and Focus on a
                             basic 8:00-12:00, 1:00-5:00 day
                             schedule at theater

        Actors will continue to work 10:00 to 5:30 at
        890 Studios. Basic concept will be work and
        notes: AM; run-thru: PM. Understudies begin
        attending rehearsals March 26.

SATURDAY MARCH 31    (if possible technically)
    8:00- 6:00    Finish Focus, Dressing and Clean-up at Theater
    11:00         Actors: Notes and Run-Thru at 890
    3:00          Break Actors/Take Furniture, etc. to theater
    6:00          Break all crew, but house heads on at 7:00
    7:00          Cast on stage: Props and work light only;
                  adjust blocking, check sightlines, answer all
                  "Is this the way it's going to be?" questions.
    11:00         BREAK

SUNDAY APRIL 1    DAY OFF

MONDAY APRIL 2/ TUES. APRIL 3
    8:00-12:00    Crew time as needed
    1:00- 6:00    Technical rehearsal    (COSTUME PIECES AVAILABLE
    7:00-11:00    Technical rehearsal      as needed for Tech)

WEDNESDAY APRIL 4
    8:00-12:00    Crew time as needed
    12:30         Half-Hour for actors and dressers
    1:00          Crew call/ Full dress/Tech of Act One
    5:30          Actors Break
    6:00          Crew Break
    6:30          Half-Hour for actors and dressers
    7:00          Crew call/Full dress/Tech of Act Two
    11:00         Break
```

```
2/22/90                ACCOMPLICE SCHEDULE              p. 2


THURS. APRIL 5
    8:00-12:00    Crew time as needed
    1:00- 6:00    Notes, fixes and any remaining tech with actors
                  OR First full non-stop dress
    7:00          Half-Hour
    7:30          First or second full non-stop dress rehearsal
    11:00         Break


FRIDAY APRIL 6
    A.M.          Clean up and clear house/Any remaining crew work
    1:00          Actors called either for work and fixes or
                  full dress
    6:00          Break
    7:30          Half-Hour
    8:00          Preview #1


SATURDAY APRIL 7
    12:00         Actors called for notes
    1:30          Half-Hour
    2:00          Preview #2
    7:30          Half-Hour
    8:00          Preview #3


SUNDAY APRIL 8     DAY OFF


THE REMAINDER OF THE PREVIEW SCHEDULE ALLOWS FOR AFTERNOON
REHEARSAL FROM 1-6 ON ONE SHOW DAYS

PERFORMANCE SCHED. FOR PREVIEWS AND RUN:

    MON.     TUES.    WED.     THURS.    FRI.    SAT.     SUN.
    8:15     8:15     2:15     8:15      8:15    2:15     DAY OFF
                      8:15                       8:15

OPENING NIGHT: THURS. APRIL 26 @ 6:45

ANY ADDITIONS, CORRECTIONS, OR CONFLICTS, PLEASE NOTIFY:
    THOMAS KELLY, PSM  XXX-XXX-XXXX or XXX-XXX-XXXX

                         THANK YOU!
```

10. Cue Lights

It is amazing how a technically intricate production can be executed by a simple system consisting of a half-dozen light switches, some colored bulbs, and a set of carefully planned cue sheets. This appendix provides an example of how a cue-light (often written as "Q-light") panel, a set of cue sheets, and a script with all the cues carefully included can make a splashy industrial run smoothly. In this case, the industrial was a show in which Oldsmobile's new car models were introduced to dealers from across the country. It was performed at Radio City Music Hall in 1984 and featured the Rockettes. Fred Travalena and Terri Klaussner were the performers/spokespersons.

Cue-Light Panel

The cue-light panel is placed on the stage manager's desk. It consists of a row of light switches, each with an indicator light underneath that becomes lit when the switch is flipped on. Every switch should be clearly marked. The cue-light panel for the Oldsmobile industrial was configured and labeled as in Figure A–1.

This particular set includes a "FLY" cue light. The switch will turn on a light(s) on the fly rail from where the flymen will fly scenery in or out. On complicated shows, there may be several fly cues in close succession, necessitating simultaneous warnings and cues. In that case, the stage manager will have various colored

Figure A–1   Cue-Light Panel

lights on the rail and label his panel accordingly ("RED FLY," "BLUE FLY," and so on). When these lights are turned on, the crew is warned, and when turned off, they execute the cue (bringing in or taking out a drop or curtain). In the stage manager's cueing script, he or she will write exactly what is done with the cue light. In other words, a warning for a fly cue in the book would read, "FLY ON," meaning turn on the fly cue light, and underneath that might be the number of the cue and what move is being warned. For example, the written warning for a cue to bring in the set piece for a scene that takes place in the county jail might look something like this in a stage manager's script: FLY ON (Q3/Jail Drop In).

When the point arrives in the script or song for the jail to drop in, the cueing script should read "FLY OFF." This indicates that the stage manager should turn off the cue light, signalling the flyman to execute the move. This basic means of backstage communication can allow huge sequences of events to happen without the stage manager having to give any spoken cues, freeing him or her to continue verbally calling the lighting cues.

The rest of the panel indicates similar cueing switches: for two travelers (#1 TRAV, #2 TRAV), a turntable (TT), the conductor (COND), and stage left (SL). The conductor's cue light allows the stage manager to begin a show on the same beat or count as the music. The stage left cue light, in this case, was used to signal the opposite side of the stage. Often this is referred to as the OP (opposite portal) cue light or position.

The preceding sample cue-light panel also has two switches devoted to work lights. This configuration allows the stage manager easy access to the lights that are used to illuminate fast changes that occur as soon as a curtain, drop, or traveler is in. However, never place work-light switches in the middle of a cue-light panel. It makes it too easy to cause accidental flashes of light onstage during a performance. Always keep them to one end, and if they are not needed during the running of the show, tape them in the OFF position.

Flyman's Cue Sheets

Notice that the flyman has three different drops—a movie screen, a scrim, and a show drop.

OLDSMOBILE—1984		1
FLY Q's	MOVE	NOTES
PRESET	RADIAL ↓ LO SHOW DROP ↓ LO SCREEN ↓ ½ WAY SCRIM ↑ HI	
DURING 1ST Q TAPE **1** (LITE) (8 MINS)	SCREEN ↓ LO	EASY
END SANCHEZ Q **2** (LITE) (4 MINS)	SCREEN ↑ HI	EASY
AFTER 1ST CAR Q **3** (LITE) (IMMED.)	SCREEN ↓ LO	MEDIUM
Q **4** (LITE) (IMMED.)	SCREEN ↑ HI	FAST
Q **5** LITE	SCREEN ↓ LO	MEDIUM

Flyman's Cue Sheets (cont.)

OLDSMOBILE—1984		2
FLY Q's	MOVE	NOTES
END FILM Q 6 (LITE) FAST	SCREEN ↑ <u>HI</u>	<u>FAST</u>
↓ Q 7 (LITE) 10 SECS	SCRIM ↓ <u>LO</u>	<u>FAST</u>
END FILM Q 8 (LITE) – LONG TIME –	SCRIM ↑ <u>HI</u>	<u>FAST</u>
AFTER 88 REVEAL Q 9 (LITE) – IMMED –	SCREEN ↓ LO	<u>MEDIUM</u>
AFTER FILM Q 10 (LITE)	SCREEN ↑ HI	<u>FAST</u>
DURING FRED – PRESET W/ WORK LITES ON	SHOW DROP ↑ HI SCREEN ↓ LO	WAIT FOR CAR MOVES Q FROM TOM OR LEE

Turntable Operator's Cue Sheets

OLDSMOBILE—1984		1
TT Q's	MOVE	NOTES
PRESET	WAGON w/ ← COVER	US FULL RAMPS IN
FIRST SONG FLASHDANCE 20 MIN IN SHOW	1) WAGON EXIT 2) TERRI EXIT 3) WAGON RESET	ADJUST FOR CAR IF NEEDED
END ROCKS I LOVE N.Y. Q1 LITE	3/4 DS + REV SR	DS LIMIT # 1
DURING REVOLVE Q2 LITE FLASH WILL STAY ON: WARN US + REV.	STOP AT:	
30 SECS. Q3 LITE	US + REV.	
TRAV. CLOSE WORKS (1 MIN)	REV TO: WAGON OFF SL SUPREME ON FROM SR ROCKETTES ON TT	1 MIN. FOR THIS

Turntable Operator's Cue Sheets (cont.)

OLDSMOBILE—1984		2
TT Q's	MOVE	NOTES
END FILM ROCKETTES EXIT Q4 LITE	DS (SUPREME →)	LIMIT 1
END FILM Q5 LITE IMMED.	REV. SL 360°	
END JOHN Q6 LITE (8 MINS)	US	TRAY CLOSE W/ CLEAR
DURING PIANOES	1) SUPREME OFF SL 2) WAGON OVER + OFF SR to SL 2) 88 ON SR (88 ←) + REV. TO ↩	
END PIANOES Q7 LITE	DS / REV. 180 SR to (88 →)	
"FLASH" LEAVE ON WARN REV. 180 (IMMED)	STOP AT 88 →	

First Traveler Operator's Cue Sheets

The light for traveler 1 was also used to cue the prop and carpentry departments at several points in the presentation.

OLDSMOBILE—1984		1
#1 TRAV (DS) Q's	MOVE	NOTES
PRESET	CLOSE	DURING ½ HR WAIT FOR Q WHEN PRESET READY
END 1ST SPEECH Q1 LITE (8 MINS)	OPEN	FAST (NOT IN VIEW OF AUD.)
1) SONG 2) ROCKETTES 3) CAR Q2 LITE (1 MIN)	CLOSE	FAST
END FILM Q3 LITE – 3 MINS –	OPEN	MED. FAST
FOR PROPS Q4 LITE –6 MINS–	SET PIANOS	
END PIANO # FOR PROPS Q5 LITE (5 MINS)	STRIKE PIANOS	

First Traveler Operator's Cue Sheets (cont.)

OLDSMOBILE—1984		2
#1 TRAV (DS) Q's	MOVE	NOTES
ROCKETTES END COUPE + FILMS ROCKETTES INTRO SPEAKER Q6 LITE (—15 MINS-	CLOSE	MEDIUM
END SPEECH Q7 LITE —3 MIN—	OPEN	FAST
DURING SONG PROP + CARP. Q Q8 LITE	STEPS + CAR COVER OFF SR	FAST

Second Traveler Operator's Cue Sheets

#2 TRAV (US) Q's	OLDSMOBILE—1984 1 MOVE	NOTES
PRESET -12 MINS -	OPEN	ON STAGE MARK (EDGE OF TT)
DURING FIRST SONG — "FLASHDANCE" Q1 LITE (30 SECS)	CLOSE	FAST WAGON OFF
Q2 LITE (10 SECS)	OPEN	FAST TO ON STG MARK
Q3 LITE (2 MINS)	CLOSE	FAST GIRL ON TT
END ROCKETTES Q4 LITE (2 MINS)	OPEN	RESET WAGON FAST REVEAL WAGON
END CAR + Q5 LITE (1 MIN)	CLOSE	MEDIUM WAIT FOR CAR US + WORKLIGHT

Second Traveler Operator's Cue Sheets (cont.)

OLDSMOBILE—1984		2
#2 TRAV (US) Q's	MOVE	NOTES
END FILM + ROCKETTES Q6 LITE – 2 MINS –	OPEN	FAST TO OFF STAGE MARK
– ROCKETTES – – FILM – CAR Q7 LITE 8 MINS	CLOSE	<u>WHEN</u> <u>CAR</u> <u>CLEARS</u>
END PIANO MEDLEY Q8 LITE 15 MINS	OPEN	FAST (REVEAL 88)
PRESET DURING FRED T. – 5 MINS –	CLOSE	WHEN CATS SET ✓ W/ SM
1) FRED 2) FILMS 3) ROCKETTES Q9 LITE (3 MINS)	OPEN	FAST (REVEAL COUPE)
1) CAR 2) FILM Q10 LITE	CLOSE	WHEN CAR CLEAR

Sample Pages—Oldsmobile Cueing Script

The following are sample pages taken from the stage manager's actual cueing script for the Oldsmobile industrial. The sections filled with numbers represent the bars in the musical dance segments.

                         TERRI

                    "WHAT A FEELING"

FIRST, WHEN THERE'S NOTHING BUT A SLOW   SPOT TO PARTY
GLOWING DREAM
THAT YOUR FEAR SEEMS TO HIDE DEEP INSIDE
YOUR MIND   WARN   SPOT TERRI
ALL ALONE I HAVE CRIED SILENT TEARS FULL OF   LQ 105.5
PRIDE   106
IN A WORLD MADE OF STEEL-MADE OF STONE
TEMPO CHANGE
      1 2 3 4 5 6 7 8

      1 2 3 4 5 6↑7 8   ⎡LQ 105.5
                TERRI POINTS   ⎣SPOT TO TERRI
WHILE I HEAR THE MUSIC CALL ME
FULL OF RHYTHM
WRAP AROUND
TAKE A HOLD OF MY HEART   5 6 7 8   #2 TRAV. ON
                                              (Q1 / CLOSE)
WHAT A FEELING
BEIN'S BELIEVIN'
I CAN HAVE IT ALL
NOW I'M DANCING FOR MY LIFE
TAKE YOUR PASSION
AND MAKE IT HAPPEN
PICTURES COME TO LIFE
NOW YOU DANCE RIGHT THROUGH YOUR LIFE

BAR_____   **1**   2   3   4   5   6   7   8 ⎡LQ 106
              2   ② 3   4   5   6   7   8
              3   ② 3 CAR #5 (ON #2 SL) BACKS IN #4 SL
              4   CAR #2 (ON #2 SR) BACKS IN #4 SR
                      2   3   4   5   ⑥ 7   8
                                       ⎡#2 TRAV OFF
I HEAR THE MUSIC CALL ME   CARS CLEAR   (Q1/CLOSE)
I AM RHYTHM
IN A FLASH
IT TAKES HOLD OF MY HEART

WHAT A FEELING
BEIN'S BELIEVIN'
I CAN HAVE IT ALL
NOW I'M DANCING FOR MY LIFE

WARN: LQ 108 109   2

BAR_____   **1**   2   3   4   5   6   7   8

         2   2   3   4   5   6   7   8

         3   2   3   4   5   6   7   8   #2 TRAV ON (Q2/OPEN)

         4   2   3   4   5   6   7   8

WHAT A FEELING
(I AM MUSIC NOW)
BEIN'S BELIEVIN'
(I AM RHYTHM)

PICTURES COME ALIVE
YOU CAN DANCE RIGHT THROUGH YOUR LIFE
WHAT A FEELING
I CAN REALLY HAVE IT ALL
WHAT A FEELING

BAR_____   **1**   2   3   4   5   6   7   8

         2   2   3   4   5   6   7   [8]   #2 TRAV ON

         3   2   3   4   5   6   7   8   (Q3/CLOSE)

         4   2   3   4   5   6   7   8

BAR_____   **5**   2   3   [4]   5   6   7   8   LQ 108 #2 TRAV OFF (Q3/CLOSE)

         6   2   3   4   5   6   7   [8] LQ 109

         7   ROCKETTES ENTER (WITH ROX ANNOUNCER)

          2   3   4   5   6   7   8   'LADIES +

         8   I LOVE N.Y.   GENTLEMEN,

          2   3   4   5   6   7   8   THE RADIO CITY MUSIC HALL

ROCKETTE'S I LOVE NEW YORK   ROCKETTES

BAR_____   **1**   2   3   4   5   6   7   8   RESET WAGON ON TT

         2   2   3   4   5   6   7   8

         3   2   3   4   5   6   7   8   WARN LQ 110

         4   2   3   4   5   6   7   8   #2 TRAV ON (Q4/OPEN)

BAR_____   **5**   2   3   4   5   6   7   8   TT ON (Q1/DS, 3/4 SR)

         6   2   3   4   5   6   7   8

         7   2   3   4   5   6   7   8

11. Actors' Equity Association Work Rules

AEA, the actors' union, puts out pamphlets detailing the "agreement and rules governing employment" for every type of union contract under which their members work. Included here are the work rules concerning rehearsal hours for the production contract (expires June 28, 1992) and the LORT contract (expires Sept. 1, 1991), and the acceptable dance floor criteria as set forth in the LORT contract. Any stage manager wishing to work professionally would do well to read through all the rules contained in these AEA pamphlets.

Production Contract—Rehearsal Hours (pp. 79–81)

(1) Rehearsal Hours.

(a) Prior to First Paid Public Performance. Except for the final seven (7) days of rehearsal prior to the First Paid Public Performance, rehearsal hours shall not exceed seven (7) out of eight and one-half (8½) consecutive hours per day (including breaks required by Rule (2)(a) below). However, Producer may elect, at Producer's sole option, to rehearse eight (8) out of nine and one-half (9½) consecutive hours per day in lieu of the seven (7) out of eight and one-half (8½) hour schedule provided the Actors receive two (2) days off in each week. These days off need not be consecutive. If the Producer elects a five-day schedule, pro-rated calculations shall be made in fifths for partial weeks. The Producer will be entitled to switch schedules only twice during the permitted rehearsal period. The Actors must receive at least one week's notice for any such change in schedule.

(b) Final seven days of rehearsal prior to First Paid Public Performance. During the final seven (7) days of rehearsal prior to the day of the first paid public performance, rehearsals shall not exceed ten (10) out of twelve (12) consecutive hours per day (including breaks required by rule (2)(a) below). On the day of the First Paid Public Performance, rehearsals and performance may exceed ten (10) hours and may encompass more than twelve (12) consecutive hours so long as applicable rest period and break requirements are met. If a Pre-Point of Organization Try-out does not use all seven (7) days of the "ten out of twelve" hour rehearsal days provided for in this paragraph, it may, when it returns to the Point of Organization, use the remainder of those seven (7) days prior to the First Paid Public Performance at Point of Organization. On a day of travel, rehearsal and travel time combined shall not exceed ten (10) hours excluding rest periods.

(c) Rehearsal and Performance Hours During Try-out Away from Point of Organization and Previews at Point of Organization. For any ten (10) out of the first twelve (12) weeks after the First Paid Public Performance during try-out away from Point of Organization and/or Previews at Point of Organization but before the Official Opening at the Point of Organization, rehearsal, travel and performance shall not exceed ten (10) out of twelve (12) consecutive hours in any one day, except as follows:

(i)   Once per week during any five (5) of the ten (10) "ten out of twelve hour" weeks, each Actor may be called for ten (10) out of thirteen (13) consecutive hours. This may not be done on a two (2) performance day.

(ii)   If the Actor is called as provided in (i) above, there shall be a rest period of not less than eleven (11) hours between the end of the Actor's employment on the preceding day and the Actor's call on the "ten out of thirteen hour" day.

(iii)   It is understood that the "ten out of thirteen hour" day, if used, need not be on the same day for all Actors, but that each Actor may be called for no more than five (5) such days.

During the remaining two (2) weeks of such twelve (12) week period, rehearsal, travel and performance may not exceed seven (7) hours out of eight and one-half (8½) consecutive hours in any one day (including breaks required by Rule (2)(a) below).

(d)   Following the first twelve weeks after the First Paid Public Performance, rehearsal hours shall be governed by Rule (D)(1)(e) below, with the following exception:

If Producer uses "ten out of twelve hour" days (as described in (c) above) during no more than nine (9) out of the first twelve (12) weeks after the First Paid Public Performance, up to a maximum of six (6) such days may be used within any single week before the Official Opening at Point of Organization, provided that in special circumstances the Producer may use them within a two (2) week period with the consent of Equity, which consent will not be unreasonably withheld.

(e)   After Official Opening at Point of Organization or First Paid Public Performance on Tour. Rehearsals after Official Opening at Point of Organization or First Paid Public Performance on Tour shall be limited to eight (8) hours weekly, except that Actors signed to Understudy may be called to rehearse their own Understudy assignments for an additional four (4) hours per week. Rehearsals shall be limited to two (2) hours on two-performance days; however, absent special circumstances, there shall be no rehearsal between the matinee and evening performances except for Understudy rehearsal and/or emergency cast replacements.

(f)   Overtime shall be paid for all rehearsal hours in excess of those permitted herein.

(g)   Rehearsals after Performance. Rehearsals shall not be scheduled after an evening performance. However, notes may be given for a period not to exceed one

(1) hour after curtain, such time to be chargeable as rehearsal hours.

(h)   Rehearsal hours for each Actor shall be computed from the time of rehearsal call for that Actor.

(i)   Absent special circumstances, rehearsals may be called only upon twenty-four (24) hours' written notice.

Resident Theatres—Work Week (p. 30)

(G) Work Week.

(1)   During non-performance weeks rehearsal hours shall not exceed seven (7) out of nine (9) consecutive hours per day (including breaks required in paragraph (H) below). The total work week for Musicals shall not exceed forty-five (45) hours, of which no more than forty-two (42) hours shall be allotted to rehearsal.

(2)   Where there is a rehearsal period of more than four (4) weeks (none of which may be tech week), the total work week, in the next to the last week prior to the first paid public performance, shall not exceed forty-seven (47) hours, of which no more than forty-five (45) shall be allotted to rehearsals. In that week, the Theatre shall have the option of seven (7) out of nine (9) or eight (8) out of ten (10) consecutive hours per day (including breaks as required in paragraph (H) below).

(3)   In the seven (7) days prior to the first paid public performance, the total work week shall not exceed fifty-two (52) hours, of which no more than fifty-one (51) shall be allotted to rehearsals. The fifty-two (52) hour week shall fall either in the last full week of rehearsal or the week of the first paid public performance, but not both. This seven (7) day period may include:

(a)   three (3) ten (10) out of twelve (12), and three (3) seven (7) out of nine (9) consecutive hour days (including the breaks as required in paragraph (H) below); or

(b)   two (2) ten (10) out of twelve (12), three (3) eight (8) out of ten (10), and one (1) seven (7) out of nine (9) consecutive hour days (including the breaks as required in paragraph (H) below).

(c)   There must be a day off within this seven (7) day period.

(4)   During combined rehearsal and performance weeks, the total work week shall not exceed fifty (50) hours.

(5)   All other rules for Dramatic productions in Rule 44 shall also apply to Musicals.

(H) Rest Periods During Rehearsals.

Except during dress rehearsals, there shall be a rest period of five (5) minutes after no more than fifty-five (55) minutes of rehearsal or ten (10) minutes after no more than eighty (80) minutes of rehearsal for each Equity member. For each failure to give such rest periods, the Theatre shall pay each Actor one (1) hour of overtime.

Resident Theatres—Dancing Surfaces (p. 60)

(G) Dancing Surfaces.

(1) Actors shall not be required to rehearse dances or dance on concrete or marble floors or on any other surfaces which Equity shall deem to be injurious or unsafe, or on wood or on any other substance laid directly over such similar surfaces which do not provide air space of at least one and five-eights ($1\,^5/_8$) inches between the concrete or marble or similar supporting surface and the dancing surface.

(2) Where a portable stage is used, platforms must be fastened securely and the stage completely covered by a level deck or decks of such material as wood or masonite. The edge of all decks must be clearly visible or protected be securely fastened guard rails.

(3) Pits not in use shall be covered completely by a firm material.

12. Performance Report Forms

A stage manager's responsibilities include the keeping of an accurate performance log. This appendix offers two forms. The first is a completed daily performance report. In this case, it is the final performance of the 1990 Broadway run of *The Merchant of Venice.* The second form is a blank weekly report that should list company members present and absent, as well as any overtime charges incurred. The last row would normally be for Sunday performances, but in the case of this production, there were none. Both forms should serve as part of the permanent record of the production and eventually be filed in the producer's office.

Sample Daily Performance Report

THE MERCHANT OF VENICE

STAGE MANAGER REPORT   46th STREET THEATRE

DAY: SAT. MAT. | DATE: MAR. 10, 1990 | PERFORMANCE # 80/FINE

ACT I Up 2:06

ACT I Down 3:43

Running Time: 1 Hr. 37 Mins.

Intermission: 18 Mins.

ACT II Up 4:01

ACT II Down 5:05 (w/speeches, etc.)

Running Time: 1 Hr. 4 Mins.

Total Running Time: 2:41

Total Elapsed Time: 2:59

WEATHER/AUDIENCE/FOH

Great House

ABSENT, ILL, ACCIDENT

REHEARSAL, WORK CALLS, P.R.

1) Load-out / Mon. + Tues. 8-5
2) Save props, costumes, drops
3) Lose set –
TV shoot in lobby w/ Dustin after show.

NOTICES, OFFICE NOTES

I doubt people will put in for over-time – the "show" was over by 5:00. The rest was part of the party.

PERFORMANCE & TECHNICAL NOTES

1) Wonderful show – a real "event" for everyone. A good way to end – great spirit and energy on stage, backstage and in house. Speeches and much affection during curtain call – Dustin + Leigh – very nice –

STAGE MANAGER: Tom Kelly

Weekly Performance Report Form

T H E   M E R C H A N T   O F   V E N I C E

WEEKLY REPORT

Week Ending _____

DATE	OUT	ON	CREW/CAST O.T.
MONDAY / /			
TUESDAY / /			
WED. MAT / /			
WED. EVE / /			
THURSDAY / /			
FRIDAY / /			
SAT. MAT / /			

STAGE MANAGER: Tom Kelly

13. Production Schedules for Touring/Closing a Show

The following production schedules are more detailed than those in Appendix 2. The first is for the national tour of *A Day in Hollywood/A Night in the Ukraine.* The schedule covers the load-out from the New York scenic shops, the load-in to the theater in Wilmington, Del., and the subsequent move to Toronto. It serves to illustrate the complexities of stage managing a production on the road. The second schedule included in this appendix is the schedule for the closing and subsequent move of *I'm Not Rappaport.* Although the play closed only to move to Broadway, several blocks away in New York, it also demonstrates the careful planning necessary for such a seemingly simple move.

Touring Production Schedule

A DAY IN HOLLYWOOD/A NIGHT IN THE UKRAINE
National Company
PRODUCTION SCHEDULE

THURS NOV 12	8:00 am	TRUCK LOADS OUT NEW SET, UNIT DECK, CRATES, ETC. FROM METRO SCENIC AND NOLAN'S.
	9:30 am	ERIE TRUCK BRINGS ROAD BOXES TO ROYALE FOR REPAIR WORK
	10:00 am	COMPANY REHEARSAL/ROYALE THEATRE
	1:00 pm	BREAK
	2:00 pm	RUN-THRU/ROYALE THEATRE
FRI NOV 13	8:00 am to 5:00 pm	LOAD OUT ROYALE—PIANO CRATES DELIVERED BY PROPIANO—TRUCK #1—UNIT, DECK, DOORS & CRATES TO WILMINGTON TRUCK #2—HANGING GOODS & PROPS, WARDROBE, PORTALS TO WILMINGTON TRUCK #3—ROYALE UNIT, DECK & PORTALS TO METROTRUCK #4— PICK UP 4-STAR FOR WILMINGTON—PICK UP MASQUE FOR WILMINGTON
	10:00 am to 6:00 pm	COMPANY REHEARSAL AT 890 STUDIOS
SAT NOV 14	10:00 am to 10:00 pm	COMPANY REHEARSAL AT 890 STUDIOS MID-DAY PRODUCTION CREW TRAVELS TO WILMINGTON
SUN NOV 15	NOON	SPOT CREW/WILMINGTON
	3:00 pm to MIDNIGHT	ELECTRIC CREW—UNLOAD TRUCK #4 AND HANG OVERHEAD ELECTRICS AND START SOUND PERFORMING COMPANY/DAY OFF
MON NOV 16	10:00 am to 10:00 pm	COMPANY REHEARSAL AT 890 STUDIOS— JOE CRANZANO TO MEET WITH COMPANY AT 10:00 am RE: MAKE-UP
	8:00 am to MIDNIGHT	LOAD-IN FULL CREW/WILMINGTON TRUCK #2 UNLOAD FIRST TRUCK #1 SECOND UNLOAD BY MIDNIGHT SHOW HUNG, DECK DOWN/ASSEMBLING UNIT

HOLLYWOOD/UKRAINE (National Company) - PRODUCTION SCHEDULE

TUES NOV 17	10:00 am to 6:00 pm	COMPANY REHEARSAL AT 890 STUDIOS T. TUNE AT REHEARSALS/T. KELLY & L. BALL IN WILMINGTON
	6:00 pm	JIM DAWSON STRIKE ANKLE STAGE AT 890 STUDIOS
	8:00 am	CONTINUE SET-UP AND ASSEMBLING UNIT, ETC. PM—START FOCUS AS EARLY AS POSSIBLE ON ACT I SET BY MIDNIGHT—FINISH ACT I FOCUS
WED NOV 18	8:30 am	CAMPUS COACH BUS LOADED AT 890 STUDIOS
	10:30 am	KING DISPLAYS DELIVER CUT-OUTS, ETC. TO SHUBERT ALLEY
	NOON	COMPANY TRAVELS TO WILMINGTON— ASSEMBLES 45TH STREET SIDE OF SHUBERT ALLEY
	8:00 am	FINISH ANY ACT I FOCUS—ASSEMBLE ACT II UNITS—SHIFT TO ACT II AND FOCUS ACT II
	10:00 am	LEONARD HARTZELL—PIANO TUNER IN TO WORK ON PIANOS
	4:00 pm	FINISH FOCUS ACT II—SHIFT TO ACT I, DRY TECH TRAVELLERS, SET FOCUS AND ACT I LITE Q's.
	6:00 pm	LATEST BREAK LOAD-IN CREW
	7:00 pm to 11:00 pm	COMPANY CALLED—ACT II SET ON STAGE RUNNING CREW—TECH AND RUN ACT II WITH COMPANY
	11:00 pm to MIDNIGHT	COMPANY NOTES/SHIFT TO ACT I BREAK
	MIDNIGHT	FLAMEPROOFING BEGUN BY CHARLES BRANCH—4 to 5 HOURS TO COMPLETE, HOWEVER, STILL TO BE DETERMINED IF IT WILL ALL BE DONE ONE NIGHT OR CONTINUED THURSDAY NIGHT.
THURS NOV 19	8:00 am to NOON	FINISH & CLEAN-UP ON ACT I SET

HOLLYWOOD/UKRAINE (National Company) - PRODUCTION SCHEDULE

	NOON	COMPANY CALLED/INTO COSTUME & MAKE-UP
	1:00 pm to 5:00 pm	TECH/DRESS ACT I
	5:00 pm	ACTORS BREAK, CREW NOTES, TOUCH UP, ETC.
	7:30 pm	RESUME TECH ACT I
	10:00 pm to MIDNIGHT	FINISH ACT I TECH & RUN ACT I AND CHANGE SET TO ACT II
FRI NOV 20	8:00 am	CREW NOTES & CLEAN UP AS NEEDED ON ACT II SET
	1:00 pm	WORK AS NEEDED IN ACT II SET WITH COMPANY
	2:00 pm	SET-UP ACT I
	2:30 pm	DRESS REHEARSAL ACT I
	3:30 pm	CHANGE TO ACT II
	4:00 pm	DRESS REHEARSAL ACT II
	6:00 pm	BREAK (CHANGE TO ACT I END OF REHEARSAL, IF POSSIBLE)
	8:00 pm	FIRST PREVIEW
SAT NOV 21	2:00 pm	SECOND PREVIEW
	8:00 pm	THIRD PREVIEW
SUN NOV 22		COMPANY DAY OFF
MON NOV 23		TRUCK #3 LOADS OUT METRO & 4 STAR AND HEADS TO TORONTO WITH MANIFEST TO BE IN TORONTO READY TO UNLOAD SUNDAY, NOVEMBER 29 AT NOON
	8:00 pm	OPENING NITE PERFORMANCE/WILMINGTON
TUES NOV 24	8:00 am to NOON	WORK CALL—ALL DEPARTMENTS—DO FOCUS CHARTS
	1:00 pm to 5:00 pm	PICTURE CALL—ON STAGE—MARTHA SWOPE

HOLLYWOOD/UKRAINE (National Company) - PRODUCTION SCHEDULE

OUTLINE FOR TORONTO MOVE

SAT NOV 28   11:00 pm   LOAD OUT WILMINGTON (APPROXIMATELY
                           6 to 8 HOURS)

SUN NOV 29   5:00 am**   SPOT LINES

               1:00 pm*   TORONTO—UNLOAD JUMP TRUCK, HANG
               to   OVERHEAD ELECTRIC & START DECK
               MIDNIGHT   *(OR 9 HOURS FROM CONCLUSION OF
                            "CHILDREN")

               2:00 pm   COMPANY DEPART WILMINGTON EN ROUTE
                            TO TORONTO

MON NOV 30   8:00 am   LOAD-IN CONTINUES
               to
               MIDNIGHT

                            COMPANY DAY OFF

TUES DEC 1   9:00 am   FINISH ACT I SET UP—SWITCH TO ACT
                            II BEFORE LUNCH SET & FOCUS ACT II

               10:00 am   FINISH SET—BEGIN FOCUS ACT I

               1:00 pm   BREAK

               2:00 pm   SET ACT II

               3:00 pm   FOCUS ACT II

               4:00 pm   ACTORS ON ACT II SET

               5:00 pm   ACTORS ON ACT I SET

               7:00 pm   BREAK

               8:00 pm   HALF HOUR

** CREW TO DEPART ON A 9:40 AM FLIGHT OUT OF PHILADELPHIA

Closing and Move Production Schedule

I'M NOT RAPPAPORT - SCHEDULE

MOVE AMERICAN PLACE TO BOOTH

Week Ending October 20th

1. Scenery shops begin
2. Electric shop bids finalized

Week Ending October 27th

1. Sound order complete and to shops for bids
2. Production Meetings with American Place regarding load-out and Electrics at Booth regarding load-in

Week Ending November 3rd

1. Electric shop begin work Monday, October 28th
2. Finalize all trucking
3. Finalize all Booth Theatre dressing room assignments and necessities (telephones, power, ice boxes, painting, furnishing and fixing)
4. Finalize load-out and load-in crews
5. Possible flame proofing at American Place

Week Ending November 10th

1. Sound shop pull equipment and dupe show tape
2. All boxes, crates, etc. for move delivered to American Place - Fri. by T. Kelly in van - Wardrobe boxes, Stage Manager desk, etc. Also deliver all tools and materials as discussed with T. Walsh and B. Scales to Booth for load-in and/or American Place for load-out
3. Friday, November 8th - Spotting call at Booth Theatre
   Joe McCarthy to set call and coordinate with Don Beck, etc.
4. Sunday, November 10th -
   3:00 FINAL AMERICAN PLACE PERFORMANCE
   6:00 - 12:00   Begin load-out American Place - Set & Electrics
   a. Re-wire lampposts
   b. Additional sound proofing underneath platform & steps
   c. Salvage deck carpet for bridge covering at Booth
   d. Wardrobe sent to cleaners for clean and store until delivery to Booth on Monday, Nov. 18th and/or packed in Wardrobe boxes in Wardrobe room. Shoes and supplies packed in Wardrobe room.
   e. All make-up, hair and personal dressing room supplies (refrigerators, phones, etc.) packed and stored in Wardrobe room

I'M NOT RAPPAPORT - SCHEDULE

MOVE AMERICAN PLACE TO BOOTH   2

        f. Portals #2 & 3 FIRST UPSTAIRS ready for
            shop pick-up MON. NOV. 11TH
        g. All props packed and stored in Wardrobe
            room. SAVE THE FLAMEPROOFED TRASH FROM
            TRASH CAN!
        h. Trees stored in safe place with
            extensions unbolted; to be walked over
            Tues. Nov. 12th

Monday November 11th

    1. 9:00 – 1:00   Finish Load-Out American Place
        2:00 – 6:00   "   "   "   " - Later if
        necessary
    2. 9:00 – Shop pick up portals
    3. 45-ft. truck arrive 10:00 A.M.
            LOAD - 1. All bridge & stone work BLANKETED
                      2. Benches & lampposts & sewer pipes
                      3. Portal #1, pipes and plexi-facing
                      4. Deck & escape stair SL & backstage stairs
          STORE - 1. Steel Framework
          LOSE - Cyc, scrim, SR stairs & SL platforms
    4. 12:00 Production Arts Truck start electrics pick-up

BY 6:00 - (Later if necessary)
        1. 45-ft. truck loaded and parked, either on 46th Street or
            in lot next to theatre
        2. Electrics returned
        3. Steel framework, props, wardrobe, personal make-up &
            dressing room boxes, Stage Manager's desk, etc. in
            loading dock ready for 9:00 A.M. TUESDAY Walton truck #2

Tuesday, November 12th

    8:00 Walton truck #1 at Electric Shop, pick up electrics
    9:00 – 12:00 – Load-In begin at Booth Theatre
        1. Electric truck (Walton #1)
        2. Shop truck #1 with Portal #2 (new) and all additional set
            pieces and new pipes
        3. Shop truck # 2 with cyc and scrim
        4. 45 ft. truck from 46th St. - at Booth by 9:30
        5. Walton #2 at American Place - 9:00 - Load steel, props,
            wardrobe, etc. - deliver to Booth, then pick up sound &
            deliver to Booth
        6. Begin Electrics, cyc, scrim & portals hung on stage
        7. During morning - trees walked to Booth

    12:00 – 1:00 – BREAK AT BOOTH
            Completely out of American Place

Glossary

act curtain   The front curtain in a proscenium theater, usually raised when the show begins and brought in for the end of each act; also referred to as the "grand drape."

arena stage   Any stage set-up or configuration that places the audience on all four sides of the stage action.

bits   The term used to describe small pieces of stage action that often do little to advance the plot or play but may enhance character or relationships. They might include little foibles that a character develops due to being short-sighted, hard of hearing, or clumsy. Quite often bits are added by the actors during the course of a run to keep their creative juices flowing at best and to get a cheap laugh at worst. There are also "bit parts" which would refer to characters—a messenger or delivery boy, for example—that only have one or two lines.

blackout   The moment at which the entire playing area goes dark, usually in a sudden fashion, often to mark the end of a scene or musical number.

blocking   The term given to the staging of the actual movement of each cast member actor; it is the stage manager's responsibility to carefully record the blocking and see that it is strictly followed.

boxes   The seats on the sides of a theater that may hang over the edge of the audience; they have separate entrances, and usually seat six to eight people. They often have poor sightlines and offer a limited view of the stage.

break-away   Costumes that are designed to do just what the word describes, allowing a fight scene to include a shirt or a jacket or dress to be ripped and then repaired easily because the tear is already built into the garment and either velcroed or loosely stitched beforehand. Break-away clothes are also designed and used for quick changes so costumes can be switched in an instant.

bridge   A term left over from the days of theater/ship vocabulary, it usually refers to a level backstage that is maybe ten feet off the deck (stage level) and often holds dimmer or sound racks.

brush-up rehearsals   Rehearsals often used to take out the actors' "bits"; on a long-running show these rehearsals seek to return the play or musical to its original form or intent, sometimes involving the whole cast, sometimes just one or two actors or scenes.

cables   There are all kinds of cables backstage: electric cables powering lights and dimmers, sound cables connecting microphones and communication systems, and steel cables that support huge pieces of scenery.

call   The time at which performers or crew members must arrive for a rehearsal or performance.

callboard   The place in the theater where the sign-in sheet, all schedules, and any other vital information for cast and crew are posted.

clip lights   These are used to provide illumination necessary to run a performance backstage. Usually rigged with low-wattage blue bulbs, they are aimed down at the floor and away from the stage, helping to light the backstage passages for actors and crew. The "clip" is a strong clamp that allows these lights to be placed anywhere—scenery, the edges of curtains, stair railings, etc.

contact sheets   The address book of a production, comprised of sheets that contain the phone and address of everyone working on a show.

costume plot   A list and description (breakdown) of every costume piece worn by every actor and character in a play.

covers   Actors or singer dancers who "cover" certain scenes, songs, or small parts. Simpler than understudying, covers may often already be in the scene or number, and when covering, may have to perform additional lines or movement for the absent performer.

crossover   A passageway behind the set used by actors to cross the stage unseen by the audience. On Broadway sets, often there isn't one, and crossovers must be made through the basement.

cue   Technically, a cue is the execution of a move or effect in lighting and sound. For the actors, a cue is the line that immediately proceeds their line of dialogue. As a verb, the word may be used by the stage manager, who "cues" all technical personnel either verbally or on a light, and "cues" actors by giving them their line when they have forgotten it.

cue light   A light that when turned on functions as a warning to a crew member to perform a cue or to an actor to make an entrance, and when turned off signals them to GO.

cue sheet The written record of every technical cue in each department, it should include the cue number or letter, how it will be cued (either verbally or on a cue light) and what will happen in the cue (either scenery move or light or sound effect).

cue-to-cue A technical rehearsal that focuses on getting the physical production caught up with the acting by skipping over scenes or dialogue that have no technical cues in them in order to run the next cue.

cyc Short for "cyclorama," it refers to a large drop or curtain that usually hangs at the back of a set and is often used by the lighting and set designers to represent the sky.

deck The stage level, derived from ship terminology.

deck cues The cues that happen on the stage level, i.e. the moving on and off of scenic elements, platforms, etc.

drops Pieces of scenery that are hung over the stage and often "fly" in and out; often painted but can also be full wall units with doors, windows, etc.

dressers The wardrobe crew members who actually help actors in and out of their costumes and supervise the cleaning and distribution of the costumes on a regular basis. They also organize and assist all quick changes that happen backstage when there is no time for returning to dressing rooms.

dry tech Basically a "cue-to-cue" without actors.

escape stairs The steps, unseen by the audience, that an actor uses to "escape" after an upper-level exit; also used to get in place for an entrance from upper platforms or doors.

fight director The person who stages, with an eye for safety and the actors' ability to repeat the actions, any fight scenes, duels, etc. in a play or musical.

first-call sheet A cast list with the first time every actor is called for rehearsal or performance.

flash-pot A small box that will cause a noisy explosion of smoke; it is set by crossing two wires with opposite polarity that then short out when cued, igniting a gunpowder-type substance with the spark.

floor plan The accurate detail of the way the set lays out on the stage with all walls, platforms, stairs, furniture, and moving pieces indicated.

fly floor The level from which the "flies" or flown scenery and drops are run.

focus The period of time during which the lighting designer instructs the electric crew where to aim and shutter (focus) each lighting instrument. Lighting instruments can be focused to illuminate a small or large area of the stage. For an actor or director, "focus" refers to where the audience's attention should be during a scene, often called the "point of focus." In large scenes it is important to watch that crowd-scene actors don't "pull focus" with some "bits" they may have devised.

gels   In the old days the color filters for stage lights were made of a gelatin substance, hence the term gels for these filters used to create dramatic lighting effects.

green room   It is a room or area in the theater in which the actors may relax and gather before and during a rehearsal or performance; the term harkens back to the Greeks, who would go off to a leafy bower or grove to relax when offstage.

grid   A matrix of iron or heavy wooden beams at the top of every theater building from which the hanging pipes for lights and scenery are suspended.

ground plan   *See* floor plan.

hanging plot   This refers to one of two plots. There is the lighting designer's hanging plot that shows where every lighting instrument is to be hung, either backstage or in the house; and there is the master hanging plot that will assign pipes and hanging positions to every lighting, sound, and scenic element in the show.

hospitality   The basic care and comfort offered by the stage manager to the cast and crew on as high a level as can be squeezed from the budget. If you don't know how to offer this, don't be a stage manager.

house   The term used to describe the area of a theater where the audience customarily sits.

house lights   The lights used to illuminate the audience areas, they are dimmed out as the show begins and the stage lights take over, drawing focus to the stage.

light board   The control board run by the electrician that cues the lights; most are computerized these days and involve nothing more complex than pushing a button . . . until something goes wrong.

load-in/out   The time a show goes into or out of a theater; also called "take-in/out." Large crews are usually assembled just for this period.

notes   The endless process of recording comments on performance quality, technical conditions, etc.; making sure they are communicated clearly is the stage manager's continuing job from beginning to end of a show. "Notes" is also the term given to the period of time when the director gathers a cast to discuss the performance or rehearsal. It is vital that a stage manager be at every note session to record the notes to avoid any confusion later.

off-book   The term used to describe when the actors put down the script in the tenuous but brave belief that they now know their lines well enough to be "off-book."

pacing   The speed at which a play is performed is called its pace. Pace can be achieved by speaking the lines faster and also by cutting down the time between lines (also called "picking up the cues").

palette A thin piece of plywood or masonite (often a section of a room covered by a rug with furniture on it) that can be used to quickly change sets without having to handle each piece of furniture separately.

perishables Props that must be replaced constantly—food, broken bottles or glasses, ripped up documents, or anything else that "perishes" on a nightly or weekly basis.

pipes Long pieces of iron, usually ³/₄ or 1 inch in diameter, that hang above the stage from the grid and from which are hung lights and scenery.

places The term used backstage to announce to the company that an act or scene is beginning. It literally means, "Kindly come to your places for the commencement of the act or scene about to be run or performed." In England the term "beginners" is used.

practical props/appliances Any object that is actually used by an actor on the set—a lamp, a stove, a cigarette lighter.

preproduction The planning period that takes place before rehearsals begin.

preset The pre-show setting of all physical elements of the production before the action begins. There is usually a lighting preset that warms the curtain or, in situations with no curtain, highlights the set slightly. On stage, the preset is the positioning of all scenery and props for the opening of the act.

preview A performance before the official opening; often these are rehearsals with an audience, and a time when new material is tested and tried.

prompt What you hope actors are; also the act of giving a line to the actor when they go "up" or forget a line, which is also referred to as "drying."

props The elements on a stage that are not scenery or furniture, including everything that is handled and used by actors, as well as all set "dressing" and ornaments.

prop tables Tables in the wings on which the actors' props can be preset for them and to which they should return the props after they use them; they should be carefully marked and labeled so each prop has its proper place.

proscenium Latin for "in front of the scenery," the word refers to the arch or frame that actually goes around the stage.

quick-change booth Temporary backstage dressing rooms used for quick changes of costume, wigs, etc.; it may be used by many different actors at different times during the show.

raked stage The practice of setting the stage floor on a "rake" so that the downstage edge is considerably lower than the upstage edge; this aids with sightlines and also gives the set designer the opportunity to use the floor as a scenic element.

replacement   Any performer who replaces another.

running crew   The actual crew that is required for the operation of each performance.

running order   The order in which a show's scenes and songs are performed.

run-throughs   The first attempts at performing a show all the way through without stopping; after opening, they are used for brush-up or replacement rehearsals.

scene breakdowns   Careful annotations of each scene in a play, with all necessary actors listed and some indication of the action and setting.

scrim   A gauze-like curtain that, when lit from the front, is opaque (cannot be seen through), and when lit from behind becomes translucent and seems to disappear.

shops   The various work places where the physical production is assembled or built; there are scenery, light, costume, sound, and prop shops.

special effects   Any effect out of the ordinary—storms, fire, explosions, blood, etc.

stage combat   Any stage fighting, from a slap to a battle.

stand-by   A performer who is an understudy but who does not report to the theater unless called to perform, and may perform one or two shows on a regular basis.

strike   What the producers hope the unions never do; also, the term for the removal of any item of the physical production either temporarily between scenes or permanently (the load out).

tableaux   A grouping of performers to make a pretty stage picture, often used for curtain calls.

tech rehearsal   The rehearsal or rehearsals where the physical elements of production are integrated with the performed elements.

theater-in-the-round   Like arena stages, the audience sits on four sides of the stage, but the stage is round.

thrust stage   Any configuration of the playing area in which the stage projects into the seating area.

trap doors   Sections of the stage floor that open, allowing actors to enter or exit.

travelers   A curtain that opens as opposed to "flying" in and out.

truss   An additional or extra system of pipes from which light and sound equipment can be hung.

turntable   A section of the deck or stage that can turn, bringing scenery and actors on.

understudy An actor who is prepared to go on for another actor in case of emergency.

wagon A rolling or tracked platform that goes on- and offstage with actors and/or scenery on it.

wardrobe department The crew members who deal with costumes.

warning The stage manager "warns" all cues either verbally or by turning on a cue light.

winch The device by which wagons are moved onto and off of the stage; basically, a large drum around which steel cables are wound or unwound by means of a crank.

wings The area directly offstage.

work call The time period during which the crew is called to work on any technical element of a production without actors or rehearsal.

Suggested Reading

Stage managers should read anything about the theater, whether technical text-books, design handbooks, guides to acting and directing techniques, or theater diaries and novels. Here are some basic suggestions.

Design/Technical

The Backstage Handbook, Paul Carter. New York: Broadway Press, 1988.
A basic guide to theatrical terms and backstage services.

The Dramatic Imagination, Robert Edmond Jones. New York: Theater Arts Books, 1969.
My favorite theater "bible," this essay collection is filled with the author's vision of an ideal theater. Jones, one of the great twentieth-century theater artists (he designed many of O'Neill's plays and the set for John Barrymore's 1922 production of *Hamlet*), believed the artform should encourage the audience's imagination, not bombard it with excess.

A Method of Lighting the Stage, Stanley R. McCandless. New York: Theater Arts Books, 1978.
The longstanding text that still offers the best basic information on how to design and execute theatrical stage lighting.

From Option to Opening: A Guide to Producing Plays Off-Broadway, Donald Farber. New York: Limelight Editions, 1988.
An excellent text on the complexities of theater from the management perspective.

Scenery for the Theatre, 2nd, rev. ed., Harold Burris-Meyer and Edward C. Cole. Boston: Little, Brown and Co., 1971.
The text that explains the fundamentals: stage terminology, basic building and rigging techniques, scenery construction and painting, and lighting rudiments. If you read only one technical book, make it this one.

Stage Lighting, Richard Pilbrow. New York: Applause Theatre Books, 1990.
A good text with excellent insights into the use of lighting and its creation.

Stage Manager's Forms and Formats, Barbara Dilker. New York: Drama Book Publications, 1982.
Many valuable forms and ideas for organization.

Stage Manager's Handbook, Bert Gruver and Frank Hamilton. New York: Drama Book Publications, 1972.
Contains helpful hints on setting up and organizing the show. Mainly geared toward the commercial New York theater and touring.

A Stage Manager's Manual, Edward C. Cole. New Haven: Yale University Department of Drama, 1937.
Old-fashioned and out-of-print but pure gold and worth a trip to the library. The advice remains sound and the methods haven't changed that much, because as the technical complexity of theater has grown, so has the need for clear, human leadership and organization.

Stage Specs: A Guide to Legit Theaters. League of New York Theaters and Producers, 226 W. 47 St., New York, NY 10036.
A thorough reference to theaters across the country, detailing dimensions, seating capacities, load-in and load-out procedures, union requirements, and more. A must for anyone considering touring a show.

Acting and Directing

Actors on Acting, rev. ed., Toby Cole and Helen K. Chinoy, eds. New York: Crown Publishers, 1980.
Interviews with many accomplished actors who discuss their approach to the creation of a character.

Building a Character and *My Life in Art,* Constantin Stanislavsky. New York: Routledge, Chapman, and Hall, 1989.
The architect of a new approach to theater at the turn of the century, Stanislavsky's thought became the foundation for Lee Strasberg's Method, as well as other acting techniques.

The Director's Voice, Arthur Bartow. New York: Theatre Communications Group, 1988.
Interviews with many of the leading directors in the theater today.

A Dream of Passion: The Development of the Method, Lee Strasberg. Evangeline Morphos, ed. New York: New American Library, 1988.
The authoritative text on "The Method" acting technique, developed by the author at the Actors' Studio.

Great Directors at Work: Stanislavsky, Brecht, Kazan, Brook, David Richard Jones. Berkeley: Univ. of California Press, 1986.
An examination of the director's art as practiced by four of the most accomplished in this century.

On Directing, Harold Clurman. New York: MacMillan, 1974.
A detailed and illuminating discussion of the director's craft by one of the Group Theatre's founders.

Respect for Acting, Uta Hagen with Haskel Frankel. New York: MacMillan, 1973.
Excellent descriptions of sense memory work and exercises used by many actors.

Sanford Meisner on Acting, Sanford Meisner and Dennis Longwell. New York: Random House, 1987.
Written by an original member of the Group Theatre and the founder of The Neighborhood Playhouse, this book details Meisner's influential actor training process.

Stage Directions, John Gielgud. New York: Theatre Arts Books, 1979.
A great lesson in acting style and approach from a master.

The Technique of Acting, Stella Adler. New York: Bantam Books, 1988.
One of the best acting texts, this is an in-depth study of behavioral acting.

Backstage Accounts and Fiction

Act One: An Autobiography, Moss Hart. New York: Random House, 1976.

Diary of a Mad Playwright, James Kirkwood. New York: Dutton, 1985
Difficult stars, a play that isn't working, and the rigors of a national pre-Broadway tour. You can learn a lot here.

Peter Hall's Diaries, Peter Hall. John Goodwin, ed. New York: Limelight Editions, 1985.
Incisive insights into the process of putting on plays, running a theater, and trying to maintain a life while existing on the creative edge.

Understudy, Elia Kazan. New York: Scarbrough House, 1975.
This novel uses the theater and its workings as the setting for its story. It offers a stage manager interesting insights into some of the emotional and philosophical motivations of theater people.

Index